TO WILLIAM ODELL

GOOD READING!

Profiting in Bull or Bear Markets

Profiting in Bull or Bear Markets

George Dagnino, Ph.D.

McGraw-Hill

New York   Chicago   San Francisco   Lisbon   London
Madrid   Mexico City   Milan   New Delhi   San Juan   Seoul
Singapore   Sydney   Toronto

Library of Congress Cataloging-in-Publication Data

Dagnino, George.
    Profiting in bull or bear markets/by George Dagnino.
        p. cm.
    ISBN 0-07-136706-3
    1. Investments. 2. Investment analysis. 3. Business cycles. I. Title.

    HG4521 .D113 2001
    332.63'2—dc21   00-048171

McGraw-Hill

A Division of The McGraw-Hill Companies

1 2 3 4 5 6 7 8 9 0   DOC/DOC   0 9 8 7 6 5 4 3 2 1

ISBN 0-07-136706-3

This publication is designed to provide accurate and authoritative information in regard to the subject matter covered. It is sold with the understanding that neither the author nor the publisher is engaged in rendering legal, accounting, futures/securities trading, or other professional service. If legal advice or other expert assistance is required, the services of a competent professional person should be sought.

—From a Declaration of Principles jointly adopted by a Committee of the American Bar Association and a Committee of Publishers.

The sponsoring editor for this book was Kelli Christiansen, the editing supervisor was Paul R. Sobel, and the production supervisor was Elizabeth J. Strange. It was set in ITC Garamond by M M Design 2000, Inc.

Printed and bound by R. R. Donnelley & Sons Company.

McGraw-Hill books are available at special quantity discounts to use as premiums and sales promotions, or for use in corporate training programs. For more information, please write to the Director of Special Sales, McGraw-Hill, Professional Publishing, Two Penn Plaza, New York, NY 10121-2298. Or contact your local bookstore.

 This book is printed on recycled, acid-free paper containing a minimum of 50% recycled, de-inked fiber

Contents

Foreword

This book had to be written—eventually! And that time is now! In this new age of universal, instantaneous financial information, with virtually no limits on who gets it and how they act on it, someone had to make sense out of the mostly unexplained rhetoric on the financial networks and nightly business news. The "secret codes" for business and financial cycles have eluded too many people for too long. *Profiting in Bull or Bear Markets* cracks that code, heretofore reserved exclusively for the financial elite.

Economists have long tried to forecast the future by explaining the relationships among economic indicators and business cycles; *investors* have extolled the virtues of price/earnings ratios and company growth dynamics; *futures traders* the merits of technical analysis and systems strategy back-testing; and *politicians* the importance of monetary and fiscal interventions. All of these disciplines make sense individually, but the results of these individual efforts often give us less than adequate results. For example, "buy and hold" and dollar cost averaging, sacred mantras within an investing community that nobody—repeat—nobody, until now, has brought these various disciplines and disparate viewpoints together into a coherent, logical, and practical understanding of how markets work. George Dagnino, however, has finally accomplished this elusive goal.

If there is a Holy Grail in financial investing and trading, it is "Following the Market." Using his 20-plus years in studying the business and financial cycles, and drawing on his proven track record as a profitable market timer, Dr. Dagnino leads the reader through a step-by-step analysis of dynamic market forces. Market forces that many try to control, but few understand. He demonstrates which economic indicators are important and why, how these indicators determine the current and future phases in the cycles, and most importantly, what action should be taken by the individual investor or trader to gain a strategic advantage no matter what phase of the economic cycles we are dealing with. In short, how to become a beneficiary of the current economic cycle phase rather than a helpless victim.

Profiting in Bull or Bear Markets is break-through work. This book is an important contribution to the vast body of financial literature. It is a

valuable resource for the professional financial manager and amateur
investor alike. Business and financial cycles have been explained
before, but never from the practical viewpoint and unique perspective
that Dr. Dagnino brings to the party. He is a master market weaver. This
work spins complex market elements into an easy-to-understand market whole.

As an investor, trader, or consumer, you should care how business and
financial cycles affect you, and what actions you can take within this
framework to positively change your economic life for the better. You
should constantly question whether your spending, savings and investment patterns are in sync, or in conflict with the business and financial
cycles. Only by understanding the cause and effect relationships in each
phase of these cycles can you make profitable financial decisions within your own level of risk tolerance. In this context, *Profiting in Bull or
Bear Markets* gives you the tools necessary to increase your odds of
winning. The markets can be timed, and Dr. Dagnino shows you how in
this historic work.

Ronald M. Brandt
Private Investor and Trader

Preface

This book is the result of more than 20 years of studying the behavior of business and financial cycles and their impact on investment management. My viewpoint has been influenced by my graduate work at Case-Western Reserve in Cleveland, Ohio, where I received a Ph.D.

Case was well known for its advanced studies and research in the field of management science, information systems, and artificial intelligence. For several years after graduation I reflected on the meaning and implications of what I learned. Finally I realized that the entire program was about "the engineering of thinking." It was about the logical, structured thought process that is typical in the field of artificial intelligence.

The main assumption of this branch of computer sciences is that human thinking can be duplicated. Anything produced by the mind is the outcome of a sequence of logical steps that, when taken all together, can be recognized as thought.

As I was investigating the forces acting on the financial markets and asset prices, some relationships turned out to be more reliable than others. The most reliable ones were those relating turning points and trends. The use of levels (such as, sell if indicator A rises to 50) made my conclusions and the resulting strategy less reliable. However, relationships between trends (such as, rising interest rates have a negative impact on stock prices) have crucial strategic value.

The main concept of this book is presented in a step-by-step process. At the same time I tried to keep everything tied together. As I added new ideas, I made sure they improved the logical model of the previous pages and made it more understandable. My challenge was to identify dependable and profitable patterns. The next step was to tie all of them together in a way that would provide only one answer for each configuration of patterns. In order to do so, I had to reach conclusions that do not reflect conventional wisdom. For example, the Federal Reserve does not control interest rates; the markets do. Interest rates rise because the markets force the price of money to go higher. The markets have the same effect on the price of burlap, aluminum, and most other commodities. The Fed has an impact on interest rates, but the process is not as direct as commentators would lead you to believe.

The same can be said about the price of crude oil, which is also driven by the markets. OPEC, like the Fed, is a cartel. One impacts the price of oil and the other the price of money. Cartels only add to the volatility of prices; they do not establish a rising or declining trend. The markets do.

I fully realize these statements are unconventional. But I believe strategists and investors have to be open-minded. If the issue is to forecast interest rates, investors have to find the true causes of their cyclical movement. These causes may eventually be the Federal Reserve itself, but not in the way conventional wisdom approaches the issue of predicting interest rates and stock market trends. The same can be said about crude oil and other asset prices.

This book provides a logical framework, based on the relationships between patterns of data involving many economic and financial variables. It is the result of a lifetime of research, studies, successes, and failures in predicting financial markets.

This is not a theoretical book. It is based on more than 20 years of editing *The Peter Dag Portfolio Strategy and Management,* an investment advisory that has gained national and international recognition.

My experience with the top management of the Goodyear Tire and Rubber Company also allowed me to formalize the concept of strategy. My role was to advise the treasurer and the CFO on the optimum fixed-to-floating ratio for the company's debt, and manage 3 billion dollars in interest rates derivatives and 1 billion dollars in currency hedges.

These experiences provided me with a great opportunity to test my ideas and learn from the challenges of developing investment strategies required to deal with sophisticated and complex markets. Managing money for clients and facing the markets every day remain a continuing learning endeavor. More information can be found on my website, www.peterdag.com.

George Dagnino

Acknowledgments

Baldwin-Wallace in Cleveland, Ohio, a liberal arts college, offered me the opportunity to teach without constraints. I was very lucky. The college let me teach economics and financial markets for management using my experience in business—practical experience and very little theory. My students were challenged with hands-on assignments and made to think on their own, to make sense out of all the information they were exposed to.

They liked my approach and my pragmatism. In fact, many months after the completion of the course, they would come to me and tell me how much it all made sense. They thanked me, even though my tests were extremely complicated. What else can I ask? My thanks goes to them for their exchange of ideas and their enthusiastic appreciation of the subject.

I am grateful to the administration of Baldwin-Wallace for allowing me to exercise my intellectual freedom. The way the information is presented in this book reflects many years of teaching at Baldwin-Wallace College.

Teaching assignments at Kent State University and Ashland College further stimulated my desire to communicate my ideas and to improve them. These ideas have also been shared with many audiences in the United States and Europe. Wherever I went, I was pleased to find that my work was accepted.

As I grew professionally, I had unique mentors like Jack Klingel, Jack Higgins, and Jim Boyazis. They were very patient with me every time I asked for advice and guidance. I would like to thank them and all the people who listened and shared their valuable time with me.

Warm thanks go to Jan Shillingburg for typing the manuscript with its numerous revisions and for her dedication in assisting me and recognizing the importance of this effort.

Special thanks go to Susan Baun, who was instrumental in organizing my work and helping me meet my schedule. She was a reliable sounding board and provided the important feedback I needed to help me focus on the essential ideas of the book and their practical use.

Finally, my deep appreciation goes to my wife, Kathi, for her patience and support. And to my children, Simone and Barbara, thank you for giving me the inspiration to achieve.

About the Author

George Dagnino, Ph.D., is chairman of Peter Dag Strategic Money Management, a lecturer at Kent State University, and a former professor at Baldwin-Wallace College. He was chief economist and risk manager for The Goodyear Tire & Rubber Company. Dr. Dagnino has been an invited lecturer at over 150 organizations and universities on how business and financial cycles impact investment and business strategies. He is regularly quoted in newspapers and magazines from *Barron's* to *Investor's Business Daily*, on news services including Reuters, and on financial TV networks including CNBC and CNN.

Introduction

The purpose of this book is not to provide you with a get-rich-quick scheme. It is not a way to invest play money. What this book offers is the knowledge required to manage all your money. We all seek security and must plan for a secure retirement. This book will help you learn how to achieve your goals in bull and bear markets. You will learn how to increase your odds of winning and decrease the risks inherent in this game of strategy.

The author has had over 22 years' experience in managing money—from a few thousand to more than 4 billion dollars in interest rates and currency derivatives—and has edited the highly acclaimed investment advisory, *The Peter Dag Portfolio Strategy and Management*, since 1977.

During these years the author has had successes and, indeed, some failures, and he has always made an attempt to learn from both his mistakes and his successes. Successfully managing money is closely related to managing the volatility of the returns of a portfolio. To achieve financial success, investors must follow the rules of the game so that their investment performance becomes predictable. Once you know all your available alternatives and the likely payoff, you can determine the best sequence of moves to achieve your goals—you map out your strategy. This, of course, is a very difficult task and requires very tight discipline.

The main objective of business and financial strategies is to maintain a desired level of financial performance. Understanding how to build these strategies is crucial to your success. This book will share with you the lessons the author has learned, the approach he followed, and the framework he used to achieve low volatility and investment performance. That success has been reported by organizations such as the American Association of Individual Investors, *Forbes*, the *New York Times*, and the *Washington Post,* with data provided by the Hulbert organization.

In reading this book, you will gain the knowledge and an appreciation of what it takes to invest by making returns more predictable; in order to do so, the author has utilized concepts related to economic and financial fluctuations. The investor must invest in tune with the times. Understanding the inherent economic forces is crucial to developing your strategies. If the times are highly inflationary, it makes sense to buy

1

real estate, gold, or commodities. However, if the times are noninflationary, these investments are not going to provide high returns.

It is very important to recognize the type of economic and financial
times we are experiencing, to recognize inflationary pressures, and to
measure the likelihood that these trends will continue. In order to do so,
it is important to learn how economic and financial cycles drive the
prices of most assets such as stocks, bonds, commodities, currencies, real
estate, and precious metals.

Using the blueprint outlined in this book, you will achieve more predictable returns by minimizing losses. The material presented in the following pages also will assist you in identifying what the sources of risk
are, and where they appear in these cycles, and what their impact on
your investments will be. These forces, present in all economic and
financial cycles, happen anyway, so why not take advantage of them?

In order to bring together the different elements needed to develop an
investment strategy, investors need to look at various disciplines in the
investment field. They need to learn about economics, fixed-income
securities or bonds, and the stock market. They need to know how the
central bank of a country operates, how trends in the commodity markets develop, and what impacts currencies. Trends in economic and
financial cycles are the unifying force acting on all these markets.

This book is like a mosaic. It deals with each aspect of the market.
Gradually, everything will come together, and you will be ready to apply
the content to your specific investment interest and goals. To achieve this
objective, the book is broken into 15 chapters.

Chapter 1 deals with investment risk. The importance of this concept
is that it points up the need for an investment strategy and the formal
process of developing it. We will cover such issues as forecasts, risks,
and game theory—what can we learn from how a successful poker player plays the game? How do we make decisions as risk changes? We will
examine the concepts of averaging down and of buy and hold—strategies that are not as profitable as some investors might believe.

In Chapter 2, we will investigate the growth phases of the economy—
why does it grow rapidly, then slow down, then grow very slowly again,
and then accelerate, and what happens to the financial markets when the
economy goes through these phases? To do so, we will look at the most
important economic data available from various sources and discuss how
to interpret them.

Chapter 3 shows how all these measures and economic data are related. If sales are growing rapidly, consumer confidence must be very high.
When consumer confidence is very high, it is likely because employment

growth is very strong. If employment growth is strong, then the economy must be expanding at a rapid pace. The chapter ties all these relationships together and explains the implications of these relationships.

The concept of leading, coincident, and lagging indicators is introduced in Chapter 4. These indicators greatly simplify the analysis of cyclical forces and make it easier to understand what is happening in the economy.

In Chapter 5, we will talk about the concept of the business cycle and growth potential. What kinds of problems arise in the financial markets during each growth phase of the business cycle? Problems and opportunities occur at the same time, depending on the economic phase. Chapter 5 helps us assess how to determine the impact of growth on the overall markets.

Chapter 6 will explore current economic times and show what has been happening in the economy. Why, for instance, after 1982, did we have declining and low inflation? Why did we have rising inflation in the seventies? And why did the fifties and sixties look more like the eighties and nineties? This has important implications for the kind of investment strategy we should follow. Understanding why there has been a transition in economic times from the fifties and sixties and then from the seventies to the eighties and nineties provides clues to recognizing changes in the economic and financial climate. The chapter will give you precise data and guidelines to follow in order to achieve this objective.

One of the main themes of this book is that the Fed, our central bank, has a major and fundamental impact through the implementation of its policies on business and financial cycles. Short-term interest rates and the money supply play a crucial role in changing the risk of investing in stocks and bonds. Chapter 7 deals with the impact of how and why the central bank affects trends in short-term interest rates depending on changes in business activity, how inflation impacts the price of bonds and stocks, and how it relates to the returns of investments in hard assets.

Contrary to popular belief, it is the author's opinion that the Federal Reserve does not control interest rates. Rather, the Federal Reserve manages the orderly rise and decline in interest rates, which are directly impacted by the markets alone. What the Federal Reserve has the power to control is the growth in liquidity in the financial system. This theme is explored throughout this book. In particular, we will explore the crucial impact of changes in liquidity on financial cycles and how they affect the behavior of the economy and all markets. It is this knowledge, that will greatly enhance your capabilities of managing the risk of your portfolio and help you develop successful investment strategies.

Chapter 8 investigates the process of inflation and the impact inflation has on economic and financial cycles and currencies. The reason for looking at currencies is that the success of investing in foreign markets depends greatly on the value and trends of the U.S. dollar relative to the currencies of other countries.

In Chapter 9 we will explore bonds within the context of the business and financial cycles. There are two important reasons for discussing bonds. Bonds are an excellent investment instrument at specific points of a financial cycle. And like short-term interest rates, they have an impact on trends in the stock market. The chapter presents indicators to determine the high-risk and low-risk times for investing in bonds.

Beginning in Chapter 10, we will zero in on the stock market. We will look at its trends and how it behaves within the financial cycles, and we will examine how business cycles impact the stock market. The chapter will provide indicators that allow us to measure risk and foresee financial opportunities. This will help us determine how much money we should invest in specific assets and will introduce the concept of dynamic asset allocation.

One of the major points emphasized in this book is that the stock market is an integral part of the economic and financial system. As economic growth changes from very slow to rapid and then to slow again, it impacts the way the financial markets behave by releasing powerful forces. The stock market is not immune to these forces. However, there is a school of thought that says the market provides information about itself, and a careful analysis of this information provides important input for developing profit opportunities in stock. The field of technical analysis focuses on the study of these forces, and an overview of the most widely known indicators is presented in Chapter 11.

Chapter 12 analyzes the issues of portfolio management using stocks and provides guidelines on how to build a stock portfolio and use strategies to manage the risk involved in equity investments. We will learn how to manage volatility, select stocks, and determine what stocks to buy and sell.

Experience has shown that the issues related to improving shareholder value and management decision making can be greatly enhanced by considering the impact that business and financial cycles have on a corporation. In Chapter 13 we will explore how the decision process used by an investor is very similar to that of a corporate executive. We will see how several areas of corporations have "a portfolio management issue" and "risk management challenges." This chapter will analyze and suggest approaches to improve the process and therefore greatly enhance shareholder value using the same techniques, analyses, and tools developed in this book.

How can investors best develop a strategy using information discussed in the book? In Chapter 14 we will see how everything is tied together. We will recognize the basic logic behind the information presented in the previous chapters. The chapter will show us how to organize the information, how to develop a strategy—from analyzing the data to selecting the various investments. We also will gain an appreciation of the importance of applying the dynamics of the investment game and how the game itself is played.

Chapter 15 brings together the major elements of this book in a simple way and provides guidelines for implementing the process of investing using the approach followed in this book. This chapter is written in a question and answer format. The spirit of the questions is to lead a step-by-step implementation of what has been discussed in this book.

Chapter 15 is the starting point in implementing what you have learned in this book. The approach followed in this chapter is to specify and discuss the charts the investor should use to begin the investment process. These charts are the same ones that have been used throughout this book. They are the ones, in the author's experience, that have proved to be effective in predicting financial markets and developing investment strategies. These charts should continually be updated and analyzed to determine new patterns and relationships between financial markets and financial cycles. This is a never-ending process. These relationships among economic, financial, and market cycles can be further enhanced by using techniques that in the field of artificial intelligence are called pattern recognition.

Chapter
1

USING RISK TO MANAGE YOUR MONEY SUCCESSFULLY

Games and Strategies

The main objective of business and financial strategies is to maintain a desired level of financial performance. The challenge is to achieve this performance in a consistent way while minimizing volatility of returns. Consistency requires the ability to anticipate the action of competitors and financial markets. At the same time it is important to balance return and risk as business and financial conditions change. How can this be achieved? What are the main parameters that drive business and financial strategies? Is there a general framework to guide the strategist? How good are your instincts?

There is no telling where your business or portfolio will end up. Look for a simple formula and you will discover that none exists. If it did, everyone would be running a successful business and be rich. Still, certain guidelines have proved themselves to be the soundest over time.

A technique that is often used in developing business and financial strategies is to think of them as a game. Every individual plays against all the other individuals or against the markets. A strategy can be visualized as a series of moves to win the game against competitors or other investors.

Game theory was developed in the 1940s to help the military design and execute successful strategies. War poses the problem of maximizing return—that is, winning at the lowest cost without knowing exactly what the enemy, who is also trying to win, is likely to do. This procedure parallels that of a successful business decision maker or financial strategist. Learn the enemy's strengths, weaknesses, and approximate position. Then assign odds on the enemy's next move. On the basis of these odds, establish the best moves you need to make in order to win.

Once we know all our available alternatives and their likely payoff, we determine the best sequence of moves to lead us to victory. After our moves, the enemy's response might send us back to the drawing board to establish the next set of strategies, and so on. Business and financial strategies face similar problems: (1) No one knows precisely what the markets—the enemy—will do next. (2) The odds of success and the size of the returns can only be guessed. (3) Strategies depend on the required returns, the perceived risk, and the acceptance of a personal risk level to play the game.

The content of this book could be considered as one set of rules to play the game. Other participants—that is, investors—may have a different understanding of how things work. As a result, they play the game in a different way. But one thing is sure—the more knowledge the player has about the rules of the game, the more likely that player is going to win.

Assessing Risk and Using It to Manage Money

The reason we are talking about risk is because forecasts aren't reliable. It is highly unlikely that what you think will happen next or what people say will happen next to the stock market, or to interest rates, or to the economy, will pan out exactly as predicted. If the forecasts were reliable, if they were a sure thing, if we really knew what was going to happen, then people would not talk about strategy, because the best strategy would be to bet everything on those forecasts. But since we don't know if a forecast is going to be accurate, we cannot bet all we have, because chances are we will lose it—therefore we need to think about strategy.

The reason a forecast can never be totally accurate is because it is developed through many steps, and at each step a new element of uncertainty is introduced. The most important part of a forecast is the assumptions that the forecaster makes. Those assumptions are based on both what the forecaster believes and what the forecaster has experienced in similar situations. For instance, the forecaster may make the assumption that with a given policy of the U.S. government—the level of taxation and the level of real interest rates—inflation cannot rise much above current levels. This is an important assumption, because, as we will discuss in detail later in this book, if inflation is stable, the odds are that there will not be major financial disturbances. That means the economy will remain stable and jobs are likely to be plentiful. An assumption of low or stable inflation also suggests that interest rates will not rise and that the stock market will probably remain in a rising trend. As you can see, assumptions are a very important step in creating a forecast.

The second step in making a forecast is to understand the relationships between economic variables on a historical basis. For example, when short-term interest rates rise, the odds favor a more volatile and selective stock market and poor price performance. This relationship is something the forecaster will have experienced and will likely make use of again in the future. Understanding this history provides a logical connection between economic variables.

The third step in developing a forecast is to understand what is happening now. The forecaster, for instance, can recognize whether interest rates are declining or are stable and is alert to signs pointing to a weak economy, giving a clear indication of what is happening now. Sometimes, as you probably already know if you follow the commentaries on television or the radio, not all economists agree on what is happening now, let alone what will happen. Is the money supply growing too rapidly? Are orders for durable goods too strong or too weak? An assessment of what is happening now is a crucial aspect in achieving an accurate forecast.

In the fourth step, the forecaster puts together all the previous steps— the assumptions, the historical connections of all the economic forces, and an understanding of the current economic climate. This leads the forecaster in the direction of determining what is happening. What is important to recognize is that there is a strong element of uncertainty in each one of these steps. Therefore, errors can be introduced with every progression in the development of a forecast. And this implies risk. The forecast is likely to be incorrect. Therefore, it is essential to recognize that an element of uncertainty exists and that investors need to protect themselves from the error of these forecasts. All the components of a forecast have to be clearly understood. As mentioned above, it is important to recognize the assumptions that have been made, the historical connection between the economic variables and what is happening now, and the process of extrapolation.

The more comfortable you are with the steps used, the more accurate the forecast will be. However, no matter how careful you are with your own forecast, it is important to remember there is always a strong element of uncertainty. The best way to reduce the uncertainty is to review the forecast often—every time a new piece of information is made available by government agencies, by the Federal Reserve, or by the market itself. All the new information should be introduced into the mix and the forecast begun again. This process will reduce the element of risk as it increases your understanding of what is happening.

Another important issue from an investment viewpoint is to recognize trends; this is where the money is made—not in forecasting. Is the economy going to grow at a rate of 2 percent or 6 percent? Is the economy going to start to slow down, or continue to slow down? Are interest rates going to continue to rise, or going to rise more slowly? Setting values—for example, interest rates will rise to 6 percent, or the economy will grow at 5 percent—is of limited help to an investor. Large profits can be derived only when investors recognize broad, fundamental trends. That's because once these trends are in place, they are likely to stay in place for months or even years. These are the trends that you will learn how to recognize from this book, and these are the trends that will help you profit.

Consider this simple equation and its financial impact on your entire portfolio of assets:

$$15\% + 15\% + 15\% - 15\% = 6\%$$

Yes, if your portfolio increased 15 percent per year for three consecutive years and you lost 15 percent the fourth year, then your total return for the four-year period would be slightly higher than 6 percent per year. This simple exercise demonstrates how important it is to protect your portfolio against losses.

Markets swing from one extreme to the other, which exposes your investments and profits to continuously changing risk and volatility. To see how you can protect yourself, take a cue from games of strategy. Acquire knowledge of a game before you play it so you know your odds of winning. Before you play poker or blackjack, chances are you take time to learn something about the game, and how different circumstances such as card sequences or dice rolls change the odds. The idea is to be aware of your chances of winning.

But even more important is being aware that the games are dynamic. The odds change as the game is being played. For instance, the odds of winning in team sports change depending on shifts in morale, injuries, and what happens to the other team during the course of the game. Think of any game you like, and several examples will come to mind. The importance of acquiring in-depth knowledge of the rules of the game is to establish risk. The main idea is to determine the chances of winning with a given set of strategies.

As a result, new strategies need to be developed to improve the odds of winning the game. It is a dynamic process the strategist must evaluate continually. It is very likely that financial strategists who review their strategies on a daily or weekly basis are likely to be more successful than those who review them monthly or quarterly. Financial decision making is no different from playing a game. At the end of a recession when companies are selling for a very low price, the odds of making money through acquisitions are very high. The same situation occurs after a long decline in stock prices. The odds of making money after a prolonged decline are very high. But as more and more investors recognize the situation and buy, the market rises and stocks become less attractive because now they have become expensive. In 'other words, as the market rises, the odds of losing money increase because a rising market is getting close to overvalued levels. The risk changes as the market moves.

In 1995, the economy slowed down and interest rates peaked. The Federal Reserve, for fear of too much of a slowdown, began to inject liquidity into the economy. With declining short-term interest rates and a market that went through some wide—though not sharp—declines in 1994, investors recognized that stocks were undervalued and began to buy. The stock market began to rise, accompanied by declining short-term interest rates and rapidly growing liquidity.

As soon as these trends become apparent, it is important to begin to buy—initially investing only a small amount of money, because the uncertainty is high and investors don't really know if this is the important bottom they were waiting for. But as soon as the trend appears to establish itself, investors should continue to increase their investment and establish their positions.

Now jump ahead four years. In 1999 the economy was very strong, the liquidity in the system began to grow more slowly, and interest rates started to rise. Clearly, the market was more expensive than what it was four years earlier. At such a time, the odds of losing money increase and are very high. As you will learn in this book, in this situation it is appropriate to slowly reduce your exposure to stocks and wait for better times. These are times when it is more appropriate to be in money-market instruments than to go through the frustration of having your portfolio lose value. The important thing to note about this example is that in 1995 there was a low-risk point for the market and investors should have increased their exposure to stock. In 1999 all the characteristics of much higher risk were present, and therefore investors should have exercised more caution.

Professionals continually evaluate this dynamic process on the basis of what happened one minute, one week, and one month earlier. In any game, and especially in business and financial management, you should invest an amount proportional to the probability of being right. So when the probability of being right is low, as it is in determining a turning point, you should invest only a small amount. As the probability of being right increases, you should increase the amount you invest in a position to take advantage of the higher chances of making money.

In 1995, for instance, as soon as interest rates started to decline and the money supply began to accelerate, investors should have recognized that stock prices were very close to the bottom. Of course, it is very difficult to know for sure if the market has hit bottom. The odds of being wrong at a turning point are very high. For this reason, in 1995 the best strategy would have been to recognize that declining interest rates were the harbingers of important changes in market trends. The appropriate way to approach this situation would have been to increase investment in stocks by a small amount. If you were wrong, and the market continued to decline, you would not have lost much because you had only a small amount invested.

On the other hand, if interest rates continued to head down and the market continued to rise, then you had more money, more capital to invest. You just have to wait a short time, perhaps one month. If you see that interest rates continue to decline and the growth of liquidity rises, then you know this is an important fundamental trend and you should increase your investment with the knowledge that the odds of being right in assessing the situation are good. You can then establish an investment strategy to take advantage of those odds.

When investors have to make a decision to buy or to sell, that decision is, in most cases, made complex and complicated because there is a tendency to always think in terms of buy or sell. Instead the decision can be made easier by deciding how much should be invested in that stock or asset or how much of it should be sold? As the probability of being right increases, the amount invested in a position should be raised to take advantage of the improved chances of making money. If the analysis of current events suggests the markets are approaching a top, this translates to a simple fact: Risk is increasing. Investors should start selling an amount based on how close they believe the market is to its top. One has to enter a certain position gradually and sell gradually. Since it is difficult to know exactly what the markets will do, it is much better for the investor to think of a gradual entry into a position or a gradual exit from a position.

Understanding what is happening in the markets is one of the most difficult things to do in establishing a strategy because there are overwhelming emotions involved. The data show you what is happening, but more often than not, investors don't want to believe the data. The year 1999 offers a good example of this situation. Rising short-term interest rates, a strong economy, and slower growth in liquidity made for a deadly combination for the stock market. Furthermore, a strong economy, as you will see later in this book, forces interest rates to rise, and so this deadly combination is likely to persist for some time. As emotions take over, investors don't want to believe what they see, and they always hope they might be wrong. The greed factor is also important and makes investors ignore what is happening.

However, once you recognize the bearish combination of factors for the stock market, the most appropriate action is to slowly reduce your investments in equities and become very selective. A small move is something you can take easily. For instance, reducing your exposure to stocks by 10 percent is probably the best way to start a defensive strategy. In 1999, as the majority of stocks kept declining, it would have been appropriate to reduce stocks by another 10 percent. As the situation continues to deteriorate and as the indicators continue to suggest caution, the odds of making money decrease. As the odds of losing money increase, it is appropriate to continue to sell slowly and gradually.

Turning points, that is, those points that offer the greatest profit opportunity, are very difficult to predict, because, again, they happen very rarely. A buying opportunity seldom happens, and for this reason, the probability of the market turning up is very small. What does that mean? Using the analogy of the poker player, that means if the probability of a winning hand is small, the amount you bet has to be small. When the time has come that risk is low and there is an opportunity to buy, investors will be well served to develop a strategy that says, "I'm going to invest 25 percent of my capital and see what happens." If the market goes in the direction expected, 75 percent of the money is still available to be invested. There is plenty of time to take advantage of the expected trend. If, on the other hand, investors were wrong and the market did not go up as they expected, the losses they incurr are small because of their small exposure to stocks. This is the advantage of investing with the odds of being right. This is what it's all about.

The same concept applies in a situation when investors decide to sell. The same gradual plan that is followed in a buy situation should be followed in a sell situation. If risk is increasing and the probabilities of a downturn are increasing, which means that the probabilities of making money are decreasing—again like a poker player—the investor has to bet less. Investors have to take some money off the table. For instance, they would have to sell 20 percent of their portfolio, or 15 percent— whatever their risk profile is. If they are right, they still have 80 or 85 percent invested and they can take advantage of the market rise. If the market starts to decline, as suspected, the odds of a bear market are increasing. Investors, therefore, should start selling more, for instance, another 20 or 30 percent. They gradually adjust to the trends in the market, and by doing so, greatly reduce the risk of their portfolio.

The temptation is to ponder the question, "Should I buy or sell?" But the issue is not whether to buy or sell, but whether the situation is attractive. The issue is how much you should buy or how much you should sell in order to have a portfolio that better reflects the risk profile of the markets.

The concept of risk, as we have discussed, provides an excellent guideline on how to do this. This approach leads to maximizing returns and minimizing risk.

Again, poker offers a good analogy. Players do not bet the same amount each time. They begin with a small bet because they do not know how their hand will develop. They increase their bet only if their hand looks promising. Depending on what the other players do, they raise their bet only if the odds of winning increase. If the odds turn against them and the risk of losing is too high, they fold their hand. Investing your money offers similar challenges. Whether we like it or not, we are all participants in the investment game. The markets are your opponents, and economic and financial forces—the "dealer"—are continually changing the risk-reward profile of each market. You need to adapt your investment strategy, that is, your bet, to the changing risk so that you protect your investment against the volatility of the markets.

The Dynamics of Risk Management

In managing your money and your portfolio risk, it is crucial to establish specific times to review your portfolio and strategies. Professionals are likely to review their strategies every day—every minute—as the data come through the screens. Avid investors may review their strategies every day or every week. Others prefer every month. What is important is that you review your strategy and reassess your risk with periodicity. The closer you keep an eye on the performance of your portfolio, the more successful you will be. If you do not have the time to perform this task, odds are that you have too many investments, too many stocks, too many bonds, and too many other assets that you have to follow. Try to choose a few assets, a few stocks, and follow them very closely. And if you do not have the time, give your money to a professional portfolio manager or an administrator who provides you with a weekly summary of the value of your investments. It is very difficult to be successful without closely monitoring the performance of your portfolio.

The choice of the investment period needs to suit your comfort level and style. Some investors like to day-trade. They feel comfortable investing early in the morning and then, after a few hours or a few seconds, selling their positions. The reason they feel comfortable is because they have developed their own indicators and methodology for investing. They review their decisions every minute after they have invested their money. On a minute-by-minute basis, they decide if they should continue to hold their current position or if they should sell. The investment period for them is very short. It fits their personality and above all fits with the model they have of how and why stock prices change. They feel comfortable with that model and are willing to make important investment decisions using it.

Other investors have identified certain cycles in the stock market during which stocks rise for anywhere from one to two weeks. For instance, when the market is oversold, volume increases and breadth expands, with a larger number of stocks rising. These investors take advantage of these patterns. They have determined that the odds of investing over a week or 10-day period are very profitable for them. Different from the day trader, they review their investment position every few hours, or every day, to make sure the trend is still in their favor. This style of investing is not as active as that of the day trader, but it is still a very intense way of investing.

There are other investors who feel more comfortable with longer investment periods and recognize that a favorable trend lasts for several months. These investors need to review information every week to make sure the trends and the factors that helped them make the decision to buy or sell are still in place.

Still other investors have a trading rule of buying only between the end of October and the end of April. They believe in the strong seasonality that exists in the stock market. According to this model, the period of May to October is very unfavorable.

Individual investors have their own personalities and their own psychological requirement when investing. Investing also depends greatly on the kind of rules that investors want to follow to make a particular decision. Whatever your personality and emotional characteristics, it is important to (1) decide what your investment period is, (2) recognize that the success of your investment program strongly relies on reviewing the performance of your portfolio, (3) review what caused your decision to buy or sell, and (4) maintain the flexibility to change that decision if it proves to be incorrect. Furthermore, it is important to move in small steps to avoid painful mistakes when a change in investment posture is required.

How do you manage risk? What is the process? Step 1 is to collect information. In the following pages, you will find the most important data you should follow to assess the risk of the various markets. You also will learn about ways of organizing information so that it becomes easily understood and can be easily interpreted.

Depending on the investment approach you choose, you have to select different types of information. If you are a day trader, you would likely be interested in sophisticated, technical patterns in stock prices and resistance and support levels, in volume patterns, and in hourly cycles in stock prices. On the other hand, if your investment period is several months, you would want to rely more on economic and financial data, and you would need to review this information every week or every two weeks.

The second step in the dynamics of risk management is to develop knowledge—that is, to have a model in your mind to process the information that you have collected in step 1. The main objective of the following pages is to provide you with this model—how to process, how to interpret, and how to use the information collected in step 1.

For instance, you will learn the reasons why a strong economy is followed by rising interest rates, and how to relate rising interest rates to the stock market and overall liquidity in the economic system. You will learn to recognize that an increase in liquidity and a decline in short-term interest rates, this usually happens when the economy is fairly weak, and that these conditions create an environment favorable to rising stock prices. There are many economic and financial factors that need to be tied together. The purpose of this book is to show you how to connect all this information and therefore recognize what is happening. Just learning to do this will help you make important projections in understanding the risk involved in the financial markets.

Step 3 is the most important and difficult phase in managing the risk of your portfolio. In this step you have to evaluate, on the basis of the model and the information collected, what the level and direction of the risk for the various markets are. This is one of the main objectives of this book.

In step 4 you have to answer three specific questions. Should you increase your investment in certain assets because you have determined in step 3 that risk is decreasing? Should you start selling because risk is increasing or becoming too high and it is not worth it to have so much money on the line? Or should you just stay with your current positions and do nothing? In step 4 you make your decision. The answer you give depends on your risk profile and how actively you want to manage your portfolio. Its main purpose is to adjust the mix of assets in your portfolio to the new risk level.

Let's assume that the investment environment is such that the economy is very strong and that, because of step 2, you have determined that the economy will remain strong. Let's also assume that short-term interest rates have been rising for more than two months. And using the methodology presented in this book, you determine that they will continue to rise. The outcome of step 3 tells you that the risk for the stock market is certainly going to increase.

As risk increases, the odds of making money decrease. Given the returns offered by money-market mutual funds, it often doesn't pay to tie up your money in the stock market. So you decide that the appropriate strategy is to reduce the amount of money you have in it. Remember, when the odds of winning are decreasing, you have to decrease the amount you bet. This is the outcome of step 4.

You also have to examine the other options that are available to you. For instance, a strong economy may cause commodities to rise, including crude oil, copper, gold, silver, palladium, and platinum. In this environment, one way to invest your money is to reduce your exposure to stocks and increase your exposure to energy and other commodity-type stocks.

Perhaps, the most difficult decision that investors have to make is whether it is better to be in cash or in the stock market. It is a difficult decision because you will always come across stories of some stocks rising and making new highs, even if a bear market is under way. What are the odds of finding those stocks? Very small. When the majority of stocks decline, the odds are that the investor will lose money by owning stocks. This is a good time to fold and to wait for the time when the odds of making money are considerably better.

Finally, once you have established the strategy, you have to implement it. And based on the period of time you have determined best for you, you will need to reevaluate your strategy.

Professional investors reevaluate their strategy daily because every day there is some new information available that might require a change in their strategy. One has to check for the latest information, process it through the model, decide if risk has increased or decreased, and then develop the new strategy: to start buying, start selling, or do nothing. And so this process is repeated everyday. This is the only way to protect yourself against losses. This is the only way you can make sure that the amount of money you have invested reflects the odds of making money. Again, if the odds of making money are low, you should not invest a lot of money. It just doesn't make sense.

The important steps to manage risk can be summarized as follows:

1. Collect information after you have decided on the investment period that best suits your personality.
2. Develop knowledge—have a model in your mind to help you understand the meaning of the information you have collected.
3. Evaluate the risk of the market based on the information you have collected and interpreted. Is the risk high and increasing or low and decreasing?
4. Establish a strategy. If risk is increasing, the strategy is to reduce your exposure to stocks. If, on the other hand, risk is decreasing, you may want to consider investing more of your capital in stocks.

These steps should be repeated in keeping with the investment period you have selected. The day trader evaluates this information and goes through these steps every minute. A 10–15-day investor reviews this information every day. The investor whose investment period is several months will likely review this information every week, or, at the very least, once a month.

What's Wrong with Buy and Hold and Averaging Down?

Buy and hold is the most popular investment strategy because it requires little or no thinking about the investment process. Of course, just the thought of this should make you realize that since nothing comes easy in life, then in itself buy and hold must have some pitfalls. The major pitfall of this strategy is that people believe that if they buy and hold a stock, over the long term they will make money. This is true when you are very young and you have many decades ahead of you. The problem is when you are very young—10 years old—you don't have much money to invest. The issue becomes important when you reach an age when you have a sizable nest egg and you realize that in a few years you are going to retire.

Let's say you are 45 or 50 years old. You have your retirement portfolio and want to grow this money so that when you retire at 65 you have a nice sum of capital to live on. The problem is that when you are 50, you cannot think long term because your investment horizon is no longer like a 10-year-old person's with many decades ahead. You have only 10 or 15 years. Therefore, buy and hold has little or no meaning for an investor who is 50 years old. This investor must determine what kind of investment environment he or she will face in the next 10 to 15 years. The 10-year-old investor with $10 does not care, because this child's capital is very small, and even with a crash in the economy, the child will not lose much money. And the chances are very good that over the next 50 or 60 years the market will rise anyway. This is a reasonable assumption. Buy and hold might be meaningful for a young investor, but has little practicality for a 50-year-old, soon-to-be-retired investor.

Buying and holding a stock involves making an investment and then forgetting about it. Eventually you are going to make money. It is a very simple decision, and there is really not much work involved. Now we have to talk about returns to better understand the risk involved in thinking long term. In this type of investment approach, the market—over the long term—has provided a return of roughly 10 to 11 percent—8 percent due to capital gains and close to 3 percent in dividends. Advisers say that since you can expect 11 percent over the long term, why try to do much else? Just find a good stock and wait for the capital to grow.

There is a huge hole in this argument. And it is that the market does not provide a return of 10 or 11 percent. That is an average. This average is from periods when the market does not do anything for many, many years, and periods when the market goes up 20 to 30 percent per year. Let's look at what happened last century.

The S&P 500 in 1928 was 17.66. In 1949 the S&P 500 was standing at 16.76—for 21 years the market had actually gone down. Looking at the Dow Jones Industrial Average, in 1900 the Dow Jones was at 77.66; and in 1932 it was at 50.16. Here we have a span of 32 years where the market was not doing much. Another more recent period is 1968–1982. In 1968 the S&P 500 was 100.53, and in 1982 it was 109.65—again, a period of 14 years where the market provided no returns. In this last period, some people might suggest that stock yields were higher. However, in this period, money-market mutual funds provided returns in the 10–15 percent range, which were much higher than the yield provided by stocks.

Buy and hold is an average. If the market has provided a 10 to 11 percent return, it is because there have been periods of 10, 15, even 20 years when the market did nothing, and periods of 10 to 20 years, like the period from 1982 to 1999, when the market provided close to a 20 percent per year return. When you average these two periods, it comes out to roughly the average long-term return. Buy and hold is dangerous. Let's say a 55-year-old investor is planning to retire in an environment like we had in 1968, and he wants to invest over the so-called long-term. By 1982 he has experienced several serious bear markets with its capital declining by 20 to 30 percent each time. If he is lucky, by 1982 he breaks even. This is a nerve-racking experience indeed.

Investing blindly is not a solution. The risk is always there, whether we want to believe it or not, and the knowledgeable investor has to recognize the conditions that might create a period of well-below-average returns. Another pitfall or risk of buy and hold is that if the market, as it did in the seventies, goes down 30 to 40 percent, investors believing in long-term investing would be seriously shaken because their assets were reduced by 30 to 40 percent. Managing volatility of return is still an issue the investor has to face.

Another way of investing is averaging down. By following this strategy, investors increase their investment in stocks by a given amount of money with some regularity. For instance, an investor decides to invest $50 or $100 every month in stocks. With averaging down, people are urged to keep investing even if the market declines. By investing the same amount of money as the price of the stock declines, the investor owns an increasing amount of shares of that particular stock. This is a mechanical rule that has a lot of appeal because it requires not much work and not much understanding of what goes on in the marketplace.

This investment strategy is based on the assumption that the market always goes up; and as we saw before, the market does not always go up. There are periods, sometimes lasting 10 to 20 years, when the market provides no returns. What is the rationale of continuing to invest when the market declines 30 to 40 percent? Why keep losing money? As every poker player knows, when you have losing cards in your hand, you're better off saving your money and folding. Losing money seriously impacts the total return of your portfolio. It is considerably more profitable to wait until conditions are better and then start investing when the time seems to be more appropriate. No serious investor buys in a declining market because the probability of losing money is very high. Serious investors buy when the market is oversold and starts rising, when there are serious reasons to believe there is a turning point under way and the market is turning up. There is no easy way of making money or managing volatility. Making money, as any businessperson or investor knows, is very difficult and intensive work. It is a knowledge-based "game," and the following pages will provide you with further information on how to play it successfully.

There are no easy formulas in investing. If there were, everybody would be a millionaire. Successful investing is a process that takes time and dedication. The objective of this book is to provide a framework for you to begin managing your money, so that you can make informed decisions based on the odds you have of making money.

Chapter
2

ECONOMIC INDICATORS

The prices of all assets are impacted by changes in economic growth. As investors study the changes taking place in the economy, they are able to determine which assets are going to appreciate the most and which ones have a downside risk. Of course, as the prices of these assets change, investors need to change their investment strategy. However, we need to explore some more concepts about business cycles before we can discuss the idea of strategy in detail.

In this chapter we will examine the main economic indicators and data available from various sources, and see how to interpret them. In later chapters we will discuss the relationships between these measures of economic activity. This is important in order to make a forecast to assess the risks of the markets. Then we will analyze how these measures will impact asset prices.

Economic Indicators

The first step is to make a list of what these indicators are, what they represent, and how they should be interpreted. Most of the data are available on the Internet from the various sources listed below.

In order to make the presentation of these indicators more organized and easier to follow, we can subdivide them into indicators that measure broad economic activity, consumer activities, manufacturing and capital investment activity, construction, inflation, productivity, and profits. It's important to keep in mind, however, that in the real world these indicators are interrelated.

For instance, if a central bank increases liquidity in the economic system, this increased liquidity is used by business. This increased liquidity is usually accompanied by lower interest rates, and the combination of increased liquidity and lower interest rates encourages business to borrow, to hire people, and to make new investments. Because of this activity, income increases, employment increases, consumer confidence rises, and the economy becomes stronger. In order to have an appreciation of these relationships and all the connections between them, we first need to examine all these measures and study in detail what they mean and their various sources. Later chapters show in detail how these measures are interrelated and what the cause-and-effect relationships are between them.

Broad Measures of Economic Activity

The broadest measure of economic activity is the gross domestic product (GDP). From an investment viewpoint, it is not used very much because it is only released every quarter and does not represent timely data for investors. However, it is important to know what it is and what information we can derive from these types of data.

The GDP represents the output of goods and services produced by labor and property located in the United States. It is measured in terms of dollars and is available quarterly from the Bureau of Economic Analysis.

The GDP is the sum of four elements: (1) personal consumption expenditures, (2) gross private domestic investments, (3) net exports of goods and services, and (4) government consumption expenditures.

Personal consumption expenditures represent what consumers spend on durable goods, such as motor vehicles, parts, and furniture, and what consumers spend on nondurable goods, such as food, clothing, gasoline, and services such as utilities, transportation, and medical care. The importance of personal consumption expenditures is that they represent roughly 60 percent of the U.S. economy. It is because this sector of the economy is so large that economists spend an enormous amount of energy trying to understand the behavior of consumers.

Gross private domestic investments represent the sum of fixed investments and change in business inventories. Fixed investments represent investments in nonresidential structures and producers' durable equipment—such as machinery used in a plant. Then there are fixed investments in residential structures, such as single-family and multifamily homes.

A key element in the gross domestic product is the net exports of goods and services. This is the difference between exports and imports. It is a very important measure, because it has a major long-term impact on the dollar, and therefore on the returns of foreign investments, as we will discuss later. One of the main elements is that net exports eventually have to become positive, because a country cannot experience a large trade deficit, with imports greater than exports, for a very long time without having its currency sharply devalued.

The last element of the gross domestic product is government expenditures at both the federal and state level. Some economists say that the greater the size of the government expenditures as a percentage of the GDP, the slower the growth of the economy over the long term. The ultimate example is what happened to the Soviet Union, where government expenditures were 100 percent of GDP. The outcome was a total collapse of the Soviet Union.

The concept of growth is relative to the average long-term growth of the economy, and the average long-term growth of the economy can and does change, depending on the overall policies of the government. For instance, in the 1970s because of rising inflation and all the problems that rising inflation brought to the U.S. and the European economy, the average growth of the economy was very close to 2 percent. In the 1980s and 1990s as inflation came down, the average growth of the economy grew to 3 percent and even higher in the U.S. The question now remains, what is strong growth and weak growth?

In the 1970s when the average growth rate of the economy was close to 2 percent, strong economic conditions would materialize when GDP grew at a rate above 2 percent. However, in the 1980s and 1990s as the average growth rate of GDP jumped to 3 percent due to major improvements in productivity, strong economic growth was experienced when business conditions expanded at a rate above 3 percent. Similarly, when the average growth rate of the economy was close to 2 percent, weak economic conditions would materialize when GDP grew at a rate below 2 percent.

The point is that the concept of growth is relative and depends on the economic times. We will see how inflation is one of the major determinants to understand and recognize the type of growth the economy will have.

Consumer Indicators

The most important indicator relating to consumers' well-being is the monthly report on employment. Strong growth in employment implies the economy is strong, consumers are making money, and they are willing to spend. A decline in employment growth means that consumers will spend less due to slower growth in income, and they will be more cautious in spending.

What is strong growth in employment? In order to assess the strength of an indicator, assuming that the overall long-term growth of employment is just below 2.0 percent, depending on what period you choose and how you measure long-term growth. Suppose, for example employment grows 0.1 percent month to month. You multiply this figure times 12 to get an annual rate (this is a very rough approximation) of 1.2 percent growth in employment, which is below the 2.0 percent overall long-term growth. This tells you that business is growing slowly.

On the other hand, if employment grows 0.5 percent month to month, a rough estimate of the annualized growth rate is close to 6 percent, which is obtained by multiplying 0.5 percent by 12. Six percent is a very strong growth rate and reflects a very strong economy. The Bureau of Labor Statistics releases employment numbers in the early part of the month for the preceding month.

Another number released along with employment figures is the unemployment rate. If the unemployment rate declines, the economy is very strong; there are more people being employed than supplied by the labor force.

When the unemployment rate stabilizes at a low level, it means that labor becomes tight and the economy is expanding to close to full capacity. Wages start rising faster, and Wall Street becomes concerned about the risks of higher inflation. When the unemployment rate increases, the economy is slowing down, employment growth is slower than the growth of the labor force, and the odds favor the economy to begin to grow at a below-average pace.

The help-wanted advertising index measures the demand for labor. It is an important indicator, because when this indicator declines, it means that business has decided to hire fewer people and employment in the future is likely to grow at a slower pace. This indicator deserves special attention because it tends to lead trends in unemployment. The help-wanted index is available from the *Wall Street Journal* or *Barron's*.

Information on retail sales is also available monthly and represents how much consumers are buying at retail stores. Strong retail sales reflect strong employment growth, a strong economy, and strong income. This measure is used to confirm the strength of the overall economy. Retail sales data are released by the Census Bureau.

Several surveys measure consumer attitudes, and the Conference Board issues an index of consumer confidence. The University of Michigan makes available a survey of consumer sentiment. This survey is the result of questions presented to a select sample group of consumers regarding how they feel about the overall economy and what their attitudes are toward purchasing goods, toward purchasing autos, about the future of the economy, about the future of inflation, and about their income. The answers are ranked, and an index reflecting consumer sentiment is computed.

When the University of Michigan's index of consumer sentiment is close to 100, consumers are very positive about the economy and its outlook, and they are willing to spend. A high consumer sentiment means that the economy will stay strong, retail sales will be strong, and employment will be strong.

However, when consumer sentiment declines, the economy will slow down because of the importance of consumer spending on the overall business cycle. One has to watch consumer sentiment very closely, especially when it declines close to 80–90; the odds are that a recession or a period of very slow growth is imminent or actually under way.

Another indicator related to consumer well-being is consumer installment credit. This figure reflects the amount of money borrowed on installment credit and is released by the Federal Reserve. It is an important indicator on the finances of consumers and their capability on spending.

Strong growth in consumer installment credit indicates that consumers are willing to borrow more because they feel comfortable about the future, and therefore the economy will be stronger. During such times it is not unusual for interest rates to rise. Slower growth in consumer credit is the result of higher interest rates and an economy that is slowing down.

Closely related to all these data, and probably one of the most important measures, is personal income. Income is closely related to employment, retail sales, and consumer confidence. Strong growth in personal income suggests that consumers are feeling good about the future, employment is strong, and retail sales are robust. The growth in personal income closely mirrors the growth of the overall economy or GDP.

More liquidity in the system and declining inflation and interest rates create the necessary conditions for people to buy and businesses to invest and expand production. As the economy strengthens, employment increases, and the increase in employment is accompanied by an increase in income. The increase in income, of course, encourages consumers to spend, and therefore retail sales tend to rise.

A slowdown in personal income is usually a sign that things are cooling off, and is reflected in lower growth in employment and lower retail sales. A slowdown in the economy, which is usually anticipated by rising inflation, rising interest rates, and some tightening from the central bank, causes businesses to become more cautious about their outlook and about their production plans. By reducing employment to keep costs under control, personal income slows down. Because of the slow-down in personal income, consumers tend to be more cautious about their spending, resulting in slower retail sales. The monthly data on personal income are available from the Bureau of Economic Analysis.

An indicator that is widely followed because it is made available weekly by the Bureau of Labor Statistics is the average weekly initial claims for unemployment insurance, which measures the number of people applying for unemployment insurance. When this index increases, it is a sign that the economy is slowing down. When the number of people applying for unemployment insurance declines, the economy is strengthening, because there are more and more people finding jobs.

One way of assessing the strength of the economy is to examine the level of initial unemployment claims. If the level is very low by historical standards—a level close to 300,000—this means the economy is very strong, employment is growing very rapidly, the labor market is very tight, and economic conditions are great. These conditions are what analysts call "overheated." Under these conditions, investors should expect wages to be rising faster. The higher that initial unemployment claims go above 300,000, the more the economy is weakening. Now many people are applying for unemployment claims, the labor market is not as tight, and so business activity is very weak. Under these conditions, investors should expect wages to begin to slow down. The unemployment insurance indicator is available from the Bureau of Labor Statistics.

To sum up, a strong economy is reflected by a group of trends that are unmistakable:

- Employment growth is strong, close to 2–3 percent.

- Help-wanted advertising increases as labor demand also increases.

- Retail sales grow rapidly, above 4–5 percent, year on year, reflecting strong consumer confidence, which is usually at levels well above 90 or 100, using the University of Michigan consumer sentiment measure.

- Consumer installment credit is also rising rapidly, reflecting high consumer confidence in future income, and therefore an increased level of borrowing activity.

- Because of a strong economy and strong employment growth, personal income is increasing.

- Initial unemployment claims decline.

A slowdown of the economy can be recognized when:

- Employment growth begins to slow down below 2 or 3 percent.

- Help-wanted advertising declines, a sign that business will be hiring fewer people.

- Retail sales slow down, confirming that employment is weakening.

- The index of consumer sentiment declines, measuring the fact that people don't feel as confident about the future because of slower growth in employment and in income.

- Consumer installment credit also tends to slow down, as people borrow less because they see uncertainty in the future and in their income growth. This, of course, is the result of weakening economic conditions and lower unemployment figures.

- This situation is also reflected by a steady rise in initial unemployment insurance claims.

Manufacturing and Investment Indicators

The index of industrial production released monthly by the Federal Reserve provides a complete picture of trends in manufacturing. It is a comprehensive report showing the growth in various sectors of the manufacturing industry. The manufacturing sector is strong when growth is above 0.3 or 0.4 on a monthly basis. Accelerating industrial output is a sign that employment, sales and income are strong and the economy is robust.

A slowdown in the industrial production index is a sign that employment and income will slow down, and sales are weaker. Trends in the industrial production index, as we will see later, is also closely related to trends in overall commodity prices. A strengthening industrial sector is usually associated with firm commodities, and a weakening manufacturing index is followed by declining commodities.

Average weekly hours paid per production on a supervisory worker per week is another important indicator of economic activity, especially in manufacturing. The importance of this indicator lies in the fact that when manufacturers want to reduce output, the first thing they do is cut working hours. Eventually, they will lay off workers.

The same thing happens when the economy improves. First, manufacturers expand working hours, and then they hire workers. Average weekly hours provide clues on the future of industrial production. Changes in average weekly hours tend to lead changes in economic activity.

Another indicator that provides clues on the future of industrial activity is overtime. Average weekly overtime hours of production constitute a leading indicator of economic activity because the manufacturing sector tends to cut overtime first, when it sees economic activity or demand for goods slowing down. The same thing happens when the economy starts improving. The first action that the businessperson takes is to extend overtime hours before hiring new people. All the above data are available in the employment release. This information is available from the Bureau of Labor Statistics.

New orders for durable goods and new orders for consumer goods are important data because they provide an indication of what is on the books of manufacturers. Rising orders suggest manufacturing will have to place those orders into production and step up production activity. If, on the other hand, orders decline or slow down, there are fewer orders to be processed through the manufacturing plants, and industrial output is likely to decline.

When orders are received by an organization, they are not filled right away, because the organization or the plant is busy fulfilling previously received orders. Current orders are therefore placed in a backlog and are scheduled to be produced in the future when manufacturing capacity becomes available. For this reason, rising orders are a reliable indicator that the manufacturing sector will improve.

On the other hand, if orders begin to decline, the organization will have to reduce production. For this reason, orders are a very important leading indicator of what will happen to the manufacturing and nonmanufacturing sectors. They are an excellent indicator of future economic health.

Orders for durable goods are particularly volatile because big-ticket items are subject to consumer sentiment. The volatility of new orders is caused by the fact that most consumers react at the same time to changes in interest rates and inflation. The reason is that to purchase durable goods—items that have a shelf life of three to four years, items like automobiles, refrigerators, furniture, and so on—people have to commit large sums of money.

When economic conditions change because of rising inflation or interest rates, almost all consumers will respond to that increase at the same time, and therefore orders decline sharply. The rise in inflation produces a very important chain reaction in the business and financial cycles.

A rise in inflation has a very important effect on the income of the working and nonworking populations. Rising inflation reduces the purchasing power of consumers, and the more inflation rises, the higher the loss of purchasing power. The outcome is that consumers defend themselves against the loss of purchasing power by first reducing purchases of big-ticket items and then eventually reducing purchases of small-ticket items. The outcome of reduced spending is a decline in orders, and therefore a slowdown in economic activity.

An increase in inflation also is accompanied by an increase in interest rates, and therefore an increase in borrowing costs. This increase in borrowing costs leads to further declines in purchases on the part of consumers and in investments on the part of business.

A decline in inflation has exactly the opposite effect of a rise in inflation. A decline in inflation is welcomed by consumers because it increases the purchasing power of the working population. Also, declining inflation is accompanied by lower interest rates. So we have two positive effects on consumer purchasing power. First, lower inflation increases purchasing power, and, second, lower interest rates decrease the cost of borrowing. Both lead the consumer to purchase and the businessperson to invest. Now consumers are inclined to borrow to purchase those items they found too expensive when inflation and interest rates were rising. The outcome is an increase in orders, which results in the improved growth of the economy.

This is the reason why orders provide important information about the future of the economy. Orders for durable goods represent the willingness of business to expand capacity and improve productivity, which is an essential element for economic growth.

Another important indicator concerning manufacturing health and trends is unfilled orders, or the backlogs on the books of the manufacturing sectors. If unfilled orders increase rapidly, manufacturing does not have the capacity to produce goods, and this implies manufacturing will be busy filling these unfilled orders. It suggests that the economy will strengthen. If, on the other hand, unfilled orders decline, manufacturing will be forced to slow down and produce fewer goods. Information about orders is released by the Census Bureau.

The National Association of Purchasing Managers provides two important reports: one on the manufacturing sector and one on the nonmanufacturing sector. The index of business activity provided in the reports by this professional group indicates how the economy is doing. It is an index that oscillates above 50 or below 50. An increase in the index well above 50 implies that the economy is expanding rapidly. A decline in the index means that the economy is slowing down. If the index falls below 50, the economy is growing very slowly.

From an investor's viewpoint, this index is very easy to use. It provides simple guidelines for developing an investment strategy. When the index rises above 50, investors have to look for those events that are typically associated with a strong economy growing at an above-average pace. Investors should look for rising interest rates and upward pressure on inflation. We will see later how this could be used to develop an investment strategy.

However, when the index falls below 50, investors are warned that the economy is growing at a below-average pace, and therefore they should expect events that are typically associated with a slower growth in the economy, such as declining interest rates and declining inflation.

An important indicator released by the purchasing managers is called vendor performance. This is an index that shows the percentage of companies reporting slower deliveries. When this indicator rises, more and more companies are reporting slower deliveries, which is an indication that the manufacturing sector is very busy and the economy is very strong.

Vendor performance can be used to confirm the trends and the information provided by the overall index of the National Association of Purchasing Managers. Investors using this indicator will be warned that if this gauge rises above 50, the economy is strengthening, growing above potential. Therefore, they should expect rising inflation and interest rates. The higher the indicator goes above 50, the more pronounced the increase in inflation and interest rates is.

When this gauge falls below 50, the economy slows down and is growing below potential. Investors should expect declining inflation and declining interest rates. The more pronounced the decline is below 50, the more pronounced the decline in inflation and interest rates is.

Change in inventories is another important indicator of manufacturing health. Acceleration in inventories indicates manufacturing is building up inventories at a faster and faster pace trying to meet strong sales. A strong inventory accumulation suggests the economy is robust. On the other hand, when inventory growth declines, it signals a slowdown in the manufacturing process.

An important gauge used to gain more insight into this process is the inventory-to-sales ratio. The inventory-to-sales ratio is computed at the merchant wholesalers and the manufacturing and trade levels and is calculated by the Department of Commerce. The ratio is found by dividing total inventories in dollar terms by sales over a month. If the inventory-to-sales ratio is low and stable, inventories and sales are in balance and the economy is doing well.

A decline in the inventory-to-sales ratio indicates that sales are growing faster than inventories and that manufacturing must catch up with sales. This indicates a very strong economy.

However, when the inventory-to-sales ratio is rising, it indicates that manufacturing is building inventories at a rate faster than sales. This situation suggests that manufacturing will have to slow down output to keep inventories in balance with sales. For these reasons, the inventory-to-sales ratio is an important gauge to assess the growth of the economy and to confirm the strengths or weaknesses of business activity.

For instance, in 1993–1994, the inventory-to-sales ratio declined quite sharply from 1.45 to 1.37. The information had to be used to conclude that sales were growing much faster than inventories. Manufacturing was forced to build inventories and, therefore, increase production. A declining inventory-to-sales ratio means that the economy is strong. Usually a similar trend is found in the unemployment rate, with the unemployment rate declining as employment grows more rapidly than the supply of labor. Then, the inventory-to-sales ratio rose sharply in 1995 from 1.37 to 1.45, suggesting the economy was slowing down.

In 1997–1998, the manufacturing sector weakened due to the financial crisis in Asia: and because of the weakness in demand, the inventory-to-sales ratio increased from 1.36 to 1.40 over two years. This was an indication that business was slowing down rapidly, sales were slowing down faster than inventories, and therefore manufacturing was forced to slow down production to match the growth in inventories to the growth in sales. The continued increase in inventory-to-sales ratio indicated a weakening in the economy.

As soon as the financial crisis of Asia normalized in late 1998, business from Asia increased, demand for U.S. goods increased, the manufacturing sector improved, and the inventory-to-sales ratio declined rapidly, indicating that the economy was very strong again. The trend in the inventory-to-sales ratio is a very useful gauge to confirm other information derived from different sources.

Comparing growth in inventories to growth in sales is also a good indicator of the health of the economy. If inventories are growing slowly and sales are growing rapidly, it is clear that the manufacturer will have to increase output to build inventories to match sales. The opposite also is true. If sales are sluggish and inventories are growing rapidly, manufacturers are likely to cut back production to slow down growth of inventories until inventory accumulation matches the growth rate of sales.

As businesses increase inventories to meet increasing sales, they have to borrow more to finance inventories. During such times, business borrowing increases, placing upward pressure on short-term interest rates.

When inventories are reduced, businesses need less money to finance inventory buildup and business borrowing slows down. Slower growth in borrowing places downward pressure on the demand for money and on short-term interest rates. What is suggested is that trends in the price of money, i.e., interest rates, are greatly influenced by demand. Inventory data are available from the Bureau of the Census.

The above indicators will give you a sense that the manufacturing sector is strong if:

- The index of industrial production is rising above 3 to 4 percent a year.

- Average weekly hours are rising, which is positive in the sense that income is increasing, but also negative because it might be an indication that inflation pressures are increasing.

- Overtime hours are rising.

- There is an increase in durable-goods orders.

- There is an increase in backlogs.

- The index of the National Association of Purchasing Managers moves above 50.

- The index of vendor performance moves above 50.

- Inventories are accelerating.

- The inventory-to-sales ratio is declining.

The manufacturing sector gives signs of weakening when:

- The growth industrial production index declines below 3 to 4 percent a year.

- The average weekly hours are declining, which is negative in the sense that income is decreasing, but also positive because it might be an indication that inflation pressures are decreasing.

- Overtime hours are declining.

- There is a decline in durable-goods orders.

- There is a decline in backlogs.

- The index of the National Association of Purchasing Managers moves below 50.

- The index of vendor performance moves below 50.

- Inventories are slowing down.

- The inventory-to-sales ratio rises.

Construction Indicators

Construction indicators are important because this sector is a major source of employment. Trends in housing starts and building permits reflect the strength of the economy and provide an indication of future economic trends. Housing starts and business structures rise when interest rates are stable or declining and the economy is improving.

However, as soon as uncertainties arise and interest rates begin to increase, consumers and investors immediately curtail their purchase of houses and investment in new construction. Trends in the housing sector are closely related to trends in interest rates. An increase in interest rates raises the cost of borrowing, and therefore considerably raises the cost of buying either a house or other property. For this reason, an increase of interest rates is followed by slower growth in the housing sector and eventually in an outright decline.

The odds favor higher interest rates as long as the housing sector is strong and people borrow to buy houses. Interest rates will decline only after a prolonged decline in the housing sector, a sign that investors have decided to wait for much lower interest rates before beginning new investments in the construction business.

However, with a decline in interest rates, there is a sense that business conditions will improve, and the construction sector is one of the first to revive. When interest rates decline, which is typically preceded by a prolonged decline in the housing sector, the low cost of money again encourages investors and businesses to borrow to invest in housing and construction projects.

The housing sector revives only after interest rates have passed their peak and are on their way down. The housing sector will grow rapidly as long as interest rates are declining or are stable. The first signs that the housing sector is likely to weaken happen when interest rates bottom out and eventually begin to rise due to the strong economic environment. Information on construction activity is available from the Census Bureau.

Other important data in this sector are the level of new-home sales and existing-home sales. They provide information on the consumers' willingness to spend. Reports releasing this information also indicate the average price paid for houses and provide an indication of the level of inflation existing in the real estate business. Home sales are closely related to the behavior of housing starts. These data are available from the National Association of Realtors.

A strong construction sector is associated with a rapid growth in housing starts, in building permits, and in the level of new-home sales and

existing-home sales. A period of strong construction is typically associated with declining or stable interest rates. The construction sector weakens following an increase in interest rates and will remain weak as long
as interest rates are on a rising trend.

The main reason why the construction sector is so sensitive to interest
rate strengths is because borrowing costs are one of the main determinants used by investors to establish the attractiveness of investing in real
estate.

Inflation Indicators

The most popular measure of inflation is the increase in consumer prices
over a 12-month period. When you read in the newspaper that inflation
is 2.7 percent, it means that the consumer price index, which will be discussed in greater detail later in this section, has risen 2.7 percent in the
previous 12 months. Investors need to follow closely the trend in inflation. To do so, they need to compare the current growth in consumer
prices with what it was a month ago, two months ago, three months ago,
and so on. Later on in this book, you will be provided with ample back-
ground on how to predict the trend of inflation.

Inflation is a very important measure to follow because the economy
and financial markets thrive during times of declining or low inflation
(below 3 percent). Years when inflation is rising are characterized by
extreme volatility of the economy and the financial markets. This is true
not only for the U.S. economy, but also for any economy around the
globe—from Latin America to Europe to Asia.

As it has been shown conclusively by Milton Friedman, inflation is
solely and exclusively a monetary phenomenon. In other words, inflationary pressures depend on the monetary policy followed by the Fed.
Chapter 7 discusses in great detail how central banks can impact the
inflation of a country.

From an investment viewpoint, changes in inflation impact the financial markets and asset prices in different ways. Declining inflation is
favorable to stocks and bonds. However, rising inflation makes real
estate, precious metals, and other hard assets more attractive than stocks
and bonds.

Commodity prices are probably the most sensitive and meaningful
indicator about future trends in inflation. Commodities are raw materials to be used in the production of goods. These are commodities
such as:

- Grains and feeds—for example, barley, wheat, and corn
- Commodities classified as foods—in this category: beef, broilers, butter, cocoa, eggs, ham, hogs, pork, and steer
- Fats and oils, such as coconut meats, coconut oil, coconut palm, lard, soybean, and tallow
- Oil, which includes different types of crude oil, domestic crude grades, and refined products
- Fibers and textiles—such as burlap, cotton, and wool
- Metals, including aluminum, copper, lead, steel scrap, tin, and zinc
- Precious metals, such as gold, silver, platinum, and palladium
- Miscellaneous commodities, such as rubber and hides

All these commodities are used in the production of goods, and so a change in the price of these commodities provides very useful information on trends in the economy. Most of these commodities tend to follow the same trend most of the time. This seems to be difficult to accept. However, when the economy is strong, demand increases across the commodity spectrum.

There are two types of commodity prices. One type is called the spot price, and the other is the price of futures. In the spot market a commodity is priced for immediate delivery. In the futures market a commodity is priced for delivery at a future date. For instance, the price of oil for delivery in a month is different from the price of oil for delivery in two months, three months, and so on. The difference for all these prices is market conditions, storage costs, interest rates, and transportation costs.

Spot prices of industrial materials are the first ones to respond to acceleration or deceleration in manufacturing and overall business activity. Since it is difficult to analyze all these commodities one by one, to make the process of analysis simpler, analysts have established indexes for groups of commodities that have the same functions: grains, foods, fats, fibers and textiles, and precious metals.

Bridge/CRB publishes the most popular indexes of these commodities. This organization releases two main indexes: the CRB Index for spot prices and the CRB Index for futures prices. The CRB index for spot prices is an index that reflects the price of the components of the spot level, while the CRB index for futures reflects the futures price of the components. The CRB industrial materials index (spot and futures) can be found on the website of Bridge/CRB (crbindex.com).

Commodity prices reflect the judgment of the marketplace, the strength of the economy, and the inflationary policies of the Fed. An overall strengthening of the commodity market reflects the fact that the economy is very strong, and the increase in commodity prices will eventually be passed on by the producers of goods to the final consumer. An increase in commodity prices has an inflationary implication and as a result, investors should expect upward pressure on short-term and long-term interest rates. This is the main reason why commodity prices provide crucial information for the investor. By closely watching the trends in commodities, the investor can begin to think about the possibility of rising interest rates and the tightening of monetary policies, which will be discussed in detail in Chapter 7. Of course, such trends greatly impact the risk in investing in stocks and bonds.

Other important gauges of inflation are gold and crude oil prices. Although crude oil prices have much more volatility than gold because they are controlled by a cartel, the basic trends and turning points are the same. It is always a good assumption to believe that all commodities follow the same trend. It is very unusual, for instance, to see an increase in gold prices without also seeing an increase in copper prices and crude oil prices. Or to put it in a different way, a strong move in copper but not in gold or other commodities would make the increase in copper suspect. The reason is that commodity prices are driven by the strength of the economy, and when the economy is strong, all commodities rise. On the other hand, when commodities are weak, investors should expect a weaker economy.

The importance of following many commodities and commodity indexes is that they all tend to rise in the same direction when inflationary pressures are rising and are strong. The more that commodities rise, the higher the risk of rising inflation. If most commodities decline, the outlook for inflation is benign.

Another indicator that is important to follow to determine inflationary pressures is wages. Wages usually accelerate when the unemployment rate declines and stabilizes, meaning that the labor market is tight. These are also times when unemployment claims are low.

Acceleration in wages, as we will see below, is not necessarily inflationary, because increases in productivity absorb increases in wages. In fact, this is exactly what you want to see in a strong economy. The ideal situation is to experience wages growing at a 3 to 4 percent pace and productivity expanding at the same rate. In these conditions, labor costs (wages adjusted for productivity) are zero and wages are not inflationary. However, if productivity growth is zero and labor costs adjusted for productivity rise at a 3 to 4 percent pace, this is clearly inflationary. Information about wages and productivity is released by the Bureau of Labor Statistics.

The producer price index provides information on the pricing power of producers and manufacturers of goods. There are several measures released by the Bureau of Labor Statistics: the producer price index for finished goods; the producer price index for semifinished goods—that is, goods that need further processing; and the producer price index of raw materials. So the producer price index (PPI) is actually a family of indexes that measure the average change over time in the selling prices received by domestic producers of goods and services.

The PPI measures price changes from the perspective of the seller. This contrasts with other measures, such as the consumer price index (CPI), which measures price changes from the purchasers' perspective. Sellers' and purchasers' prices may differ, due to government subsidies, sales and excise taxes, and distribution costs. Over 10,000 PPIs for individual products and groups of products are released each month. PPIs are available for the products of virtually every industry in the money, mining, and manufacturing sectors of the U.S. economy.

New PPIs are gradually being introduced for the products of industries in the transportation, utilities, trade, finance, and service sectors of the economy. Producer price index data are widely used by the business community as well as the government. The three major uses are:

1. As an economic indicator. The PPIs capture price movements prior to their retail level. Therefore, they may foreshadow subsequent price changes for businesses and consumers. The President, Congress, and the Federal Reserve employ these data in formulating fiscal and monetary policy.

2. As a deflator of other economic series. PPIs are used to adjust other economic information for price changes to translate those data into inflation-free dollars. For example, constant-dollar gross domestic product is estimated using deflators based on PPI data.

3. As a basis for contract escalation. PPI data are commonly used in escalating purchasing and sales contracts. These contracts typically specify dollar amounts to be paid at some point in the future. It is often desirable to include escalation clauses that account for increases in input prices. For example, a long-term contract for bread may be escalated for changes in wheat prices by applying the percentage change in the PPI for wheat to the contracted price for bread.

While both the PPI and the consumer price index measure price change over time for a fixed set of goods and services, they differ in two critical areas: 1) the composition of the set of goods and services and 2) the type of prices collected for the included goods and services.

The target set of goods and services included in the PPI is the entire marketed output of U.S. producers. The set includes both goods and services purchased by other producers as inputs to their operations or as capital investments, as well as goods and services purchased by consumers either directly from service producers or indirectly from retailers. Because the PPI target is the output of U.S. producers, imports are excluded.

The target set of items included in the CPI is the set of goods and services purchased for consumption purposes by urban U.S. households, including imports. The producer price index, as its name suggests, is an index and as such is a tool that simplifies the measurement of movements in a numerical series. Movements are measured with respect to the base period when the index is set to 100. An index of 110, for example, means that there has been a 10 percent increase in prices since the base period. Similarly, an index of 90 indicates a 10 percent decrease. The typical way of expressing the increase in producer price index, for analysis purposes, is done by comparing the index of this month with the index for the same month 12 months ago. It is used by comparing the rate of change over 12 months. The PPI rate of change over 12 months is calculated by dividing the current month by the same month a year ago, subtracting 1 from the result, and then multiplying the outcome by 100.

The turning points of all these measures take place at the same time. When one of those indexes slows down, they all slow down. The difference is in their volatility. Changes in producer prices of crude materials are much more volatile than changes in producer prices of semiprocessed goods or changes in producer prices of finished goods.

A broad measure of inflation, the one that we all relate to, is the consumer price index. The CPI is a measure of the average change over time in the prices paid by consumers for a market basket of consumer goods and services. The CPI provides a way for consumers to compare the change in prices of the market basket of goods and services.

The consumer price index affects nearly all Americans because of the way it is used. Three major uses are (1) as an economic indicator, (2) as a deflator of economic series to eliminate the effect of inflation, and (3) as a means of adjusting dollar values. The CPI reflects spending patterns of the population. It is based on the expenditures of almost all residents of urban or metropolitan areas, including professionals, the self-employed, the poor, the unemployed, and retired persons, as well as urban wage earners and clerical workers.

Not included in the CPI are the spending patterns of persons living in rural, nonmetropolitan areas; farm families; persons in the armed forces; and those in institutions such as prisons and mental hospitals. The CPI market basket is developed from detailed expenditure information provided by families and individuals on what they actually bought. The CPI represents all goods and services purchased for consumption by the referenced population. The Bureau of Labor Statistics has classified all expenditure items in more than 200 categories into eight major groups:

1. Food and beverages (breakfast cereal, milk, coffee, chicken, etc.)

2. Housing (rent of primary residences, owners' equivalent rent, fuel oil, etc.)

3. Apparel (men's and women's clothing, shoes, etc.)

4. Transportation (new vehicles, airline fares, gasoline, etc.)

5. Medical care (prescription drugs, medical supplies, physician services, etc.)

6. Recreation (television, movies/theater tickets, pets and pet products, etc.)

7. Education and communication (college tuition, postage, telephone services, etc.)

8. Other goods and services (tobacco and smoking products, haircuts, etc.)

Also included within these major groups are various government user fees, such as water and sewerage charges, auto registration fees, and vehicle tolls. The CPI also includes taxes that are directly associated with the prices of specific goods and services. However, the CPI excludes taxes such as income and social security taxes not directly associated with the purchase of consumer goods and services. The CPI does not include investment items, such as stocks, bonds, real estate, and life insurance.

For each of the more than 200 categories, the Bureau of Labor Statistics has chosen samples of several hundred specific items within selected business establishments frequented by consumers, using scientific statistical procedures to represent thousands of varieties available in the marketplace. Every month the Bureau of Labor Statistics data collectors visit or call thousands of retail stores, service establishments, rental units, and doctors' offices all over the United States to obtain price information on thousands of items used to track and measure price changes in the CPI.

The CPI, like the producer price index, is used to compare the current level of the index with a given reference point. So if the index is 115 and the reference index is 100, that means that prices have increased 15 percent over the reference time. The most useful way of using the CPI is to compare the rate of change over 12 months, which is computed by taking the value of the index this month divided by the value of the index the same month a year ago, subtracting 1 from the result, and then multiplying the outcome by 100. By making this computation, one can chart the trend in inflation every month.

The Bureau of Labor Statistics also produces specialized indexes. The most common one is core inflation, which is the CPI excluding the change in prices of food and energy. Since food and energy prices are highly volatile and so provide great volatility to the overall index itself, analysts like the core inflation index because it is less volatile than the CPI.

Acceleration in the consumer price index indicates that inflation is increasing. Because the consumer price index reflects the price of a basket of goods and services, it is affected by the price of commodities. It is not unusual to see commodity prices accelerating ahead of an acceleration in the consumer price index. On the other hand, a sharp decline in commodities over a few months is an indication that the economy is weakening and that the growth in consumer price index will soon decline. Information on the consumer price index is available from the Bureau of Labor Statistics.

The National Association of Purchasing Managers releases data on prices paid by purchasing managers. This index oscillates around 50. Inflationary pressures are strong when more than 50 percent of purchasing managers report that they are paying higher prices. When this index falls below 50, it is an indication that the risk of higher inflation is decreasing and inflation is being brought under control.

This information is very useful for investors. If the odds favor rising inflation, there is a strong probability that interest rates will also rise, pointing to higher risk for the financial markets. On the other hand, a decline of the index below 50, since it provides an indication that inflation is subsiding, suggests that interest rates are likely to decline, thus providing a favorable environment for stocks and bonds.

Finally, the Bureau of Labor Statistics releases the employment cost index on a quarterly basis. This index reflects trends in both wages and benefits paid to workers, and it represents the most comprehensive figure of labor costs. The importance of following the rate of change in the employment cost index is twofold. First, an acceleration or rising growth in the employment cost index means that the labor costs for corporations and businesses are increasing. Therefore, businesses will try to pass this increased cost to consumers. An increase in the rate of change in the employment cost index is likely to be reflected in higher inflation rates. Second, the employment cost index is important because as labor costs for businesses increase, the profitability for businesses is under downward pressure. And when margins decrease, businesses can only react by cutting costs and increasing layoffs.

The employment cost index has importance as an inflation indicator and, therefore, is a gauge that will point to the direction of interest rates and also has importance in the fact that it signals a downward pressure on the profitability of business.

In summary, inflationary pressures arise only after the economy is growing rapidly. They are reflected by an increase in the growth of commodity prices, in rising growth in the producer price index and the consumer price index, and a more decidedly above 50 in the price index of the National Association of Purchasing Managers. During such times of rising inflation, the growth in the employment cost index is also rising. Declining trends in inflation are found after the economy has been slowing down for some time, commodity prices are declining, the change in producer price index and the consumer price index are declining, and the price index of the National Association of Purchasing Managers is going below 50. During these times, the growth in the employment cost index is also declining.

Productivity and Profit Indicators

Productivity is a measure of economic efficiency that shows how effectively economic inputs are converted into output. Productivity is measured by comparing the amount of goods and services produced with the inputs that were used in production. Labor productivity is the ratio of output of goods and services to the labor hours devoted to the production of that output. In other words, productivity measures the output per man-hour, or the output generated by one hour of labor. This is labor productivity. Output per hour of all persons is the most commonly used productivity measure. Labor is an easily identified input to virtually every production process. In terms of costs, it represents about two-thirds of the value produced.

Business-sector output is based on GDP, but also includes a subset of the goods and services included in GDP. The business sector accounts for about 80 percent of the GDP, since it must exclude those portions of the economy for which productivity measures cannot be constructed. General government, the output of employees of nonprofit institutions, private households, and the rental value of owner-occupied real estate are excluded. The primary source of hours and employment data comes from the Bureau of Labor Statistics, which provides data on total employment and average weekly hours of production and nonsupervisory workers in nonagricultural establishments.

Unit labor costs are calculated by dividing total labor compensation by real output, or equivalently, by dividing hourly compensation by productivity. That is, unit labor cost is equal to total labor compensation divided by output. Compensation is a measure of the cost to the employer of securing the services of labor. It includes wages and salaries and such things as bonus and incentive payments and employer contributions to employee benefit plans.

Real output is the total output of the economy after inflation, as mentioned above. Productivity growth, which is a main determinant of economic growth, depends on the economic times. For instance, in the 1970s when inflation was rising from 2–3 percent to 15 percent, productivity growth was very low (between 0 and 1 percent). However, in the 1980s after inflation started to decline from 15 percent to close to 2–3 percent, productivity growth steadily rose. In the manufacturing sector in the 1990s, it was not unusual to find productivity growth around 5–6 percent. Such strong productivity growth was the main reason why in the 1980s and 1990s the United States achieved such high levels of wealth and prosperity.

Growth in productivity is one of the most important indicators providing information on the health of the economy. Let's see why this indicator is important.

Let's say you are the only producer of a widget in a country that does not have competitors for your product. It takes an entire day to produce one widget, and you sell it for $50 at the end of the day. Your income is therefore $50 per day. Then, because of some technology that you have learned to apply to the process of building widgets, you improve the output per day from one widget to two widgets. Since you are the only producer, your income has increased to $100 per day. In other words, as you doubled your productivity, your income has also increased by the same amount.

Growth in productivity is closely related to growth in income. A country cannot hope to grow faster, or a person cannot become wealthier, if productivity does not increase accordingly.

Productivity also has an important impact on profitability. In order to increase profitability, corporations have to absorb increases in wages, raw material costs, and other costs. Let's say that productivity increases by 4 percent and all these other costs also increase by 4 percent. The impact on profits after productivity is taken into account is zero. In other words, costs have not increased, because the improvement in productivity has absorbed their impact. Productivity is a major determinant of economic growth. As productivity slows down, the economy will eventually slow down, because income, which depends on productivity, slows down. As income slows downs, sales slow down, and the whole economy suffers.

The first sign that the economy is improving is when productivity increases. The increase in productivity suggests that income and profitability are also going to increase. As a result, the whole economy will benefit. Data on productivity are released by the Bureau of Labor Statistics.

Trends in corporate profits are also an indicator of economic health and future economic activity. The reason is that as corporations' profits increase, business is likely to increase investments to expand capacity, buy new machinery, and hire more employees. Another important indicator of corporate profits is earnings per share (EPS) of the S&P 500 corporations. EPS information is available weekly in *Barron's*.

Periods of low inflation have usually been associated with strong productivity growth. Periods of rising inflation have been associated with periods of slower productivity growth. The importance of strong and rising productivity growth is in the fact that business is capable of absorbing higher wages without impacting profitability. The problem with lower productivity growth is that business will not be able to absorb increased costs, and therefore will experience downward pressure on profitability. The only line of action is to cut employment, cut costs, and cause a slowdown in the economy. For this reason, maintaining strong productivity growth is one of the paramount objectives of policymakers.

Where to Get the Data

The above indicators are readily available from several sources. (We did not discuss monetary indicators here because we will devote an entire chapter to this important and crucial aspect of the economy.) The government agencies or organizations responsible for releasing the above data make them available on the Internet. All the following organizations have websites providing ample support to obtain these data: the Bureau of Economic Analysis, the Bureau of Labor Statistics, the Census Bureau, the National Association of Purchasing Managers, the Conference Board, the Federal Reserve System, the National Association of Realtors, and all the Federal Reserve banks. They all have an exhaustive library of information with substantial help to download historical data.

The Federal Reserve Bank of St. Louis has an extensive database on the Internet called "FRED" which is easily accessible (stls.frb.org). It has all the information one would need, probably more than the average investor would require. It is an excellent source providing extensive historical data, with a superb support staff who are always ready to help when you call them.

One of the problems with economic data is that they are often revised and it becomes time-consuming to keep track of all the revisions. The attractiveness of the FRED database is that it provides you with the latest revised data that can be easily downloaded onto your computer.

The Wall Street Journal offers a complete collection of economic releases with the charts of the main indicators. *The Economic Report of the President*, the National Association of Realtors, and all the major financial institutions, such as Bank One, Bank of America, Deutsche Bank, the Bank of Tokyo-Mitsubishi, the Bank of Montreal, and Morgan Stanley, have excellent economic research and data on their websites.

Conclusion

In this chapter, we introduced you to the most important indicators and their meaning and interpretation. This is the first step in developing the knowledge required to assess their impact on the financial markets and your investments.

We have seen that strong economic growth can be recognized when:

- GDP is growing well above the long-term average growth rate.

- Employment grows rapidly above 2 percent.

- Help-wanted advertising increases.

- Retail sales rise rapidly.

- Consumer confidence rises above 90 or 100.

- Consumer installment credit accelerates, and personal income rises at the same pace as GDP.

- Initial unemployment claims decline.

Other indicators of a strong economy are:

- A rapid growth in industrial production above 3 to 3 1/2 percent
- Rising average weekly hours
- Rising durable-goods orders
- A rise in the number of unfilled orders or backlogs
- The index of the National Association of Purchasing Managers rising above 50
- The vendor performance index rising above 50
- Inventories accelerating, with the inventory-to-sales ratio declining rapidly
- Rising building permits and housing starts
- Strong growth in new-home sales and existing home sales close to 4 percent

Periods of strong economic growth place upward pressure on inflation, and this can be measured by an increase in:

- Commodity prices like the CRB index for spot and futures
- Rising prices for crude oil and gold
- Rising growth in the producer price index and its components
- Rising growth in the consumer price index
- The price index of the National Association of Purchasing Managers moving rapidly above 50
- A rise in the growth of the employment cost index

We have also seen that in order to maintain low inflation and a strong economy, it is paramount that the policies of the government are such that they lead to strong productivity growth needed to absorb rising costs.

Periods of slow economic growth are those when:

- The growth of the GDP falls below its long-term average.
- Employment slows down below 1–2 percent.
- Help-wanted advertising declines.
- Retail sales slow down and peak.
- Consumer confidence falls rapidly close to 90 or even 80.

- Consumer installment credit slows down.

- Growth of industrial production declines to 2, 1, or even 0 percent, indicating that industrial production has peaked.

- Personal income slows down or even peaks.

- Unemployment claims rise.

During such times, it is not unusual to see:

- Average weekly hours paid slowing down

- A decline in average weekly overtime hours

- Slow growth or a decline in durable-goods orders

- Declining unfilled orders

- The index of the National Association of Purchasing Managers falling below 50

- The vendor performance index falling below 50

- A rising inventory-to-sales ratio

- A weakness in the construction sector, with declining housing starts and lower new-home and existing-home sales

After a prolonged period of weak economic conditions, it is quite typical for inflation indicators to begin to decline with:

- Commodity prices heading downward

- Slower growth in the producer price index and consumer price index

- The price index of the National Association of Purchasing Managers falling below 50

- Declining growth in the employment cost index

During periods of slower growth, it is typical to see productivity growth declining.

In the next chapter, you will see how these indicators are related to each other and how their interaction creates periods of stronger economic growth followed by periods of slower economic growth. The consumer cycle, the manufacturing cycle, the real estate cycle, the inflation cycle, and the productivity and profit cycle will be explored to gain a better understanding of economic fluctuations. All this information will be brought together to show how these indicators cause business cycle fluctuations and impact prices of assets and the financial markets.

Chapter

3

RELATIONSHIPS BETWEEN ECONOMIC INDICATORS

As noted at the beginning of this book, business cycles are like a mosaic. Throughout these early chapters, all the pieces of the mosaic are slowly being put together, and eventually you will have a full view of the subject. The previous chapter discussed the main economic indicators that provide information on the direction and intensity of the business cycle.

In this chapter, some examples of business cycles will be used to develop a way of thinking and a way of looking at economic data. These examples are by no means complete and exhaustive. Their main purpose is to illustrate some basic concepts, such as why the economy accelerates after a period of slow growth through a process of positive feedback. They also will be helpful in explaining why the economy is eventually going to slow down following a period of strong growth through a process of negative feedback. These examples serve as the groundwork for the next two chapters, which deal with the overall process of the business cycle. The mosaic will then be almost complete.

In the rest of the book the focus is on how to use this information to select investment assets and develop an investment strategy that allows you to manage risk.

The Consumer Cycle

Let's consider first the indicators concerning the behavior of consumers, and see how they act during a typical business cycle (Figure 3-1). Let's assume that inventories are low. As a result, business decides to increase inventories because it expects sales to improve. The first step is an

CONSUMER CYCLE

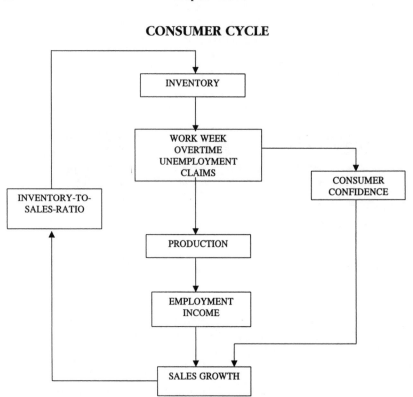

Figure 3-1. This chart illustrates a simple example of how the consumer sector impacts the business cycle. Pay particular attention to the positive and negative feedback provided by changes in the inventory-to-sales ratio.

increase in the average workweek and in overtime, because corporations want to make sure the recovery is a lasting one before increasing employment. Unemployment claims will likely decline, and because of improved conditions, consumer sentiment, which was low due to poor economic growth, starts rising.

The increased workweek and overtime result in higher production levels, which are accompanied by high employment and higher income. As consumers increase their take-home money, they spend more and sales accelerate. The strength in sales will produce a decline in the inventory-to-sales ratio as sales grow faster than inventories at the beginning of the recovery.

Of course, the increase in consumer confidence further reinforces the strength in sales. As the inventory-to-sales ratio declines, the business sector decides to further increase the workweek, overtime, and production. This process will eventually result in higher employment, further increasing income and sales.

Consumer confidence remains strong as the inventory-to-sales ratio continues to decline, and the need arises to replenish inventories. This cycle repeats itself, and the economy improves, growing faster and faster.

The question is why the economy eventually begins to slow down. The main reason is employment becomes scarcer. At the beginning, business rises rapidly after a period of slowdown because there are many people ready to be hired. As the labor force is increasingly used, there are fewer people to hire; therefore, the growth in employment has to slow down.

The slowdown in employment results in a slowdown in both income and sales. Slower growth in sales makes the inventory-to-sales ratio rise, which means business has to adjust inventories down. This downward adjustment in inventories results in a shorter workweek, less overtime, and slower growth in production.

Consumer confidence declines because there is a slowdown in overall employment and in income. As a result, sales growth continues to decline as the unemployment rate slowly increases. Even though the inventory-to-sales ratio continues to rise, the adjustment process goes on as business continues to cut inventory costs. The economy reflects this downshifting and grows very slowly. However, eventually inventories are cut so low that business decides to replenish them, because it knows that it will have to meet a certain level of sales.

Replenishing inventories triggers the business cycle again. This readjustment of replenishing inventories causes overtime to rise at first, and then employment, which translates into higher income. The upswing in the business cycle is under way again. This is a very simple model, but it helps to explain why growth at the beginning of the slowdown is fast and then is bound to slow down because economic resources become scarce. The emphasis has been placed on the inventory adjustment mechanism. In later chapters, the role of the Fed, inflation, and interest rates will be included to make the process more complete.

The evolution of the business cycle from 1991 to 1995 offers a good example of what happens in the business and financial markets, even in the absence of a recession. We will see how slight changes in economic growth can drive prices of assets in major ways.

Interestingly, the business cycle that began in 1991 was caused by the recession of 1990 and the early part of 1991. This shows that the main features of a cycle are influenced by some characteristics of the previous cycle. In 1991 a new business cycle began. An increase in the growth of the money supply was the key sign that a new business and financial cycle was under way. (The role of the Fed during this phase of the financial cycle will be discussed in detail in Chapter 7.) That was also the time when the great real estate crisis and savings and loan crisis were under way in the United States and created major disruptions.

Because of these crises, the Federal Reserve fulfilled its function of lender of last resort by providing liquidity in the system, in order to isolate the crises and keep them within the real estate and savings and loan sectors. This aggressive growth in the money supply created ripples throughout the economy. In 1994 the economy started growing very rapidly because of the aggressive easing of the Federal Reserve. The outcome was an acceleration in employment, income, and sales.

Because of strong sales and a cautious manufacturing sector, the inventory-to-sales ratio declined sharply, as sales were growing faster than inventories. Unemployment claims also were declining in response to faster growth in employment. However, the strong growth of 1994 created a series of events, such as rising interest rates, that caused consumers to become more cautious. This led to a slowdown in sales and income and employment.

In the meantime, manufacturing experienced an increase in the inventory-to-sales ratio in 1995 and slowed down production and employment. At that point, the business cycle experienced a slowdown, which created the conditions for stronger growth in 1996 and beyond.

Manufacturing and the Investment Cycle

Let's assume again that inventories are low and that business decides to increase their level (Figure 3-2). Business must then increase production and hire more people. As a result, income and sales increase, and the inventory-to-sales ratio declines. Inventory must be replenished, as sales keep growing faster than inventory at the beginning of the expansion of the business cycle.

As production increases, capacity utilization also increases, providing information on the ability of the country to produce and meet increasing demand. Capacity utilization represents the percentage of what manufacturing can produce. There is a point when business recognizes it cannot meet demand with current resources. It, therefore, needs to expand production facilities in order to meet increasing sales and improve productivity. The increase in sales and investment in new capacity results in higher orders for durable goods and consumer goods. This reinforces the need to increase production to satisfy increased

MANUFACTURING AND INVESTMENT CYCLE

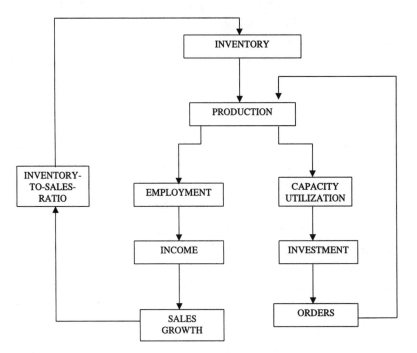

Figure 3-2. This chart illustrates how manufacturing and investment activities influence the business cycle. Production slows down as full utilization of capacity and the work force is reached. Positive and negative feedback are provided by changes in the inventory-to-sales ratio, causing adjustments in manufacturing and investments.

orders. The process continues and feeds on itself, and the economy expands strongly.

Why does the economy eventually slow down? For the same reason we mentioned in the previous section—employment is a scarce resource. But capacity is also a scarce resource. At the beginning of the cycle, when capacity utilization is low and there is a high unemployment rate, there are a lot of people to hire and a lot of capacity to utilize. Strong growth can be accommodated until scarce resources (labor and capacity) are more fully utilized.

However, when the employment rate is low and capacity utilization is high, growth cannot be supported as it was at the beginning of the business cycle. Growth has to slow down. A decline in growth in sales also will be reflected in a slowdown in investments, in orders, and therefore in production.

The inventory-to-sales ratio is a regulating mechanism guiding business to increase or decrease production and capacity expansion. As the economy slows down, borrowing for investments and borrowing by consumers to finance purchases also will slow down. The upswing in production and the investment cycle will be under way again when inventories have declined enough to justify a resumption of output. It must be noted that the strengthening and weakening in borrowing activity is connected to the inventory buildup and capacity expansion and is one of the major forces acting on short-term and long-term interest rates.

Let's look again at the 1991–1995 business cycle. The sharp decline in short-term interest rates that took place from 1991 through 1993 caused consumers to buy more aggressively and sales growth and employment growth to increase rapidly; as the inventory-to-sales ratio declined in 1994 because of the strong economy, manufacturing felt compelled to increase production.

The outcome was that capacity utilization started to increase, reflecting the increased production. The sharp growth of the economy in 1994 created disruptions, such as rising inflation, commodity prices, and interest rates, and forced consumers to be more cautious about their purchase plans.

The outcome was a sales slowdown, and the inventory-to-sales ratio rose in 1995. The manufacturing sector realized what was happening and slowed down production to bring inventories under control, and capacity utilization began to decrease again as less and less capacity was utilized to meet slower growth in sales.

The outcome of this action was to bring the inventory-to-sales ratio under control to bring inventories more in line with sales growth. Of course, this action created a slowdown in 1995.

The Real Estate Cycle

The real estate cycle starts when the economy is growing slowly (Figure 3-3). Interest rates are declining, and wages, inflation, and commodities are stable. This is the time when real estate developers recognize the opportunity provided by low costs. Believing in better business conditions ahead, and the resulting need for office space and housing, developers begin building new office space and housing with a distinctive character to attract new buyers. Borrowing activity increases to initiate these projects.

Soon, other developers recognize that something unusual is happening and maybe someone knows more than they do. They also recognize that

THE REAL ESTATE CYCLE

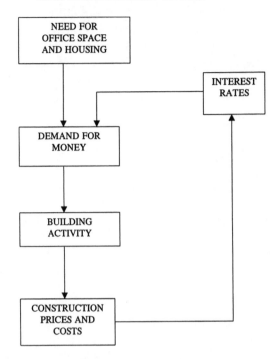

Figure 3-3. This chart demonstrates how the real estate sector grows rapidly as long as costs, such as raw materials and interest rates, remain stable. The negative feedback effect is provided by the eventual rise in raw material prices and interest rates, thus causing the real estate sector to slow down.

because of lower interest rates, this is a good time to increase construction. This involves more bank loans and employment to build new offices and new houses. Bank loans, as a result, start increasing more rapidly.

As the economy improves because of this building demand and increased overall business activity, prices of houses and offices eventually start appreciating faster. This process attracts more developers, more bank loans are therefore required, and a new housing and construction boom is under way. Initially, banks feel comfortable with these loans because of the strong construction activity, especially in light of the fact that prices for office space and housing continue to increase.

At some point, however, development becomes overextended. Interest rates begin to rise because of an overall strong economy. The new houses and office buildings are not bought or rented right away, as higher borrowing costs make new investments unattractive. Eventually, some price concession has to be made to sell the properties. Rents and prices of houses decline, and as new developers recognize that the building boom does not offer the profit potential that they realized earlier in the cycle, they stop building. Of course, this has a negative impact on the overall economy and a negative effect on employment and income.

Demand for real estate declines, caused not only by overbuilding but also by increasing interest rates. Eventually, prices of new construction actually decline. Builders find themselves overextended, and banks realize that their loans cannot be serviced anymore due to poor profitability of the construction industry. These are times when banks' insolvency begins to be an issue, an issue that becomes more acute as the slowdown continues. This is usually the time when lending officers increase the spread between the interest they charge and market interest rates to protect themselves against marginal borrowers and to improve their profitability, thus worsening the negative impact of rising interest rates.

This process causes a further slowdown in overall business activity until the cycle starts over again when interest rates decline due to the slow demand for money, not only from the construction sector, but also from the rest of the economy. Eventually, the business cycle stabilizes, and opportunities seem to be on the horizon again as the cost of raw materials, labor, and money decline to a level attractive enough to start a new real estate cycle. Examples of real estate cycles can be found in the United States in the 1980s and in Japan and Asia in the 1990s.

The real estate cycle is strongly influenced by trends in the economy and trends in interest rates and commodity prices. The strong increase in liquidity from 1989 to 1992 created a strong economy, and during that time, interest rates also were declining, with fairly weak commodity prices, particularly in lumber. However, the strong growth that took place in 1994 caused interest rates and commodities to rise from 1994 to early 1995.

The outcome was that real estate stopped expanding, reached a peak, and declined mildly in 1995, due to the sharp increase in commodity prices and interest rates. The subsequent slowdown in the economy in 1995 created the climate for lower interest rates, and therefore, the construction business revived again in 1995 and 1996 in response to lower interest rates and lower commodity prices.

The Inflation Cycle

The most important forces affecting inflation are monetary ones (growth in monetary aggregates and real short-term interest rates), as we will see

INFLATION CYCLE

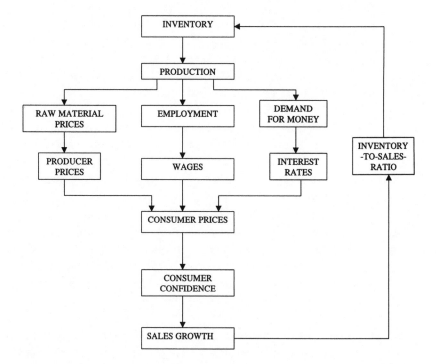

Figure 3-4. The strong growth in the economy caused by an ample supply of money, labor, and raw materials eventually declines as full utilization of resources is reached. The negative feedback effects come from the eventual rise in costs transmitted to consumers in the form of inflation. Lower real income growth caused by rising inflation has a negative impact on sales growth.

in detail in Chapters 6 and 7. However, inflation has very distinct cyclical timing (Figure 3-4).

The purpose of this section is to review how and why the forces of inflation develop, and above all, how they are part of the overall business cycle. The objective is to emphasize the positive feedback of inflation. When inflation declines, real income (income less inflation) increases and provides consumers with extra stimulus to spend. On the other hand, rising inflation sets in motion negative feedback. Rising inflation decreases real income, and therefore, consumers become more cautious about their spending plans.

Let's start again with the simple inventory cycle model. Inventories are low, but businesses recognize the opportunities for future sales, so they start planning to increase inventories. In order to do that, they have to increase production and employment. But to increase production, they need raw materials.

Since raw materials are very sensitive to changes in demand, as soon as business improves, raw material prices tend to rise. The stronger economy also places upward pressure on interest rates and wages. These increased costs are initially absorbed by business, but eventually they are passed to the consumer through higher prices.

As consumer prices increase, consumer confidence declines. The reason is that as inflation increases, income after inflation, that is real income, decreases. The decline in consumer purchasing power has a negative impact on the consumer's attitude toward the future. As a result, consumers begin to spend less. This has a negative impact on the inventory-to-sales ratio as sales slow down relative to inventory. As a result, the inventory-to-sales ratio starts rising.

Businesses recognize that inventories are out of line, and so they start cutting production. Cutting production implies that they have to cut raw material purchases and employment. Because of the decline in raw material purchases and the decline in employment, raw material prices decline, wages slow down, and eventually consumer prices also slow down.

The decline in consumer prices is good news for consumers because now their income after inflation improves. As a result, their outlook for the future becomes more optimistic, and they start spending more. Because of increased sales, the inventory-to-sales ratio declines, production is increased to replenish inventory, and the consumer cycle starts all over again.

As you can see from this and the previous cycles we have discussed, every time the economy expands, something else develops to correct the growth and eventually cause the business cycle to slow down. This is an automatic self-correcting mechanism.

In all the cycles we have discussed, the main point to focus on is that every time the economy expands, it causes developments that will correct its excessive growth (negative feedback) and eventually bring down growth of the business cycle closer to the long-term average pace of the economy, which is close to 2.5–3.0 percent. The business cycle has delicate and pervasive self-correcting mechanisms to bring back economic and financial conditions close to their long-term patterns. Higher inventory-to-sales ratios, rising inflation, rising short-term and long-term interest rates, and higher unit labor costs are the most important of these forces. It is just a matter of time before they impact the economy in a negative way.

As you can recognize from the previous examples, actions that happen at a certain point in time have a ripple effect in the economy through a cause-and-effect relationship. For instance, the strong growth in the money supply that was induced by the Fed to solve the savings and loans and real estate debacles in 1992 and 1993 caused a strong economy in 1993 and 1994. However, the strong economy in 1993 and 1994 caused raw material prices and interest rates to move higher. Eventually these same trends caused the 1995 slowdown.

This slowdown had a negative impact on employment and on income, and the economy remained soft until 1996. This allowed interest rates and commodity prices to decline again, which caused the economy to strengthen in 1997 and 1998. As you can see, current events of the period caused future disturbances that propagate. In the 1970s these ripple effects were violent because of rising inflation. Following the early 1980s, these fluctuations were milder due to declining and low inflation.

The forces of inflation increase following a period of strong growth in the economy. Depending on monetary conditions, which will be discussed later in Chapters 6 and 7, inflation could rise very much or remain muted. In the 1970s every time the economy strengthened, inflation rose considerably, from 3 percent to 5 percent in one cycle to be followed by an inflationary burst from 6 percent to 8 percent in the following cycle. The causes of these trends will be discussed in detail later.

Since 1982, these conditions have changed and inflation has remained muted. However, its cyclical timing can still be recognized. For instance, following the strong growth in monetary aggregates from 1989 to 1992, the economy strengthened considerably through 1994, resulting rising commodity prices due to strong production and strong sales. The CRB raw industrials price index (spot) rose quite sharply through 1994, and this was accompanied by much higher interest rates. What is important to recognize is that the prices of two basic assets, commodities and money, rise after a period of strong economic growth.

Unit labor costs also had a mild uptick, but very minor. The increase in these prices resulted in an acceleration in the producer price index of crude materials. This increase rippled through the chain, but in a very mild fashion, almost indistinguishable. The outcome was that consumer prices through 1994 and 1995 had a very small increase.

The slowdown that took place in 1995, caused by an increase in interest rates and inflationary pressures in 1994, kept commodities from rising further, and they remained fairly stable through 1995.

Productivity and Profit Cycles

In order to examine the behavior of productivity and profits during a typical business cycle (Figure 3-5), let's start as usual with the fact that inventories are low and business decides to increase production to replenish inventories. In order to increase production, business needs to borrow money to buy raw materials, to pay wages as employment

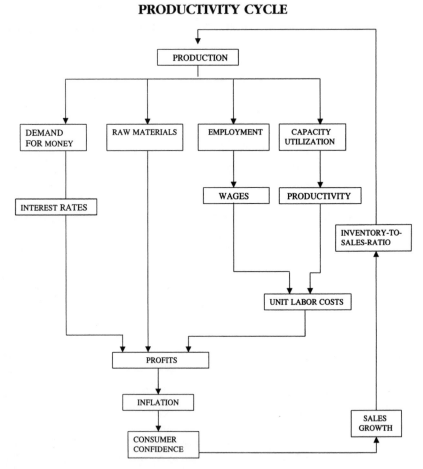

Figure 3-5. Strong economic growth places upward pressure on costs (interest rates, raw materials, and wages). As capacity becomes fully utilized, productivity growth declines, placing upward pressure on unit labor costs. The negative feedback is provided by the rise in business costs (interest rates, raw materials, and unit labor costs). As profits experience downward pressure, prices to consumers are increased, thus affecting negatively their propensity to spend. A further negative effect is provided by the cut in the costs of business to improve profitability.

increases, and to invest in new processes. As production increases, the demand for money also rises and raw material prices move up. And as employment grows, the unemployment rate declines and eventually wages start to increase faster.

Furthermore, as production increases, capacity utilization also increases. At first, business puts the most efficient machines and processes into the production line or into the manufacturing of the product. As capacity utilization continues to rise, the less productive machines and processes are utilized. Also, as the unemployment rate declines, the skill level of the residual labor force decreases. For these reasons, as the economy strengthens, productivity slows down.

As growth in productivity declines, business is not capable of absorbing the increase in wages, and so unit labor costs, which were initially stable because of strong productivity growth, start to rise faster. The increase in unit labor costs, in raw material prices, and interest rates has a negative impact on profits, which start to decline. Labor costs, raw material prices, and interest rates are in fact the main costs of running a business. The outcome is that the increased costs erode the profit margins of a company. The opposite is also true. When these costs decline, the profitability of the company improves as margins increase.

Initially, lower profits are being offset with price increases. This results in higher inflation. Of course, as we have seen in the previous section, rising inflation is followed by lower real income and slower growth in sales. Business, therefore, needs to adjust inventories downward to match the slower demand for goods.

Also, the reaction of a typical business to declining profits is to cut costs of money, raw materials, and labor. The lack of productivity also needs to be solved. Business has to think in terms of what investments have to be made to increase capacity and make the production process more effective. However, this is a long-term strategy.

In the short term, business has to cut employment to minimize the effect of rising wages, cut raw material purchases, and reduce borrowing. However, by decreasing the costs of borrowing, the decision has to be made to delay those investments needed to improve capacity at a later date. Of course, layoffs, a cut in production and raw material purchases, and less demand for money cause a slowdown in the economy.

Businesses will continue to cut until profit margins improve. And profit margins will improve when wages slow down quite sharply and raw material prices and interest rates also decline. Businesses, therefore, in spite of a weak economy, recognize that there are still opportunities in the marketplace, and they will soon start rebuilding inventories and making new investments, encouraged by the improving profitability. So the cycle of productivity and profit starts all over again.

As the economy becomes very strong, costs (wages, interest rates, and raw materials) rise, and eventually productivity slows down as business works closer and closer to full capacity. Initially, business tries to pass the increased costs, due to lower productivity, to consumers. This causes inflation to rise, and increasing inflation lowers consumers' real income. In turn, this causes the consumer to spend less and the economy to slow down. This happens at the same time as business tries to cut costs to improve profitability, due to a slowdown in profitability and higher unit costs. The new business cycle starts when costs decline because of the slow economy. At this time, profitability improves, as a result of lower capacity utilization, higher productivity, and lower inflation.

Profitability and Earnings per Share

The year 1994 offers a great example of the cyclical nature of profitability. Since an investor is worried about not only profits but profits per share, which is the main driver in the price of a stock, let's consider what happened in 1992–1994 to earnings per share of the S&P 500. The main point of the following discussion is that changes in earnings per share of the S&P 500 follow very closely the change in raw material prices. Let's see why.

The aggressive easing of the Fed caused the economy to expand very rapidly in 1994. The outcome of this growth was strong production, strong employment, strong income, and, therefore, strong sales. As sales were increasing more rapidly than costs, profitability improved. As a result, earnings per share greatly improved with other cyclical indicators, such as interest rates and raw material prices. But eventually the increase in interest rates and raw material prices had a negative impact on earnings per share. Business tried to control costs, and created a slowdown in 1995; as the economy slowed down, commodity prices and interest rates declined. Earnings per share also slowed down with overall business conditions.

It is very important to realize the cyclical nature of earnings per share and the close relationship of this measure with trends in interest rates and commodities. This relationship is important in assessing the risk of the stock market. We will see that earnings per share is not a good indicator to time the overall market, but it is a more appropriate measure for selecting stocks.

Conclusion

In this chapter we examined the interaction between various indicators. In the next chapter we will put all these different cycles under one process and see how growth and changes in business cycles take place.

As discussed in the previous example, it will become clear that the main driver of a business cycle is the financial cycle. The financial cycle represents the pattern of growth in monetary aggregates or money supply, which is controlled by the central bank. An increase or decrease in the growth of the money supply creates ripple effects through business activity and prices of assets for years to come.

We have seen that in 1992 through 1994 the Federal Reserve eased monetary policy aggressively because of problems that the economy had with the real estate and the savings and loans sectors. The Fed kept interest rates artificially lower than what the market would have set these rates. The outcome was a sharp increase in credit, a powerful stimulus for business to borrow and to invest.

The business cycle eventually started in full force, and employment, income, and sales grew more rapidly, the inventory-to-sales ratio declined to reflect strong growth, the unemployment rate declined to reflect more favorable hiring conditions, and the process fed on itself. However, in 1994 as the economy grew very strong, eventually it had an effect on prices (the price of money, the price of labor, and the price of raw materials).

In 1994, therefore, the economy experienced sharply rising interest rates and commodity prices and some upward pressure in labor costs. Because of strong sales, earnings per share grew very rapidly. However, the strong growth of the economy created the seeds for the following slowdown. This is the phenomenon of negative feedback. As costs of running a business increased—specifically interest rates, labor, and raw materials—business slowed down its investment activities and hiring. It also started to cut inventories and production. The outcome was slower economic activity in 1995 and lower earnings per share. The slowdown in the economy and the decline in the costs of running a business were the seeds for the next acceleration in the business cycle.

Later, we will analyze long-term trends and how the U.S. economy went from low inflation in the 1950s to high inflation in the 1970s and back to low inflation again in the 1980s and 1990s. This analysis will provide important information on the essential features that characterize the volatility of business cycles and their relationship with inflation and monetary policy.

Chapter
4

THE COMPOSITE INDEXES OF LEADING, COINCIDENT, AND LAGGING INDICATORS

In Chapter 1, we discussed the concept of risk and the importance of protecting your portfolio from losses. Managing your investment risk should be the primary objective of your strategy. As with games of strategy like poker, investors can learn how to develop an investment strategy centered on flexibility and sensible risk taking. Just as poker players plan their bets in light of the odds of winning the hand, the investor has to change the amount invested in each asset depending on the odds of making money in that particular investment.

One of the main objectives of this book is to show that the prices of most assets are driven by changes in economic conditions. As the economy moves from a period of fast growth to one of slower growth, asset prices change to reflect the evolving economic conditions. Understanding how and why prices change is key in developing an investment strategy leading to risk management.

We also have begun to understand the forces acting in the economy and how these forces are related to each other. Economic indicators were introduced and subdivided into categories. This subdivision did not have any specific purpose except to make it simpler to explain and introduce these indicators. They were categorized into consumer-related indicators, manufacturing indicators, construction indicators, inflation indicators, and, finally, measures related to productivity and profitability. Indicators related to interest rates and the stock market will be discussed in detail later in the book.

In addition, we saw how these indicators are related to each other in a cause-and-effect type of chain reaction. This was achieved by discussing some examples of business cycles. One of the objectives was to show how the process of feedback develops in the phase of acceleration of the business cycle and how forces leading to a slowdown eventually develop to bring growth back to its long-term average.

But the mosaic is still not complete. In this chapter, we will attempt to put the pieces together and explore how all the indicators impact the growth of the business cycle and how the financial markets react to changes in economic growth. Later, we will discuss how to develop investment strategies that take advantage of economic changes.

However, first, let's examine the concept of leading, coincident, and lagging indicators. These indicators greatly simplify the understanding of cyclical forces and make it easier to understand what is happening in the economy.

In the late summer of 1937, then Secretary of the Treasury Henry Morgenthau, Jr., asked the National Bureau of Economic Research (NBER), an organization devoted to studying business cycles and other economic problems, to compile a list of strategic indicators that would best indicate when the recession would end. Wesley C. Mitchell, then NBER's director of research, enlisted the help of Arthur F. Burns, who later headed NBER and then became chairman of the Federal Reserve.

The report presented to the secretary discussed a list of the most reliable indicators of business expansions, explained how they were selected, and included a record of their past performance. This report was published in May 1938. The first set of leading, coincident, and lagging indicators was born.

In the summer of 1938, the indicators were put to their first test. The recovery began in June, and the first signs of its appearance were registered by the leading indicators identified by Mitchell and Burns.

Many new theories relating to various aspects of business activity became available, and new findings about cyclical upturns and downturns were published. The original list of indicators was revised several times.

At present, the Conference Board maintains and updates monthly the latest data concerning the leading, coincident, and lagging indicators, and it makes these data available free through the Internet. Most industrialized countries have copied the system developed by the United States because it is one of the most sophisticated and timely ways of collecting information for developing economic and monetary policies.

Additionally, the advantage of looking at composite indexes is that instead of examining the behavior of hundreds of indicators, a composite index summarizes their action. The analysis of just three indicators provides the analyst with a fairly good idea of what is happening in the economy. However, a better understanding of what is happening is derived by examining the detailed action of the components.

Leading Indicators

The composite index of leading indicators is a summary statistic for the U.S. economy. This index is constructed by averaging its individual components in order to smooth out a good part of the volatility of the individual series. The purpose of this index is to indicate the future trend of the U.S. economy. A slower growth in this index foretells that the growth of the economy is likely to decline in the future. On the other hand, an increase in the growth of this index indicates that the growth of the economy will rise in the near future.

The composite index of leading indicators is computed using 10 measures that have the property of leading the business cycle at peaks and at troughs. The typical lead time is about 12 months at peaks and a few months at troughs.

The indicators used to compute the composite index of leading indicators are the following:

1. *Average weekly hours in manufacturing.* The average hours worked per week by production workers in manufacturing industries tend to lead the business cycle because employers usually adjust work hours before increasing or decreasing their work force.

2. *Average weekly initial claims for unemployment insurance.* The number of new claims filed for unemployment insurance is typically more sensitive than either total employment or unemployment to overall business conditions. This series tends to lead the business cycle and is inverted when included in the leading index.

3. *Manufacturers' new orders, consumer goods and materials.* These goods are primarily used by consumers. The inflation-adjusted value of new orders leads actual production because new orders directly affect the level of both unfilled orders and inventories that firms monitor when making production decisions.

4. *Vendor performance, slower deliveries diffusion index.* This index measures the relative speed at which industrial companies receive deliveries from their suppliers. Slowdowns in deliveries increase this series and are most often associated with increases in demand for manufacturing suppliers, and therefore, this series tends to lead the

---

business cycle. The National Association of Purchasing Managers provides this information, which represents the number of managers experiencing slower deliveries. An increase in this index suggests that the economy will improve.

5. *Manufacturers' new orders, nondefense capital goods.* This series represents new orders received by manufacturers in nondefense capital goods industries. As explained for the series on new orders, new orders for nondefense capital goods lead the business cycle.

6. *Building permits, new private housing units.* This series represents the number of residential building permits issued. This is an important indicator of construction activity, which typically leads most other types of economic production trends.

7. *Stock prices, 500 common stocks.* The Standard & Poor's 500 stock index reflects the price movements of a broad selection of common stocks traded on the New York Stock Exchange. Increases and decreases in stock prices, which reflect increases and decreases in overall financial liquidity, provide another good indicator of future economic activity.

8. *Money supply M2.* The money supply M2 is expressed in inflation-adjusted dollars. M2 includes currency, demand deposits, other checkable deposits, traveler's checks, savings deposits, small-denomination timed deposits, and balances in money-market mutual funds.

9. *Interest rate spread, 10-year Treasury bonds less federal funds.* This series is constructed using the ten-year Treasury bond rate and the federal funds rate, an overnight interbank borrowing rate. Changes in this spread lead important turning points in economic activity.

10. *Index of consumer expectations.* This index reflects changes in consumer attitudes concerning future economic conditions and is the only indicator in the leading index that is completely expectations-based.

The use of rate of change over 12 months is recommended when using business cycle indicators. The main reason is that trends in asset prices in the financial markets are particularly sensitive to changes in the growth rate of economic indicators. Furthermore, the use of rate of change helps to compare the growth rate of one indicator versus other indicators.

The main reason the index of leading indicators leads turning points of the business cycle is that many of the components used to compute the index reflect decisions or commitments to change output—for example, new orders, building permits, and measures of financial liquidity such as the money supply and stock prices. Stock prices respond immediately to increases in liquidity injected in the banking system by the Federal Reserve, as discussed in detail later in this book. The term *liquidity* refers to how fast the money supply is growing. Rising growth in the money supply means that the Federal Reserve is increasing liquidity in the system, while a decrease in the growth of the money supply implies the Fed is taking liquidity out of the banking system. (How this is done will be discussed in Chapter 7 concerning the operations of a central bank.) All these measures affect economic growth with a lead of at least several months. For instance, the growth of the money supply leads changes in the growth of the economy by about two years.

Orders, an important component of the index, reflect the decision of business firms to buy new machines and expand existing capacity. Since it takes time to convert orders into machines or plants, such orders tend to precede changes in the production of goods or machinery. This makes orders a good leading indicator.

Another important component of the index of leading indicators is building permits. Let's assume that building permits start rising, reflecting a commitment to build more housing due to, for instance, declining interest rates. Rising building permits will eventually be reflected in increased construction activity, in the completion of buildings, in the production of materials that are needed to build houses, and eventually, in their final sales.

It is reasonable to expect that some time will elapse from the time the building permit is granted, to the time the production of the equipment needed to build the buildings is completed, and finally to the time the buildings are sold. For this reason, changes in the growth of building permits tend to anticipate—that is lead—the growth in overall business activity.

Another important leading indicator is the index of stock prices, as represented by the S&P 500 common stocks index. The stock market is an important leading indicator of economic activity because changes in stock prices tend to lead changes in business activity by several months, and the action of the stock market is available daily. The reason the stock market is a leading indicator of economic growth is because, like the money supply, it reflects the growth of liquidity in the economic system. For instance, the growth of the money supply and the change in stock prices measured on a year-over-year basis started to increase very sharply in 1995. Economic growth resumed quite strongly toward the end of 1997 and early 1998.

Since financial liquidity reflects an expansion of credit, the more liquidity is made available, the more money is eventually used in business to build houses, to manufacture goods, to buy other companies, or to invest. A decline in the growth of stock prices signals that liquidity in the economic system is growing more slowly. The outcome is that consumers have less money to spend, investors have less money to invest in new ventures, and overall business activity is likely to slow down.

Another important leading indicator is the growth of the money supply, which measures credit expansion. We will examine in detail this type of indicator when we talk about the Federal Reserve in Chapter 7. We also will see how the central bank impacts the growth of the money supply, and as a result, the growth of the economy. For the time being, it is enough to say that the money supply also is a measure of liquidity in the economic system and is closely controlled by the Federal Reserve.

When more liquidity is made available through banks, there is more money to borrow. Consumers and businesses will then borrow and use the money to invest, thus impacting the growth of the economy. If liquidity in the banking system slows down, there is less money to borrow, and business activity will slow down because there is less money available to spend and to invest.

To sum up, the composite index of leading indicators provides an overview of the future trends of the economy. It simplifies the analysis because it summarizes trends of 10 indicators that in the past have proved to be reliable leading indicators of economic activity. Although all measures are important, investors will find that changes in the growth of the money supply provide the most reliable indication of future trends because of this measure's long lead time in predicting changes in economic activity.

Coincident Indicators

The composite index of coincident indicators provides information on what is happening now in the economic system, and is computed using four measures that reflect the current strengths and weaknesses of the economy. The growth of the index closely approximates the growth of business. Its trend reflects what is happening at the moment to business activity.

The measures included in the computation of the index of coincident indicators are the following:

1. *Employees on nonagricultural payrolls.* This indicator includes full-time and part-time workers and does not distinguish between permanent and temporary employees. Because the changes in this series reflect the actual hiring and firing of employees at all but agricultural establishments, government agencies, and the smallest businesses in the nation, it is one of the most closely watched series for gauging the health of the economy.

2. *Personal income less transfer of payments.* This indicator measures the real salaries and other earnings of all persons in inflation-adjusted dollars. This series excludes government transfers, such as social security payments, and includes an adjustment for wage accruals less disbursements. Income levels are important because they determine both aggregate spending and the general health of the economy.

3. *Index of industrial production.* This index measures the physical output of all stages of production in the manufacturing, mining, and gas and electric utility industries. This index has historically captured a majority of the fluctuations in total output.

4. *Manufacturing and trade sales.* Sales at the manufacturing, wholesale, and retail levels reflect trends in the economy and represent real total spending—that is, spending adjusted for inflation.

The economy is strong if employment, production, income, and sales are all growing rapidly. The business cycle is slowing down if the components of the coincident indicators are slowing down too.

Since the leading indicators have been chosen because they lead the economy, changes in the growth of the leading indicators also lead changes in the growth of the coincident indicators. Thus a decline in the growth of the index of leading indicators is followed after several months by a decline in the growth of the coincident index. On the other hand, an increase in the growth of the leading index is followed after a few months by an increase in the growth of the coincident index.

Lagging Indicators

The composite index of lagging indicators is constructed by averaging individual components that historically follow the turning point of the coincident index. This gauge is probably the most important of the three indicators because it provides information about the degree of excesses that there are in the economic system.

The growth of the index of lagging indicators increases when the economy is growing rapidly, usually above its long-term average growth rate of about 2.5 to 3.0 percent.

The indicators used in the computation of the index are:

1. *Average duration of unemployment.* This series measures the average duration in weeks that individuals counted as unemployed have been out of work. Because this series tends to be higher during recessions and lower during expansions, it is inverted in the computation of the index. In other words, the signs of the month-to-month changes are reversed. Decreases in the average duration of unemployment invariably occur after an expansion gains strength, and the sharpest increases tend to occur after a recession has begun. Therefore, sharp decreases in average duration of unemployment suggest the economy is overheating and investors have to begin to be cautious. On the other hand, a sharp increase in the average duration of unemployment is a sign that the economy has been slowing down quite sharply, and therefore, the excesses of the previous cycles are being corrected.

2. *Inventories-to-sales ratio, manufacturing and trade inventories to sales.* The ratio of inventories to sales is a popular gauge of business conditions for individual firms, entire industries, and the whole economy. This series is calculated by the Bureau of Economic Analysis using inventory and sales data for manufacturing, wholesale, and retail business. The data are used in an inflation-adjusted form, and are based on information collected by the Bureau of the Census. Because inventories tend to increase when the economy slows down and sales fail to meet projections, the ratio typically reaches its cyclical peak in the middle of a recession. It also tends to decline in the beginning of an expansion as firms meet their sales demand from excess inventories.

3. *Change in labor costs per unit of output in manufacturing.* This series measures the rate of change in an index that rises when labor costs for manufacturing firms rise faster than their productivity, and vice versa. The index is constructed by the Conference Board from various components, including seasonally adjusted data on employee compensation in manufacturing, which includes wages and salaries plus any supplements. These data are available from the Bureau of Economic Analysis and are seasonally adjusted for industrial production in manufacturing from the Board of Governors of the Federal Reserve System. The data are adjusted to eliminate distortion due to seasonality in the series, such as effects caused by higher manufac-

turing activity in winter and lower output in summer. Because the monthly rate of change in this series is extremely erratic, the percent change in labor costs is calculated over a six-month span. Cyclical peaks in the six-month rate of change typically occur during a recession, as output declines faster than labor costs, despite layoffs of production workers. Troughs in the series are much more difficult to determine and to characterize. Typically, as the economy slows down and employment declines, growth in wages and labor costs tends to decline. Therefore, this series decreases following a downturn in economic conditions or a slowdown in the index of coincident indicators. On the other hand, protracted growth in the coincident indicators is followed after one to two years by an increase in the growth of labor costs, due to the low availability of labor.

4. *Average prime rate charged by banks.* Although the prime rate is considered the benchmark that banks use to establish interest rates for different types of loans, changes tend to lag behind the movements of general economic activity. The monthly data are compiled by the Board of Governors of the Federal Reserve System. There is no doubt that interest rates are one of the most important components of the index of lagging indicators because they measure the cost of credit. Although the prime rate is used in the index of lagging indicators, in later chapters we will discuss other interest rates that respond much more quickly to changes in market conditions, such as the rate on 13-week Treasury bills or interest rates tied to Treasury bond yields.

5. *Commercial and industrial loans outstanding.* This series measures the volume of business loans held by banks and commercial paper issued by nonfinancial companies. Commercial paper is high-grade unsecured notes sold through dealers by major corporations. They basically represent IOUs of major corporations. The underlying data are compiled by the Board of Governors of the Federal Reserve System. The Conference Board makes price-level adjustments using inflation data based on personal consumption expenditures, which are the same data that are used to deflate the money supply data in the leading index. This series tends to peak after an expansion peaks because declining profits usually place downward pressure on the demand for loans. Troughs are typically seen more than a year after the recession ends.

6. *Consumer installment credit outstanding–to–personal income ratio.* This series measures the relationship between consumer debt and income. Consumer installment credit outstanding is compiled by the

Board of Governors of the Federal Reserve System, and personal income data are from the Bureau of Economic Analysis. Because consumers tend to hold off personal borrowing until months after a recession ends, this ratio typically shows a trough after personal income has risen for a year or longer. The peak in this ratio follows a peak in the general economy.

7. *Consumer price index for services.* This series is compiled by the Bureau of Labor Statistics and measures the rate of change in the services component of the consumer price index. Inflation declines following a prolonged period of slower growth in the overall economy and in the index of coincident indicators, and it rises about two years after an increase in the growth of the economy and in the index of coincident indicators.

There is little doubt that the index of lagging indicators is the most misunderstood index, and despite its importance, the press and investors pay little attention to its trend. After all, why pay attention to an indicator that rises after the economy is already in full swing? Or declines following a peak in overall economic conditions? Why should anyone pay attention to an indicator that is the result of what has already happened?

However, the index of lagging indicators and all its components provide the most important information available to investors. They are the most important gauges to assess the health of the economy and the financial markets. Their trends represent a valuable tool available to investors to assess the risks in the financial markets that were caused by the business cycle. Let's explore why they are important tools for investors.

As we said above, the index of lagging indicators lags trends in business activity by about two years. Let's see why. Let's take, for instance, interest rates. Interest rates tend to decline after the economy slows down quite dramatically and rise following a period of strong economic growth. The main reason is that as the economy grows rapidly, so does the need to borrow in order to invest to expand expanding capacity and to hire people. This increased borrowing activity eventually places upward pressure on interest rates. This is why the rise in interest rates lags trends in business activity—aggressive borrowing is done after businesses recognize that the economic expansion has staying power. The same can be said when the economy weakens. Once businesses recognize that economic activity is deteriorating, they start borrowing less and interest rates decline.

Another component of the index of lagging indicators is unit labor costs—that is, the cost of labor adjusted for productivity. This gauge also rises after the economic recovery is well under way and the economy strong. At the beginning, when the business cycle goes from a slow period to a strong period, there is a lot of labor available to be hired, productivity is high, and wages are low; therefore, labor costs decline and remain stable. But as the labor supply decreases because more and more people have been hired, there is an increasing upward pressure on wages.

These are also times when capacity utilization is high and productivity declines as a result of the lower margin of productive capacity available. Productivity is a measure of economic efficiency, which shows how effectively economic inputs are converted into output. The most commonly used measure of productivity is output per hour of all persons. If productivity grows, for instance, at 4 percent and wages are growing at 5 percent, labor costs adjusted for productivity are just 1 percent. As a result, lower growth in productivity has a negative impact on labor costs. Lower growth in productivity and higher wages place upward pressure in unit labor costs, which rise well after the business cycle is growing rapidly.

These simple examples show that the lagging indicators reflect excesses in the economy and lag economic conditions at peaks and troughs in business activity. If the economy expands too strongly and there are some imbalances created by the way the economy is growing, then the index of lagging indicators starts rising. If, on the other hand, the economy slows down and slack is built into the system, lagging indicators eventually decline.

The index of lagging indicators is very important because it rises when the economy is beginning to operate at such high levels that it is producing strains on costs. An increase in the index of lagging indicators suggests that the economy is very strong and that there are strong cost pressures in the system. Rising cost pressures have two major impacts. The first is a negative impact on the profitability of corporations. The second is closely related to the first. As businesses see costs rising, they try to pass these cost increases to consumers. The outcome of this is increased inflation at the consumer level and downward pressure on real income and consumer purchasing power. An increase in the index of lagging indicators is, therefore, a sign that there are major changes taking place in business; changes that have a negative impact for business and consumers. Later in the chapter we will explore the strategic use of these indicators to determine the conditions of the business cycle.

Other Experimental and Coincident and Leading Indicators

In the spring of 1989, two economists, James S. Stock and Mark W. Watson, published a paper entitled "Indexes of Coincident and Leading Indicators" in the *NBER Reporter*. In this paper the two economists proposed a different approach in computing economic indicators. They selected them solely on the basis of their reliability. They devised the experimental coincident index and the experimental leading index.

The experimental coincident index is a weighted average of broad monthly measures of U.S. economic activity. These measures are:

1. Industrial production

2. Total personal income, less transfer payments adjusted for inflation

3. Total manufacturing and trade sales adjusted for inflation

4. Total employee hours in nonagricultural establishments

These measures, as we discussed above, represent what is happening in the economy at any particular point in time, and reflect the strengths and weaknesses of the overall economy. The weighted average used to compute the experimental coincident index is determined using current and recent values of the growth rates of the four measures. This weighted average in growth rates is then cumulated to create an index in levels. This index was constructed in July 1967, so that it equaled 100. The average monthly rate of growth in the experimental coincident index is 3 percent at an annual rate. Thus, the experimental coincident index has approximately the same trend growth rate as real GDP, which grew at an average rate of 3.1 percent from 1960 to 1988. The experimental coincident index is approximately 1 to 1 1/2 times more volatile than real GDP.

The experimental leading index proposed by Stock and Watson is a forecast of the growth of the experimental coincident index over the next six months (that is, for the six months subsequent to the month for which the data are available). The forecast is stated in percentage terms on an annual basis. Thus, for example, the experimental leading index for April represents a forecast of the percent growth in the experimental coincident index between April and October at annual rates.

The experimental leading index is a weighted average of seven leading indicators:

1. Building permits for new private housing

2. Manufacturers and field orders in the durable-goods industry, adjusted for inflation

3. Trade-weighted index of nominal exchange rates between the United States and the United Kingdom, Germany, France, Italy, and Japan

4. Number of people working part time in nonagricultural industries because of slack work

5. The yield on a 10-year U.S. Treasury bond

6. The difference between the interest rates on 3-month commercial paper and the interest rates on 3-month U.S. Treasury bills

7. The difference between the yield on a 10-year U.S. Treasury bond and the yield on a 1-year U.S. Treasury bond

Stock and Watson developed another indicator called the *experimental recession index*. The experimental recession index is an estimate of the probability that the economy will be in a recession six months from the date of the index. For example, the experimental recession index for April gives the probability that the economy will be in a recession in October. The experimental recession index is computed using the four monthly series in the experimental coincident index and the seven monthly series in the experimental leading index.

The experimental recession index represents a probability. For example, if the experimental recession index is 25 percent, then the probability of the economy being in a recession in six months is 25 percent. The lowest possible value of the experimental recession index is 0 percent and the highest is 100 percent.

Since the experimental leading index was too dependent on financial information, Stock and Watson developed an alternative experimental recession index, This one is based on seven leading indicators that exclude interest rates and interest rate spreads. The method used to construct the alternative experimental recession index is the same as the one used for the experimental recession index. The difference between the two is the underlying series to construct the two indexes. The seven series used in the alternative experimental recession index are:

1. Building permits for new private housing

2. Manufacturers and field orders for durable-goods industries, adjusted for inflation

3. Trade-weighted index of nominal exchange rates between the United States and the United Kingdom, Germany, France, Italy, and Japan

4. Index of help-wanted advertising in the newspapers

5. Average weekly hours of production workers for durable-goods industries

6. Percentage of companies reporting slower deliveries, as determined by the National Association of Purchasing Managers

7. Capacity utilization rate in manufacturing

The two economists publish the latest information on these indicators on their website (HTTP://www.KSGHOME.Harvard.edu). For more details and a discussion on how these indicators are computed and how they are used, the reader is referred to their original paper published in the spring of 1989 in the *NBER Reporter.*

Although not used in either the Conference Board or the Stock-Watson indicators, the ratio between BAA bond yields and 10-year Treasury bond yields is also an excellent leading indicator. This ratio is very closely correlated with the growth in the money supply and stock prices. Because of this cyclical timing, the ratio has an important strategic value when used in conjunction with other business cycle indicators.

Conclusion

The purpose of this chapter was to bring together all the economic indicators discussed in the previous pages and introduce the concept of composite indicators. We also reviewed the history of these indexes and their importance for investors when monitoring the performance of the U.S. economy and the financial markets.

The crucial feature for investors is that these indicators can be subdivided into three main categories: leading, coincident, and lagging indicators. The index of leading indicators and its components need to be followed closely because they provide information on the future pace of the economy.

However, the index of lagging indicators is probably the most important of the three gauges for developing a successful investment strategy. Investors should be particularly cautious and vigilant about the outlook of the economy and financial markets when this index begins to rise. A rise in the index of lagging indicators reflects excesses in the economy, which eventually will have to be brought under control by a visible economic slowdown caused by slower growth in liquidity.

In the next chapter, we will look in detail at how the leading, coincident, and lagging indicators are related to each other and how they impact the business cycle.

Chapter

5

THE BUSINESS CYCLE: A PRACTICAL USE OF ECONOMIC INDICATORS

The system of leading, coincident, and lagging indicators allows the investor to follow the progress of the business cycle through its various phases. It also provides an important way to assess the risks and opportunities offered by various assets. We now know that an increase in the index of leading indicators—for instance, growth in the money supply, orders, building permits, or profits—is followed after several months by an increase in the coincident index—for instance, production, employment, and income.

A protracted and strong increase in the coincident index is followed by an increase in the lagging index—that is, inflation, labor costs, and interest rates—a sign that the economy is strong, that it is working close to full capacity, and that price and cost pressures are intensifying.

The length and volatility of the business cycle, and therefore, the investment risk, depend on how rapidly and how soon the lagging indicators rise. The reason is that a rise in the growth of the lagging indicators is followed after several months by slower growth in the leading indicators. For instance, an increase in interest rates makes the building and purchase of real estate more expensive, and therefore discourages the development of this sector. This is a typical example of a rising lagging indicator, such as interest rates, followed by slower growth in a leading indicator, such as housing starts or building permits.

The same applies to profits. An increase in costs has an almost immediate negative impact on profits, forcing profits to grow more slowly. Or a rise in interest rates is followed by a decline in the growth of the money supply or stock prices. Eventually, the slowdown in the leading index causes, after several months, a decrease in the growth of the index of coincident indicators. The point is that these three types of indicators (leading, coincident, and lagging) are closely interconnected to one another by very precise and logical relationships.

Only after a protracted decline in the growth of the coincident index does the index of lagging indicators begin to decline. A peak in the growth of the lagging indicators follows a protracted slowdown in the coincident indicators, which is reflected by poor growth in various sectors of the economy. As a result, unemployment rises, labor becomes more available, and wages do not increase as fast anymore. On the other hand, because of slower economic growth, demand for money declines and interest rates also decrease.

A few months following a decline of the index of lagging indicators the index of leading indicators rises again. The reason is that the decline in costs (wages and interest rates) makes it attractive again to invest in a new house, or to build new productive capacity. The money supply accelerates in response to increased demand for funds due to the decline in interest rates, and stock prices rise.

The importance of the system of leading, coincident, and lagging indicators is that they are closely tied together (Figures 5-1 and 5-2). The lagging indicators are the most relevant ones because an increase in the lagging indicators forewarns both investors and businesspeople that the leading index will decline and the economy will eventually worsen. On the other hand, a decline in the lagging index tells investors and businesspeople that the leading indicators will soon rise and that business conditions will improve.

As mentioned earlier the S&P 500 index, which is an index used to measure stock market performance, is a component of the index of leading indicators; short-term and long-term interest rates are lagging indicators; and the stock market is a leading indicator of the business cycle because it reflects the liquidity available in the system. Since the stock market is a leading indicator, its risk decreases when the index of lagging indicators—for instance, inflation, short-term interest rates and long-term interest rates—decreases or remains stable. This is a good time to be in stocks. However, the odds favor a peak in the stock market when inflation, short-term interest rates, or long-term interest rates begin to rise.

The financial cycle that took place from about 1989 to 1995 can also be used to explain the relationship between leading, coincident, and lagging indicators. In 1989 the growth of the money supply began to expand rapidly (the growth of the money supply is a leading indicator). This was also the time when stock prices bottomed and then started to grow faster. The index of industrial production began to grow faster in

LEAD-LAG RELATIONSHIP BETWEEN LEADING, COINCIDENT, AND LAGGING INDICATORS

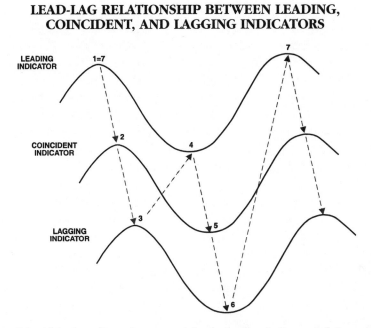

Figure 5-1. This chart shows how a peak in the leading indicator is followed by a peak in the coincident indicator, which is then followed by a peak in the lagging indicator. A peak in the lagging indicator is then followed by a trough in the leading indicator, which is then followed by a trough in the lagging indicator. And the cycle starts all over again. Note the negative feedback induced by the rise in the lagging indicator. The importance of the negative feedback is in its impact on measuring stock market risk and predicting the market's important peaks.

TURNING POINTS IN CYCLICAL INDICATORS BOX CHART

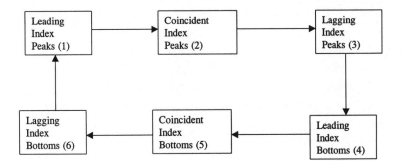

Figure 5-2. This is a different way of representing Figure 5-1. It also emphasizes that a leading indicator is predicted by using a lagging indicator, a coincident indicator by a leading indicator, and a lagging indicator by a coincident indicator.

1991 due to the generous injection of liquidity in the economic system. The economy strengthened, and in 1994 interest rates and commodities began to rise because of the very strong growth of the economy. The increase in interest rates (a lagging indicator) was followed by a slow-down in the growth of the money supply and also a decline in the growth of stock prices. The financial cycle ended in 1995 when the pro-tracted decline in the money supply, going from 1992 to 1995, caused the economy to slow down in 1995. A new financial cycle began in 1995.

A decline in the growth of stock prices (a leading indicator) is fol-lowed by a slowdown in the economy and eventually by a decline in the lagging indicators and a decline in interest rates (a lagging indicator). A decline in interest rates cannot take place without a protracted weakness in stock prices. Stock prices will start rising again after a few months of declining interest rates (lagging indicators). In other words, it takes a few months from a peak in interest rates to a bottom in stock prices and sev-eral months from the trough in interest rates to a peak in stock prices.

The importance of the system of leading, coincident, and lagging indi-cators is that it ties together business and financial indicators. Their rela-tionship is a very important tool in determining the level of risk for investors in the financial markets. The basic relationships can be sum-marized as follows:

- An increase in the growth of a leading indicator (for example, the money supply) is followed after about two years by an increase in the growth of the coincident indicator (for example, industrial production).

- A prolonged increase in industrial production is followed after 1 1/2 to 2 years by an increase in the lagging indicators (for example, inter-est rates).

- An increase in the growth of the lagging indicators is followed after several months by a peak in the growth of the leading indicators (for example, the money supply).

- A decline in the growth of the leading indicators (for example, the money supply) is followed after about 1 1/2 to 2 years later by a decline in the growth of the economy (for example, industrial production).

- A decline in the growth of industrial production is followed after sev-eral months by a decline in the growth of the lagging indicators (for example, interest rates).

- A decline in the growth of the lagging indicators (for example, inter-est rates) is followed after a few months by a rise in the growth of the leading indicators (for example, the money supply).

And the business and financial cycles start all over again.

The Phases of the Business Cycle

The economy is a very sensitive and delicate mechanism. Small changes in growth rates put in motion forces that have a major impact on economic behavior, from changes in business profitability to the value of assets. Everything from commodities to stocks, from interest rates to precious metals and currencies, is affected. Oil or lumber may soar one year and decline the next. Gold and real estate were the hot investments in the 1970s and the dramatic losers in the 1980s and 1990s. Bonds collapsed in the 1970s, but provided returns up to 40 percent after 1982.

As a business and financial strategist, how do you predict when and in which direction these changes will occur? The essential driving force that moves the prices of all assets is how fast the economy grows relative to its long-term growth rate.

Asset prices change depending on how fast the economy is growing relative to its long-term average pace. The long-term growth rate of an industrialized country is usually around 2.5 percent. The average long-term growth for the U.S economy after 1982 is somewhere between 2.5 and 3.0 percent. We also call this *growth potential*. The average growth of 2.5 to 3.0 percent represents how fast the economy can grow on average during normal conditions.

But growth is very rarely at its 2.5 to 3.0 percent potential. Sometimes it speeds up above this range and other times it slows down below it (Figure 5-3). We will further investigate the reasons for this variation

PHASES OF BUSINESS CYCLE

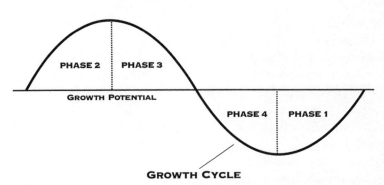

Figure 5-3. The business cycle goes through four phases, releasing forces that drive asset prices and financial markets.

later. Values of assets respond to whether business growth is above or below its long-term potential. In order to develop guidelines that can be used for investment strategies, it is useful to follow what happens to the business cycle as it moves through four main phases.

Phase One

Phase one of the business cycle occurs when the economy comes out of a period of slow growth that has been well below its growth potential. The growth rate increases but does not exceed the growth potential. When the economy grows at a pace below the long-term average pace, the economy could well have been in a recession. But investment strategies developed over a period of very slow growth or a recession are the same because asset prices act in the same way in both cases.

Phase Two

Phase two of the business cycle occurs when growth rises above the growth potential. For instance, if the average long-term growth of the economy is assumed to be 3 percent, phase two of the business cycle takes place when growth of the economy rises above this level. These are the boom periods when everything seems to be going right and terms such as *Goldilocks economy* are used, as during 1995–1999.

Phase Three

In phase three, economic growth returns to the typical growth potential. This phase identifies the beginning of a correction, as a result of the policies followed by the Fed in phase one and phase two.

Phase Four

In phase four, growth declines below the average growth potential. All the excesses created in phases two and three are brought under control in this period. This is the time to pay the piper. And it is the time that offers the greatest investment opportunities for the astute investor. Although this is also the time when economic conditions are very poor, unemployment is rising, and the mood of the nation is typically depressed, the financial markets are rising quite strongly, with both the stock and the bond market growing in value quite appreciably. Historical evidence shows quite clearly that as the economy strengthens and grows more rapidly, the financial markets begin to perform more sluggishly. However, as the economy slows down to the point when interest rates start declining, the financial markets provide some attractive returns. Opportunities and risk change as the growth of the economy shifts from slow growth to strong growth to slow growth again. For instance, in 1995 interest rates (a lagging indicator) began to decline, the money supply (a leading indicator) immediately started to grow much more rapidly, and stock prices soared. Eventually, in 1996 growth in industrial production (a coincident indicator) began to rise.

Investment risk changes as the business cycle moves steadily from phase one to phase four. Economic growth above its long-term potential is accompanied by rising lagging indicators, such as interest rates, inflation, and labor costs. These times have been high risk for the stock market because returns from equities in this period have been well below average. Investment risk declines, and the prospect of considerably higher profits in stocks and bonds materializes when the economy grows more slowly, its growth falls below its long-term average, and interest rates and inflation decline. As the economy accelerates, as we have seen in previous chapters, it nurtures the forces that will make it grow at a slower pace. However, in spite of all these dynamics, the long-term average growth of the economy is 2.5 to 3.0 percent.

This is similar to what happens to a jogger. If the jogger's natural pace is nine minutes per mile, any attempt to speed up will result in a faster pulse rate, higher temperature, shortness of breath, and increased fatigue. Before long, the jogger will have to slow down and coast until strength returns. Competitors know that the faster and longer joggers run above their average pace, the more likely they will have to slow down to rest and the longer it will take to recuperate.

The economy behaves exactly the same as a jogger. If the economy grows much faster than the growth potential, its temperature rises too. For the economy, this rising temperature equates with inflation, higher interest rates and commodities, accelerating wages, high-capacity utilization of machines and human resources, and eventually lower business profitability as productivity slows down. Like the jogger, the economy has to slow down under this pressure if it is to regain strength. To do this it must grow at a pace below its growth potential. Only then will inflation, interest rates, wages, and capacity utilization decline and business profitability improve as costs decline and productivity improves.

As the growth of the economy changes, profitable trends develop. Before we examine them, however, let's look at what makes the economy accelerate and slow down. Later we will discuss how to predict these changes and how to time specific investment strategies.

What Happens in the Phases of the Business Cycle?

As you read the following pages, a question will emerge. If the long-term average growth rate is so important, what can we do to make it rise? Substantial research in this area indicates that increasing the country's productivity is the only answer. And this can only be accomplished through improved education, increased investments, and low inflation. It is both that simple and that enormously difficult to achieve.

What Happens During Phase One of the Business Cycle?

This phase is signaled when the economy finally comes out of a period of recession or slow growth below the growth potential and starts improving again.

Any change from one phase to another is a direct consequence of what happened in the prior phase. When the economy grows very slowly, inflation declines because consumers recognize they are going through difficult times and they become cautious buyers. People find it difficult to find jobs as unemployment rises. As a result, growth in wages declines, and income grows very slowly. For this reason consumers watch prices very carefully, keeping inflation under control. Of course, with the economy very slow, borrowing is also subdued, and interest rates decline. A slow growth period is also characterized by slow production, and therefore, there is less need for raw materials, the price of which weakens as slow production lessens the demand for them.

But there is good news during a period of very slow growth. The decline in wages, interest rates, raw materials, and inflation is reflected in lower costs for business. As a result, business profitability begins to improve at the moment when most people consider this to be the worst time of the business cycle. So the costs go down, business profitability goes up.

It is important to note that the growth in wages, the decline in interest rates, and the decline in the growth of borrowing are all lagging indicators, and a decline in lagging indicators means that the cost pressures—the excesses that were generated by the previous growth—are finally being brought under control. Therefore, businesses anticipate some improvement in the business cycle. In fact, as slow growth begins to bring costs down, and the effects of efforts to improve productivity implemented during the slow growth period kick in, profits begin to improve. For this reason, profits are an important leading indicator. Their improvement encourages business to be more aggressive in its outlook for the future and in its investment plans.

What we are beginning to see is a very important aspect of the business cycle. A decline in a lagging indicator is followed by an improvement in leading indicators—that is, a decline in cost factors is followed by an improvement in profitability. A typical example of this relationship is what happened during the financial cycle that began in 1995. At that time, the economy slowed down and interest rates began to decline from a level close to 6 percent. The decline in interest rates brought about more borrowing, and the Federal Reserve accommodated this need for money by letting the money supply grow more rapidly. The strong growth of the money supply which began in 1995 was eventually followed by very strong growth in the economy in 1997 and 1998. By mid-1998, the pressures on inflation were rising, and inflation gradually moved higher from a low 1.5 percent in 1998 to about 2.7 percent in 1999. At the same time, as inflation was rising, long-term and short-term interest rates also began to rise. The increase in interest rates during 1998 and 1999 discouraged borrowing, and as a result, the growth of the money supply peaked in early 1999. In this example, inflation, interest rates, the money supply, and the economy behaved exactly how investors should have expected.

The reason interest rates decline during phase four of the business cycle is due to the slower growth in the demand for money, because business is discouraged to borrow due to the slow growth in business activity typical of this period. However, as soon as profitability improves, demand for money increases. The Fed encourages this process by creating the necessary liquidity needed by business (the process of liquidity creation will be discussed in detail in Chapter 7 when we will review the functions of the Fed).

In phase one, you see not only an improvement in liquidity, but also an increase in the growth of the money supply because the Fed has made money more available to business as well as to consumers. During a period of slow growth, as inflation declines, long-term interest rates also tend to decline, reflecting lower inflation expectations.

Furthermore, since the stock market thrives on liquidity, equity prices bottom out and start rising. There is no doubt that phase one represents a very important time in the business cycle as far as financial markets are concerned. In phase one the economy slows, interest rates decline, and the Federal Reserve injects money in the system to favor expansion. The increase in liquidity goes partly into the real economy. However, another part of this liquidity goes into the financial markets, and that's why the financial markets perform extremely well in this phase.

As profits continue to improve and costs remain under control, business begins to expand capacity and production and hire more people to take advantage of the opportunities. More jobs lead to more income; more sales lead to more production and even more jobs. The economic growth keeps on rising as the process feeds on itself, with business increasing its profitability, the money supply expanding strongly, interest rates declining, bond yields declining, and the stock market rising. The dollar, reflecting the confidence of the international financial markets and the future of the U.S. economy, strengthens. This is the phase where the jogger—that is, the economy—is finally well rested and able to begin running faster.

The major developments that take place in phase one can be summarized as follows:

- The growth of the money supply is rising rapidly.

- The dollar is improving.

- The stock market is rising.

- The growth of the economy, as measured by the growth in production, sales, income, and employment, stabilizes and improves but remains below its growth potential.

- Profits bottom and then improve.

- Commodities continue to weaken and eventually bottom.

- Short-term interest rates continue to decline and eventually bottom.

- Long-term interest rates continue to decline and eventually bottom.

- Inflation continues to decline and eventually bottoms.

It must be kept in mind that although short-term and long-term interest rates have the same cyclical turning points, short-term interest rates are more volatile than long-term interest rates. For this reason, moves in short-term interest rates can provide investors with useful insights on money-market conditions and trends.

What Happens During Phase Two of the Business Cycle?

In this phase the momentum of the economy is so strong that growth rises above the long-term potential. Employment, production, income, and sales continue to rise rapidly. As unemployment continues to decline, it becomes difficult to find skilled workers, and so wages begin to rise faster. Increased production places upward pressure on raw materials. Favorable economic conditions, coupled with growth in income, lead to aggressive consumer buying resulting in an increasing pace in borrowing. Eventually, higher growth consumer borrowing and business borrowing cause interest rates to rise.

In fact, this is the time when capacity utilization is reaching high levels and business feels more and more compelled to borrow to increase capacity. But, of course, as capacity utilization increases, productivity improvements slow down, as discussed earlier.

At this point in the cycle, business can no longer absorb the rising costs of commodities, labor, and interest rates. The lagging indicators are finally raising their ugly heads and warning investors that the economy is overheating and risk is increasing. The implication is that profitability is now at stake, with profit margins under pressure because of rising costs.

The rise in costs is a signal that the strength of the economy is at risk because an increase in costs will force the leading indicators to decline. How? An increase in costs means that business profits are at risk and business will have to cut costs to maintain profitability. During this phase, characterized by strong growth in the economy, investors need to pay attention to those variables (mostly lagging indicators) that have an impact on decisions (leading indicators) that would cause the economy to slow down. For instance, when the growth in wages and overall labor costs begin to rise, accompanied by rising interest rates (all these measures are lagging indicators), investors need to follow closely the impact of these indicators on the economy.

The most immediate impact of these indicators is on profitability, which is an important leading indicator, and on housing starts, which is also another important leading indicator. For instance, the rise in interest rates will cause construction activity to slow down and orders for heavy equipment to weaken because business finds investing in construction and heavy equipment less attractive as a result of the increased costs of borrowing.

As interest rates and inflation rise, they will have a negative impact on other important leading indicators, such as consumer sentiment and consumer expectations. As interest rates and inflation rise, income for consumers declines, thus affecting consumer attitude in a negative way. The main reason is that as inflation increases, it erodes the purchasing power of consumers, and thus has a negative impact on their outlook for the economy. Furthermore, the increase in interest rates raises the cost of borrowing for consumers, and this also has a negative impact on their attitude. A period of strong growth, accompanied by increasing lagging indicators, will force a series of decisions that will eventually lead to slower growth in the economy.

Like an overconfident jogger, the economy in phase two tries to run faster than it should. When this happens, the Fed eventually acknowledges that the economy may be overheating and that too much growth would bring a higher rate of inflation. Interest rates are, therefore, allowed to rise even further, discouraging business and consumers from borrowing. This action will cause a decline in the growth of the money supply and in overall liquidity. Slower growth in liquidity, accompanied by rising interest rates, has a negative impact on the stock market, which peaks and becomes very selective. The strong growth that we have in phase two eventually triggers a slowdown and anticipates the events in phase three of the business cycle. As the economy downshifts, the dollar is likely to weaken, anticipating slower growth in the future.

The major developments that take place in phase two can be summarized as follows:

• The money supply continues to rise very rapidly and eventually peaks.

• The dollar remains strong and eventually peaks.

• The stock market continues to rise and eventually peaks.

• The economy, as measured by the growth in production, sales, income, and employment, grows very rapidly above the growth potential.

• The growth in profits rise rapidly.

• Commodities are very strong and rise.

• Short-term interest rates rise.

• Long-term interest rates rise.

• Inflation rises.

What Happens During Phase Three of the Business Cycle?

Phase three is the most treacherous phase of the business cycle. Growth in sales is at the highest level in years, profits are beginning to soften, but the recognition that interest rates and inflation have been rising for some time tends to lag behind. As costs accelerate and sales slow down due to businesses cutting costs and the Fed reducing the growth in liquidity, there are downward pressures on income, sales, employment, and production. The reason is that as the growth in the money supply declines, less liquidity is available to consumers and businesses to spend. This lower level of liquidity and rising inflation and interest rates force businesses and consumers to cut spending. The ultimate effect is a slowdown of the economy.

Of course, as costs keep rising, businesses are forced to cut them. The negative feedback between lagging and leading indicators is clearly visible at this point. Businesses will not be satisfied to cut costs until the factors that created declining profits are brought under control. In other words, businesses will stop cutting costs only when the lagging indicators finally decline. A decline in the lagging indicators (for example, inflation, interest rates, growth in labor costs) is a signal that costs are finally under control. It is a signal that labor costs, commodities, and interest rates are on the way down. This is an important indication for businesses that their margins are likely to improve in the near future, and therefore encourages them to start spending again. Phase three represents this adjustment, and the slowdown will continue until the lagging indicators begin to decline. This is the crucial development that investors have to look for in this phase of the business cycle.

The important developments that take place in phase three are the following:

- The growth of the money supply continues to decline.

- The dollar is relatively weak.

- The stock market is weak.

- The economy, as measured by the growth in production, sales, income, and employment, continues to slow down and eventually falls below its long-term growth potential.

- The growth in profits peak and eventually declines.

- Commodities peak and eventually decline.

- Short-term interest rates eventually peak and then decline.

- Long-term interest rates eventually peak and then decline.

- Inflation continues to rise and then eventually declines.

What Happens During Phase Four of the Business Cycle?

Like the jogger who has decided he just can't make it—he has to slow down—it is time for the economy to slow down, at least to below its average pace. This is phase four, a time when the growth of the economy falls below its long-term average of 2.5 to 3 percent. With tight monetary policy, as the money supply continues to slow down, and with business continuing to cut costs, the economy remains weak, and eventually in phase four the first signs of recovery begin to appear. As the economy grows very slowly, inflation peaks and then starts declining.

Consumers aren't buying much because of rising unemployment rates due to business cost-cutting programs. Interest rates, due to lower inflation and slower growth in the demand for credit, start to decline. Commodities weaken because of slow demand caused by the economy and slow growth in production. The dollar, reflecting all these uncertainties, remains weak.

It is interesting to note that the forces that caused a slowdown—higher costs, inflation, and interest rates—are now reversing. In other words, the lagging indicators are now declining. But as cost factors decline, profit margins tend to improve again. At the same time, since the Fed has now achieved its purpose of controlling inflation, it will start easing again and let the growth of the money supply expand.

The Fed decides to provide more liquidity because it has achieved its purpose. More liquidity, lower costs, lower inflation, increasing profitability—now the economy is back in a position to start all over again. The jogger has rested and has the strength to start running at a faster pace, and the economy is ready to start all over again with phase one. The dollar, reflecting an improved mood, begins to strengthen.

The developments that take place in phase four can be summarized as follows:

- The growth of the money supply continues to decline, and as soon as short-term interest rates peak, it begins to rise again.
- The dollar declines and eventually strengthens.
- The stock market remains weak but eventually strengthens.
- The growth of the economy, as measured by the growth of production, sales, income, and employment, continues to slow down.
- Profits continue to remain weak.
- Commodities are weak.
- Short-term interest rates decline.
- Long-term interest rates decline.
- Inflation declines.

Investment Implications

In the prior sections we reviewed the concept of leading, coincident, and lagging indicators, how they are computed, what they mean, and how they can be used. We also looked at how the business cycle evolves from a period of slow growth, to stronger growth, then slower growth again, going through four distinct phases. As the business cycle moves through these phases, the economic indicators maintain precise relationships, as discussed above. In particular, we have noticed how rising lagging indicators, such as change in unit labor costs, inflation, and interest rates, provide crucial information for investors. These lagging indicators warn investors to look for a peak in the leading indicators, such as stock prices and changes in the growth of the money supply.

The purpose of this section is to see how the evolving economy creates different situations, to which you must adjust your investment portfolio. We will examine the process from the investor's viewpoint in order to recognize the strategic implications derived from changes in the growth of the economy.

At the beginning of phase one the economy grows very slowly, and as we have seen, the posture of the Fed is to let the money supply grow faster in order to accommodate the demand for credit. The increased availability of credit is a measure of the liquidity in the economic system. The money supply accelerates and this increased liquidity has an immediate positive effect on stocks. Profit margins start improving because of the declining cost of money, cost of labor, and raw material prices.

With an improved tone in the economy, the U.S. dollar strengthens. This is an important barometer of the health of the economy. The stronger dollar confirms that all the trends in place are likely to continue. Production at this time is still weak, and so are commodities. Because of the slack in the economy, the unemployment rate is high, capacity utilization is low, commodities are weak, inflation is declining, and short-term interest rates are heading down or are stable, while bond yields decline due to lower inflation.

This is the phase of the business cycle that is most favorable to stocks. Investment in commodities and hard assets is not particularly attractive due to low inflationary pressures. Because of lower inflation, bond yields decline, making bonds an attractive investment.

As the economy strengthens in phase one, several developments take place. Initially, they are not easy to discern because they occur gradually, but then they become more and more visible. Commodities stop decling as rapidly as they had been and eventually stabilize for several months. Then they start gradually rising. The upward action of commodities is followed closely by a rise in short-term interest rates. Bond yields do not decline as rapidly, and eventually they bottom. For instance, in 1994 when the economy strengthened quite visibly, commodities rose quite sharply, accompanied by a rise in interest rates from 3 to 6 percent and also by sharply rising bond yields.

This gradual change in trend suggests the economy is slowly moving into phase two when growth becomes quite strong. The business cycle moves into phase two when the economy grows beyond potential. Risks are beginning to increase for some assets, while others become more attractive. As the economy grows above potential, commodities start growing quite rapidly. Therefore, investments in commodities, real estate, or industrial types of assets that are commodity driven become attractive.

Inflation bottoms out at the beginning of phase two, and the odds favor higher inflation as resources become more fully utilized. Because of increasing inflation, bond yields bottom and possibly rise. Bonds, as a result, become less attractive.

This is the time when risk begins to shift. Investment in stocks becomes riskier because the business cycle is in a strong growth phase, with yields too high to justify the current price-earnings ratio. Commodities also remain an attractive investment. With inflation rising, real estate investments are beginning to offer a good opportunity as prices of real estate reflect the underlying inflation and tend to rise at a faster pace than inflation. Due to rising inflation, bond yields are rising, thus making bonds a high-risk investment.

In phase two, when the economy becomes very strong, the Federal Reserve recognizes that the strong growth in credit is causing the economy to overheat, generating strong inflationary pressures. Therefore, the Fed will attempt to slow down the growth in credit to achieve slower and more sustainable growth in the economy. Two developments usually happen at this time. One is that the money supply slows down, a sign that the liquidity in the system is decreasing. The second is that stocks peak and become more selective due to slower growth in the money supply as short-term and long-term interest rates continue to rise.

The dollar weakens, as we mentioned above, thus making foreign investments more attractive. Profits decline as costs rise and productivity slows down. The business cycle now moves into phase three, with the financial markets at a high-risk level while hard asset investments (energy stocks, gold stocks, commodities, real estate, art, etc.) provide more attractive returns.

In phase three, the leading indicators, such as the growth of the money supply, stocks, and profits, decline. The dollar is weak as the economy slows down and tries to readjust. Bond yields keep rising, production slows down, and commodities do not rise as rapidly and eventually decline. Inflation is still rising, short-term interest rates continue rising, and the Fed is firm in controlling the growth in credit. The Fed will continue this policy until there are signs that inflation will decline. Bond yields will eventually follow inflation down.

Phase three is a very unfavorable period for financial instruments and is more favorable for hard assets. Eventually, the economy enters phase four. The economy is slow, the Federal Reserve has finally achieved its objective of slowing down the economy below potential, and investors begin to see signs that inflation is declining.

Phase four is a very important phase because all the indicators that created a slowdown are now reversing themselves and create new investment opportunities. Inflation peaks and starts declining. Bond yields peak, wages slow down, and costs decline. Bonds offer good investment opportunities at this time. The Federal Reserve recognizes that inflation has been brought under control and the economy is likely to stabilize.

Low inflation and lower bond yields make stocks attractive again. Short-term interest rates decline because now the Fed is gradually easing the growth in credit, and the financial instruments become attractive again. Commodities are weak, inflation declines, and short-term rates and bond yields continue to head downward. The dollar finally improves as the excesses generated in phases two and three are brought under control.

The Fed recognizes business conditions are normal again and allows liquidity to increase. The business cycle is close to entering phase one, with all the financial markets in an uptrend.

The major developments that take place in phase one can be summarized as follows:

• The growth of the money supply is rising rapidly.

• The dollar is improving.

• The stock market is rising.

• The economy, as measured by the growth in production, sales, income, and employment, stabilizes and improves but remains below its growth potential.

• Profits bottom and then improve.

• Commodities continue to weaken and eventually bottom.

• Short-term interest rates continue to decline and eventually bottom.

• Long-term interest rates continue to decline and eventually bottom.

• Inflation continues to decline and eventually bottoms.

The major developments that take place in phase two can be summarized as follows:

- The money supply continues to rise very rapidly and eventually peaks.

- The dollar remains strong and eventually peaks.

- The stock market continues to rise and eventually peaks.

- The economy, as measured by the growth in production, sales, income, and employment, grows very rapidly above the growth potential.

- Profits rise rapidly.

- Commodities are very strong and rise.

- Short-term interest rates rise.

- Long-term interest rates rise.

- Inflation rises.

The important developments that take place in phase three are the following:

- The growth of the money supply continues to decline.

- The dollar is weak.

- The stock market is weak.

- The economy, as measured by the growth in production, sales, income, and employment, continues to slow down and eventually falls below its long-term growth potential.

- Profits continue to remain strong and then eventually decline.

- Commodities peak and eventually decline.

- Short-term interest rates eventually peak and then decline.

- Long-term interest rates continue to rise and then eventually decline.

- Inflation continues to rise and then eventually declines.

The developments that take place in phase four can be summarized as follows:

- The growth of the money supply continues to decline, and as soon as short-term interest rates peak, it begins to rise again.

- The dollar declines and eventually strengthens.

- The stock market remains weak and eventually strengthens.

- The economy, as measured by the growth of production, sales, income, and employment, continues to slow down.

- Profits continue to remain weak.

- Commodities are weak.

- Short-term interest rates decline.

- Long-term interest rates decline.

- Inflation declines.

The rest of this book will examine in more detail the various aspects of the financial markets, and we will discuss which indicators are most suitable to assess the risk and predict the trend of each asset.

First, however, we must deal with a very important issue, and that is to examine the important changes in the economy in the financial markets that took place since 1955. Why did these changes take place? What can we learn from them? How can we use the lesson of history to protect our portfolios? What happened after 1955 has an invaluable and profound impact on how to establish a long-term investment strategy. This is the subject of the next chapter.

Chapter
6

LONG-TERM ECONOMIC AND INVESTMENT TRENDS

The challenge in managing investment risk deals with two basic issues. The first one is selecting the asset that investors think offers the greatest opportunities. History shows that stocks are the asset of choice in declining and/or low inflationary periods. Hard assets, such as real estate and commodities, have proved to provide superior returns during times of rising and/or high inflation. The second issue is deciding how much money the investor should invest in a particular asset. The amount of money to be invested initially and in the future depends on the assessment the investor has of short-term and long-term economic trends.

In previous chapters we examined indicators that help investors recognize important economic trends and possible areas of risk and opportunities. At the end of the analysis of the main economic indicators, they were summarized in three main groups: leading, coincident, and lagging indicators. It was also suggested that the growth of the economy, relative to its long-term average, has an important impact on the financial markets and the overall investment climate. The relative movement of the leading, coincident, and lagging indicators, and of the economy in relation to its growth potential, affects short-term investment decisions. These decisions are the outcome of the answer to questions such as "What should I do now?" "What should my strategy be in the coming months?" "What is the asset that offers the greatest opportunities and least risk, depending on the phase of the business cycle?"

In the following chapters, we will analyze in more detail each particular asset and how its price is affected by the business cycle itself. However, before beginning that discussion, it is important that investors gain an appreciation and understanding of the broad, long-term eco-

nomic trends. The first thing investors need to understand is the kind of
economic times in which they live.

Learning from History

There is a lot to learn from history. And while it is beyond the scope of
this book to analyze all the historical events that took place in the last
century, in this section, we will look back at some economic and financial history of the second half of the last century and try to extract the
most relevant information that directly impacts the investors' assessment
of the financial markets. What we will learn from that are some basic
trends that are useful in identifying basic strategic choices of assets and
the long-term risks of certain economic developments.

To begin, we can subdivide the history of the past decades into three
basic periods: the 1950s to 1968, 1968 to 1982, and the years following
1982 to the end of the twentieth century. These three periods offer great
lessons for investors and provide important guidelines for them to follow to assess the major economic and financial trends that will impact
their investment performance. A study of these periods will be useful in
determining which kinds of assets were the most attractive, and which
were the least, during these times and why.

The main distinction between the three periods is the rate of inflation.
In the 1950s up to 1968, inflation was well under control. From 1968 to
1982, inflation in the United States and overseas soared and reached
unprecedented levels. Then in 1982 inflation started to decline. We will
examine the reasons for this transition and obtain some useful guidelines
as they apply to investing.

Policymakers operate the levers that control these huge movements in
prices from the 1950s to the 1970s and following the 1980s. These levers
are very powerful and effective. Ultimately though, it is the opinion of
the author that it is we, the people, who have great influence in driving
the actions of the policymakers.

In the 1950s, following World War II and the Korean War, the United
States was the economic leader of the world and the most powerful
nation in the world. We realized our power and our dominance of world
events. The peace and prosperity that that America felt beginning in the
fifties created a sense of optimism and wealth, also shared by Europe.
As the world and the population of the industrialized world recognized
the great well-being that they enjoyed, they tried to seek more of it.
Toward the end of the 1960s and into the 1970s, the population of both

the United States and Europe became more sensitive to the suggestion that government could provide even more wealth than what people had already attained.

As people called on their governments to provide and share more and more wealth, the governments in the industrialized world became bigger and bigger. It is not to pass judgment, but it is a fact of human life that when an organization becomes very big, it eventually becomes inefficient, especially because of the size of the bureaucratic apparatus. This inefficiency of the governments and their increasing expenditures created inflationary pressures that were beyond control. Eventually, toward the end of the 1980s, people realized that large governments were not the answer they expected. Instead of more well-being, they were getting less and less wealth as inflation soared.

People in the United States demanded that inflation in the country be brought under control. The experiment that lasted the whole decade of the 1970s, an experiment based on providing the country with social programs and regulations that went beyond what the country could afford, had created serious problems. Government bureaucracy increased, inflation steadily rose, and the country soon realized that the price to be paid for all the social programs and the multitudes of regulations that were instituted was higher inflation. Of course, rising inflation was a major price to pay because it had the immediate effect of reducing income. As a result, toward the end of the 1970s the country elected leaders who promised in a credible way to bring inflation under control and bring back solid economic times, which is what happened after 1982.

This same experiment of the 1970s also took place in Europe. The same inflationary pressures that were experienced in the United States were also a major issue in Europe. European inflation had a more structural problem. Many laws had been passed in Europe providing protection on the surface for the workers. This created a rigidity that the U.S. economic system did not have. In fact, even when inflation began its long-term decline in the early 1980s, the economy in Europe did not enjoy the kind of vitality the U.S. economy had, because of the rigidities in labor laws that were designed more to protect the people who worked than those who were seeking new jobs.

Since 1982, lower inflation created other strains but also created great wealth. Countries that had extremely large governments had difficulty in managing themselves, and they strove to survive. The collapse of the Soviet Union is ultimate proof that very large bureaucratic systems cannot survive. They have within themselves the seed of collapse and high inflation. As the U.S. population asked for lower inflation, government shrank, inflation came down, and new opportunities arose. The leaders elected in the United States were successful in bringing down inflation in the country and initiating a very positive process. Of course, as inflation came down, it forced people to become more efficient. Inefficiencies could not be tolerated, as the country was committed to keeping inflation under control. It's no coincidence that governments were forced to become leaner and reflect the mood of the country.

As the environment in the last century moved from one of low inflation to one of high inflation and back to one of low inflation again, the population had a major impact in initiating these changes. Great wealth was created in the 1950s and the 1960s, destroyed in the 1970s, and attained again in the 1980s. The savvy investor would have recognized these trends and taken advantage of them.

How could an investor have detected these huge changes from the available data? We will identify the main parameters that would have shown the astute observer that policymakers were following policies that would have a major impact for many decades.

Real Short-Term Interest Rates

In order to recognize the overwhelming changes in the investment climate since the 1950s, it is crucial to appreciate the impact of real short-term interest rates on the economy and inflation. They play a major role in the way the U.S. economy, and for that matter any economy, performs. Their level has a close relationship with the performance of the financial markets and the price of hard assets. They also can be used to assess strengths and weaknesses of foreign economies, and as a result, to evaluate the attractiveness of foreign investments. This will be discussed in more detail later in this chapter.

Short-term interest rates represent the price of money when it's borrowed and repaid in a period of less than one year. In our discussion, we will use the rate on 13-week Treasury bills, which represents the interest paid by the U.S. government when it borrows money over 13 weeks. The reason for using this rate is that it moves quickly when market conditions change. It also has the property of moving ahead of Federal Reserve announcements. Later, we will see the relationship between the Fed and interest rates. For the time being, let's accept the fact that the Fed has a major role in impacting the trend and the level of short-term interest rates, and in particular the rate of 13-week Treasury bills.

The difference between the level of short-term interest rates and inflation is called *real short-term interest rates*. Inflation is measured as the change over 12 months in the consumer price index or in the core consumer price index (over the long term, these numbers are the same). These data are readily available from the Bureau of Labor Statistics. The Fed, since it can manage the level of short-term interest rates, also impacts the level of real short-term interest rates. The level of real short-term interest rates has an impact on the level of real long-term interest rates, that is, the price of money when investors and businesses borrow over the long term. The evidence shows that the 1970s, a period of low real short-term interest rates, was also accompanied by low real long-term interest rates, well below the average for the century. On the other hand, the 1950s and the years following 1982 were periods when real short-term and real long-term interest rates were well above their long-term average.

Real short-term interest rates oscillated around the value of 1.4 throughout most of the twentieth century. The historical evidence strongly shows that the 1.4 value is an important number to follow when developing long-term investment strategies. The history of the last century since 1955 shows that as long as real short-term interest rates stayed close to 1.4 or higher, inflation remained under control.

Real short-term interest rates were close to this value from the early 1950s to 1967, and inflation oscillated between zero and 3 percent most of the time. However, real short-term interest rates began to decline quite sharply after 1968 and fell from 1.4 to as low as -7. That meant that interest rates were kept below the level of inflation through most of the 1970s. For this reason, in that decade people used to say that it paid to borrow—that inflation was going to bail you out. The cost of money was lower than inflation.

In 1980–1981, real interest rates rose dramatically and moved well above the level of 1.4, hovering close to 5 in the 1980s. In other words, short-term interest rates were kept 5 percentage points above the level of inflation. The outcome was very expensive money and this was a major determinant for inflation to decline from roughly 15 percent to 2–2 1/2 percent. Since the early 1980s, real short-term interest rates have been above the important 1.4 level, except for a short period in 1992–1993, when the price of money was kept artificially low to reliquefy the banking system because of a severe real estate crisis.

But after 1994, real short-term interest rates moved up again above 1.4, and inflation moved close to 2 to 3 percent. The main lesson of the last century has been that in the 1970s inflation moved dramatically higher from close to 3 percent to 15 percent, as real short-term interest rates were kept by the Fed well below the 1.4 level. The other times prior to 1968 and following 1982, when real short-term interest rates were close to or above 1.4, inflation hovered close to 2 to 3 percent.

Real long-term interest rates behaved very much like real short-term interest rates during the twentieth century. For most of the century, real long-term interest rates, computed as the yield on 10-year bonds less inflation, hovered around the 2.75 level. Since 1955, as it happened for short-term interest rates, one can distinguish three main periods when real long-term interest rates behaved like real short-term interest rates.

From 1955 to 1966–1967, real bond yields were very close to 2.75 as the yield on 10-year bonds stayed close to 4 percent. From 1965 to 1982, real bond yields declined sharply below the 2.75 level to drop as low as -4. During this time, when yields on long-term bonds were below the level of inflation, inflation soared. The outcome, which will be discussed in more detail in later chapters, was that bond yields jumped from 5 percent to 15 percent during the 1970s.

However, beginning in 1982, as it has happened for real short-term interest rates, real bond yields soared to well above the 2.75 level, moving close to 7 percentage points above the level of inflation. Since 1982, the level of real bond yields was constantly above the 2.75 level as bond yields declined from 15 percent to close to 6–7 percent.

There are various theories on how real short-term and real long-term interest rates relate to the level of inflation and the level of productivity. What is important to recognize, however, is their strong relationship with inflation trends in the last century. As noted earlier, there have been three important periods:

- Prior to 1967

- From 1967 to 1982

- Following 1982

The experience of the 1970s shows that sharply rising inflation and sharply rising bond yields were accompanied by very low real interest rates. The other two periods were similar in many respects. But their main feature was low or declining inflation and high real long-term and short-term interest rates. The experience of foreign countries confirms this relationship. Countries with low real interest rates are usually countries that have much higher inflation than the countries with high real interest rates. Real long-term interest rates are also related to the growth of the economy and the growth of productivity of the country. Trends in long-term interest rates and their role in your portfolio will be discussed in a later chapter.

When we speak about real short-term interest rates, we assume the Fed has an important role in determining their level. From our perspective, the issue is not why real interest rates are high or low. Our objective is to relate their level to economic and inflationary conditions.

Why do real interest rates have such an impact on the economy? The answer is quite simple. The level of real short-term interest rates determines whether the price of money is cheap or expensive. When the price of money is high relative to inflation, money is expensive. And this makes consumers, businesses, and investors more cautious about the use of their funds. On the other hand, when real short-term interest rates are low, money is inexpensive, and it is easy to borrow and spend.

Why are low real interest rates inflationary? Let's consider an example. When real interest rates are low, as in the 1970s, the price of money is close to or below the level of inflation. Since the price of real estate grows roughly as inflation grows consumers and investors in the 1970s borrowed heavily to buy real estate. There was little to lose. The price increase in the asset was enough to repay the borrowed money. There was no risk. More and more people thought that this was an easy way to protect their capital. As a result, the real estate sector boomed, and prices rose sharply with it. In more general terms, low real short-term interest rates stimulated inflation through excess demand for goods due to inexpensive money.

Real interest rates also impact businesses and their decisions to invest and the type of investments they choose. For instance, high real long-term interest rates force businesses to invest in projects with a high rate of return. However, investments with a high rate of return require large financial commitments and have a high technological content. Let's assume that a manufacturing company has the need for more production capacity and the company plans to have a plant expansion. The project has to pay for itself to be implemented. That is, the savings that a project will provide, or the return of the project, has to be greater than the cost of the money that is needed to implement that particular project. Let's assume that long-term interest rates are 8 percent and inflation is 7 percent. The project can be implemented only if its return is greater than 8 percent, which is the cost of borrowing the money. But since inflation is 7 percent, that means that the company can increase prices by 7 percent a year; offsetting 7 percent of the cost of the money. As a result, the project only has to return at least 1 percent to make it viable. Clearly, a project with only 1 percent improvement is not difficult to achieve. Any small adjustment to existing machinery can provide a 1 percent return, thus making the project profitable.

However, let's assume now that long-term interest rates are 8 percent but inflation is 2 percent. The project can be implemented only if its return is greater than 8 percent, which is the cost of money. The company can increase prices at a rate of 2 percent a year, which only takes care of 2 percent of the cost of borrowing. The overall project, therefore, has to return at least 6 percent to make it profitable after inflation. Clearly, the effort needed for this kind of project has to be much more involved than for the previous one, because now the project has to return at least 6 percent. In order to achieve this goal, the company has to allocate specialists to study productivity improvements of at least 6 percent, and they are likely to be achieved only if there is heavy usage of computers, programming efforts, and other technical innovations.

The point of these two simple examples is to show that the level of real interest rates has an impact on the type of projects that can be implemented. The higher the real cost of money, the higher the level of sophistication of the project, because the project has to provide a higher return. The high productivity of the project is a major reason why inflation during times of high real interest rates is kept under control.

We have discussed an example of one company, but high real interest rates affect all the companies in the country. When all the companies are trying to achieve the same goal, that is, to implement projects with a high rate of return because of the high real cost of money, the whole country becomes more productive. This is the reason why as inflation declines, the productivity of the country increases. Declining inflation does not allow businesses to raise prices at will, thus squeezing margins. On the other hand, high real interest rates force corporations to implement high-rate-of-return, high-productivity projects. The outcome is that the whole country has a productivity boom, as experienced by the United States after the 1980s.

The opposite happens when real short-term interest rates are low and real long-term interest rates are also low. Businesses does not have to invest in high rate of return projects because money is cheap and any project is easy to justify from a financial viewpoint. This leads necessarily to low productivity and higher inflation. As discussed above, low real interest rates do not stimulate innovation because any slight improvement in efficiencies will make the project viable. Since low real interest rates are accompanied by rising inflation, a company will find it easier to improve margins by raising prices rather than going through involved technological projects. Again, what the 1970s showed in the United States and Europe is that high levels of inflation are associated with ever-decreasing levels of productivity, growth, and low real interest rates.

High real short-term interest rates in the United States (or any country in the world) are a sign the Federal Reserve or any particular central bank is committed to keeping money expensive. This situation forces consumers and investors to use money more carefully, thus keeping inflation under control and forcing productivity to rise.

Productivity rises when inflation declines because business cannot raise prices. As a result, the only way to improve margins and profitability is to improve productivity. This is the reason why technology stocks boom in periods of very low inflation. In fact, the technology boom that we had since the 1980s did not occur in the 1970s because margins in the 1970s could be easily improved simply by raising prices and so there was no need for technology. There is no doubt that as inflation declines, business pricing power decreases; and as a result, businesses cannot raise prices to improve margins. The only way to increase margins is by improving productivity to absorb and cut costs. It's no coincidence that as inflation declined in the 1980s and 1990s, productivity growth soared in the United States, both at the overall economic level and at the manufacturing level. One can also say that low inflation is good not only for overall corporate America, but especially for the technology sector because of the strong reliance on technology to improve both productivity and profitability.

Low real short-term interest rates suggest money is cheap, and therefore, consumers and businesses do not have the self-discipline to spend it carefully. As a result, they create inflation and a low-productivity environment. Let's see now how these concepts may help in explaining the huge changes in the economy and asset prices we experienced since 1955.

Assessing Changes in Long-Term Investment Trends

The dramatic developments in the U.S. economy and financial markets since 1950 can be explained in terms of what happened to the level of real interest rates. Of course, there have been many other factors at play, including, just to name a few, wars, changes in government policies from smaller governments to bigger governments, and an increase in the welfare state. Quite often it is easy to be misled by headlines proclaiming specific ideas and specific political trends. Sometimes it seems appropriate to have a government leaning more toward a welfare state, where the government is the caretaker of the problems of the citizens, from insurance, to medical assistance, to day care, and so on. But all these trends have a price, and politicians don't seem to know, or for that matter no one seems to know, when to stop. The only time people recognize that they have to stop is after the problem is so big that it has to be dealt with.

A typical example is what happened in the 1970s in the United States. The trend in the 1970s was to provide more government assistance to the citizens. At the same time, the United States was also involved in a war. It was difficult for the average person to recognize what was happening, and difficult for the average citizen to evaluate the impact of certain decisions when the commitment was *not* to raise taxes—although there was a commitment to fighting a war and implementing President Johnson's Great Society. Inflation was the only solution. Of course, inflation had ravaging effects on the financial markets, and investors were severely penalized by the policies that led to unprecedented increases in prices. Because of the impact on inflation and on investment returns and investment strategies, the average investor needs to have an impartial framework to assess and develop an investment strategy. The investor needs a precise number and something to follow to make decisions. The only number that can accurately depict what happened is the level of real short-term interest rates, rates that mainly have been driven by the policy of the Federal Reserve. Clearly in the transition from the 1960s to the 1970s, average investors would have realized that something was happening when gradual inflation kept rising and real interest rates started to decline. As inflation began its decade-long rise, the dollar slowly and steadily began to weaken.

In the 1970s, when real short-term interest rates declined sharply below 1.4, it was a clear signal to the investor that the seeds for an inflationary environment were planted. Remember, inflation was stable when real short-term interest rates were kept close to 1.4 or above this level. In the postwar era (World War II), the only time inflation rose sharply was when real short-term interest rates declined below 1.4.

Dr. Henry Wallich, a governor of the Federal Open Market Committee in the 1970s, often noted that real short-term interest rates were too low in the 1970s, even at a time when short-term interest rates soared from 3 percent in the late 1960s to 20 percent in 1982. His point was that money was too cheap and that was inflationary. Of course, the Fed could not raise real short-term interest rates because cheap money was necessary to finance the Great Society and the war in Vietnam since the government did not increase taxes to finance those efforts.

In order to fight inflation the Fed let interest rates rise in 1968, causing the recession of 1969–1970. Inflation declined because of very slow growth in the economy, but money was still kept cheap, as real interest rates were kept low.

The next expansion, which started toward the end of 1970, saw inflation grow from 4 to 6 percent from 1972 to 1974. Worried that rising inflation might go out of control, the Fed increased interest rates again in 1972, causing the recession of 1973. Again, inflation declined, from 6 to 4 percent, because of slow economic growth. However, because of very low real short-term interest rates, the next expansion was accompanied by even higher inflation, which soared to 15 percent in 1982.

The lesson of the 1970s was that low real short-term interest rates were accompanied by soaring inflation and a very volatile economy because the Fed had to induce a recession every two years to try to keep inflation under control (Figure 6-1). Commodities soared, with the price of gold rocketing from $35 to $800 an ounce and the price of crude oil rising sharply from $25 to $40 a barrel. Wages jumped because of rising inflation and also lower productivity. As a result, unit labor costs (the difference between wages and productivity) rose rapidly. Not surprisingly,

INFLATION AND BUSINESS VOLATILITY

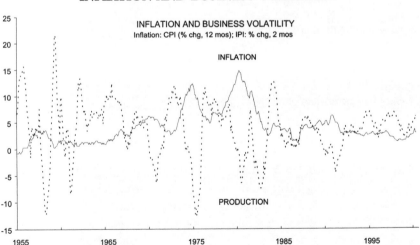

Figure 6-1. Some readers may recall that the 1970s experienced extreme business fluctuations as inflation rose from 3 percent to 15 percent. Business cycles were much more stable in the 1960s and after 1982 as inflation declined to 1960 levels.

corporate profitability was dismal. The dollar, which reflected soaring inflation and poor economic conditions, collapsed. The exchange rate between the German mark and the dollar went from 3.20 German marks to the dollar to only 1.50 German marks to the dollar in 1990. The yen also gained great strength relative to the dollar, going from 340 yen to the dollar to just about 85 yen to the dollar.

While returns from hard assets were simply fantastic as prices of commodities, such as gold, crude oil, industrial metals, real estate, and just about anything, soared, the returns from investments in financial assets in the 1970s were dismal. Bond prices collapsed as the yield on 10-year Treasury bonds soared from 5 percent to 15 percent in 1982. The stock market finished at the same level as it was in 1968, mirroring the dreary performance of the profitability of corporations.

Clearly, the 1970s was a special decade and provided important lessons. The 1970s can be characterized by:

- Low real short-term interest rates below 1.4 percent

- Rising inflation

- Rising commodities

- High volatile economic cycles

- Dismal productivity growth

- Corporations could raise prices because of rising inflation to improve profitability

- Low investment in technology

- Soaring real estate and land prices

- Soaring long-term interest rates

- Sagging bond prices

- Frequent protracted declines in stocks, with prices going nowhere from 1968 to 1982—an astonishing 15-year sideways market

Throughout the 1970s, the dollar also sagged, reflecting a U.S. economy in disarray. During this decade, the decline in the dollar made foreign investments particularly attractive, thanks mostly to the strength of European and Japanese currencies. If the investor looks at the years 1955 to 1968 and the years following 1982, the most crucial feature is that real short-term interest rates in this period were kept well above 1.4. In the years following 1982, they were considerably above their long-term average. By making money expensive in real terms, the Fed forced consumers and businesses to become wiser in their spending and their investments (Figure 6-2).

Lower inflation meant that businesses could not raise prices at will. Price increases had to reflect current inflation pressures, which were waning. Lacking the lever of price to improve margins, corporations had to rely on other strategies to improve their profitability. One solution was to emphasize restructuring, resulting in streamlining the operation, cutting personnel, and flattening the organization. The other solution was to improve productivity (Figure 6-3) by investing heavily in technology and advanced productive processes.

It is no coincidence that technological development was stagnant in the inflationary 1970s and boomed after 1982. Technology stocks soared as new technologies were introduced.

As productivity soared, unit labor costs remained stable, even if wages were growing at a 3 or 4 percent pace. The lesson is that as long as real interest rates stay high and inflation stays low, technology stocks will continue to perform well.

At the same time, inflation and higher productivity were accompanied by a stable economic environment, with only one minor recession in 1990–1991, mostly caused by the consumer panic over the Gulf War with Iraq.

INFLATION AND REAL INTEREST RATES

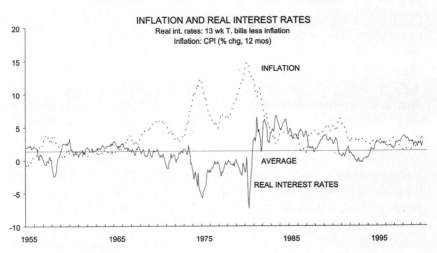

Figure 6-2. Inflation soared in the 1970s as real short-term interest rates were kept below their historical average. Inflation was low in the 1960s and after 1982 as real interest rates were kept above their historical average.

PRODUCTIVITY GROWTH IN THE U.S.

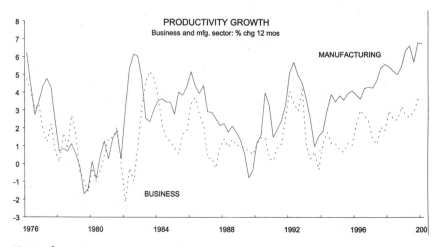

Figure 6-3. Due to declining and low inflation after 1982, business lacked pricing power to improve margins. Consequently, corporations relied on enhancing productivity as a way of absorbing costs and raising profitability. As a result, since 1982, the United States enjoyed soaring productivity growth.

As inflation declined after 1982 from 15 to 2 percent, 10-year bond yields dropped from 10 to 5 percent and stocks soared. Low inflation also meant lower commodity prices, with gold declining from $800 to $300 an ounce and crude oil from $40 to $15 a barrel. Real estate, reflecting the slower growth in inflation, did not display the phenomenal price increases of the 1970s. Financial assets were the great performers. Hard assets such as precious metals performed poorly—exactly the mirror image of the 1970s.

There is only one period when this great economic environment was disturbed. In 1992–1993, because of the real estate and savings and loan crisis, the Fed had to make money cheap to protect the U.S. economy and improve bank profitability by keeping the yield curve unusually steep. It did so by keeping short-term rates very low relative to inflation. This easy-money period was briefly followed in 1994 by the type of environment typical of the 1970s: rising inflation and bond yields, weak stock prices, soaring commodities, and a weak dollar.

The years that followed 1982 were in many respects similar to the 1950s. In the 1950s real short-term interest rates were kept above the historical average of 1.4. Inflation as a result was around 3 percent, bond yields were stable, the stock market was strong, and the dollar was the currency of choice. Gold was trading at $35 an ounce, and the economy had two mild recessions. Financial assets were definitely a solid invest-ment. In the years following 1982 both bonds and stocks provided superb returns as inflation declined, while hard assets such as precious metals and real estate did not perform as well as stocks and bonds. Although it is difficult to find a single indicator that can best give a sense of the economic times facing the investor, real short-term interest rates, with their simplicity and easy availability, explain the huge transition that took place from the 1950s through the 1970s and the years since 1982.

Using Interest Rates to Assess the Risk of Foreign Investments

The money markets are a very sensitive mechanism, causing interest rates to adjust quickly to small changes in economic growth and in the overall financial environment. Because of this sensitivity, they provide an objective view of the state of the investment environment. As Sydney Homer once said, "Interest rates are the fever chart of any economy."

Rising interest rates are the result of a strong economy, making invest-ments in stocks a risky proposition. Periods of rising interest rates have been notoriously accompanied by poor market performance. During such times investors have two basic options:

• Invest money in money-market instruments, thus providing a return equal to short-term interest rates.

• Find stock sectors that perform unusually well during those periods. This takes lengthy research and requires special tools.

On the other hand, declining interest rates provide investors with con-firmation that the economy is slowing down and the stock market again represents a good investment. The relationship and turning points between interest rates and stock prices can best be understood by remembering that equity prices are a leading economic indicator and interest rates are a lagging economic indicator.

Besides watching for the trend that interest rates indicate, it is also important to keep track of their level. Since 1955, in the United States, the average level of short-term interest rates has been about 5 to 6 per-cent. The further interest rates moved away from this range, the more the country was subjected to economic and financial disturbances in var-ious degrees of intensity. In the 1970s short-term interest rates rose to 20 percent, well above the 5–6 percent range. As they moved toward this level, the economic cycle became more unstable, inflation increased to higher and higher levels, and the unemployment rate moved to all-time highs. The country was confused by social and war issues, and it wasn't clear what was happening in terms of the economy. Political and monetary policies were in disarray. Inflation had a negative impact on investments, financial assets, and corporate performance. Without a doubt, rising interest rates to these unprecedented levels created a poor return for financial assets.

It is also true that the further interest rates move on the downside, below 5 to 6 percent, the more the country's economy is in serious trouble. Growth stagnates, the unemployment rate soars, prices of hard assets decline, deflation becomes a major issue, and corporate performance and earnings deteriorate as business attempts to survive by cutting prices. A decline in interest rates well below 5 to 6 percent is an indication that there is poor demand for money because of lack of business opportunities.

When interest rates fall close to 2 or 1 percent, the country experiences not inflation, but deflation. Deflation is that condition whereby business has to cut prices to sell. The reduction of prices has a negative impact on profitability and profit margins. Therefore, business feels compelled to aggressively cut costs. But cutting costs means laying people off, delaying capacity expansions in order to cut interest rate costs, and reducing inventories. Of course, this is a vicious circle that provides a very negative environment for any type of asset.

During such periods the currencies of countries that endure this kind of environment are very weak, as we saw in the United States in the 1930s and Japan in the 1990s. However, there is no doubt that a country with 5 to 6 percent interest rates has an economy that performs well, with a stable political environment and sound financial markets. The level of interest rates is the stamp of approval or disapproval of the financial markets on the policies followed by Congress, by the Federal Reserve, or by the policymakers of any country.

The behavior of interest rates provides important clues to the performance of any country. This information is available daily from the financial pages of most newspapers or on the Internet. It is a simple, fast, and powerful way to assess what is happening around the world. The closer that interest rates for a given country are to 5 to 6 percent, the sounder its economy is, because it reflects economic stability and low inflation. Under these conditions, it is likely the currency is firm, confirming that the policies followed by the local policymakers are sound.

However, there is another element that can easily be checked to confirm your conclusions. This element is the level of real interest rates, which is measured as the difference between short-term interest rates and inflation. For instance, if a country has a level of interest rates of 20 percent, and an inflation of 10 percent, real interest rates are very high—approximately twice the level of inflation. This indicates that the country is committed to bringing inflation down, and monetary policy is conducive to that result.

However, if a country has, for instance, short-term interest rates of 10 percent but inflation is 15 percent, real interest rates are too low because they are well below the level of inflation, and the country is not following policies conducive to lower inflation. Actually, the country's policies are leading to higher inflation because the interest rates are kept below the inflation level. Only if interest rates would go to 25 to 30 percent would the country have a possibility of bringing inflation down from the current 15 percent. The weekly publication *The Economist* makes these data readily available in each issue.

Evaluating Risk

Let's see now how to use the available data to evaluate a country's risk from an investment viewpoint. Let's say country A has interest rates of 30 percent and country B has interest rates of 15 percent. The markets are saying that country B is considerably better than country A even if both countries have interest rates well above the 4 to 5 percent benchmark range. Both countries are not following sound economic and financial policies and provide a high level of risk. Let's also assume that country A has an inflation rate of 29 percent and country B has an inflation rate of 10 percent. Real interest rates between the two countries are considerably higher in country B than in country A. The message is that the policymakers in country B are more determined than those in country A to bring inflation under control by keeping the price of money more expensive than that of country A. Country B is a better managed country than country A, and as a result it should be the country of choice.

However, another element comes into the picture, and that is the value of the currencies of country A and country B. In fact, since the currency of country B follows sounder policies, odds are the currency of country B is stronger than the currency of country A. Investing in country B provides a hedge against your own currency because your investment is denominated in a stronger currency than that of country A, and therefore, your investment will appreciate, other things being equal, because of the increase in value of the currency of country B.

To make things more interesting, let's assume the investor is in country C where interest rates are close to 4 to 5 percent and inflation is close to

2 percent. Clearly, country C is in much better shape than country A and country B, because it has higher real interest rates and interest rates are close to the ideal level. This was the situation of the United States in the 1990s. The odds are that country C will have a much stronger currency than either country A or country B. If investors are in country C, where should they invest? If investors places their money in country A or country B, clearly they will see the investment depreciate in terms of the currency of country C. Even if investors make money on their investments in country A or country B, they are most likely to lose on the depreciation of the currencies of those countries relative to the currency of country C.

The lesson here is that investors should place their money first of all in those countries with the strongest currencies. This is the first and foremost guiding principle. This is not an easy decision to make for the average investor, because predicting currencies is a very tricky and difficult business indeed. However, this example provides simple, yet useful, guidelines.

Making foreign investments is not as simple as some may make it sound because there are many decisions to consider: the evaluation of a country, the risk that the country offers, the value of the currency, and the trends of the currency vis à vis the trend of the dollar. And then there is the issue of buying stocks in that particular foreign country, and we know how difficult it is to buy successful stocks. This is a note of caution for investors who get excited about the possibility of making more money in foreign investments. Quite frankly, this is a very difficult feat.

Investment Implications

In order to establish a long-term investment strategy, it is crucial for the investor to closely follow the current level of real short-term interest rates. We have seen that if real short-term interest rates are below 1.4, or short-term interest rates are considerably less than twice the level of inflation, the following conditions are likely to happen in almost any country:

- Rising inflation
- Rising commodities
- Volatile economic and financial cycles
- Very low productivity growth
- Very poor economic growth

- The tendency of corporations to raise prices rather than invest to improve productivity

- Low investment in technologies

- Soaring real estate prices

- Soaring land prices

- Rising art and coin prices

- Soaring long-term interest rates and sagging bond prices

- Soaring short-term interest rates

- Frequent protracted declines in stock prices, with equities declining 20 to 40 percent

On the other hand, the above trends are reversed when real short-term interest rates are close to 1.4 or above this level, or short-term interest rates are close to two times the level of inflation.

The message of this chapter is that interest rates, their level and their trend, represent an important element to guide your investment strategy. Their careful interpretation provides a useful tool for developing a successful investment program. Higher-than-average real interest rates tell the investor that policymakers are determined to keep inflation under control and therefore maintain stable economic conditions. These economic conditions are usually associated with a strong currency. These are ideal times to invest in financial assets (for instance, bonds and stocks) and avoid hard assets (real estate, art, coins, precious metals and commodities). Furthermore, if short-term interest rates are close to 5 to 6 percent, the markets are confirming that the policies followed in a country are sound and there are no problems on the horizon.

If real short-term interest rates are very low, or worse, interest rates are below inflation, the implication is that the country is in serious trouble and monetary authorities are following an easy-money policy to hide the problems. This is achieved by letting the money supply grow very rapidly and keeping real interest rates very low. The odds favor higher inflation, higher commodities, unstable economic conditions, and a weak currency. Investing in hard assets is the investment strategy that would likely be successful in this environment. The simple lesson is, avoid investing in countries with weak currencies. Always give preference to countries with strong currencies.

Clearly, we can see that there are many forces that impact investment strategies. The trend in the economy, its growth, and its momentum are the major determining factors to consider when developing an investment plan. The level and trend, not only of interest rates, but also of real short-term interest rates and long-term interest rates provide crucial clues about the risk and opportunities of stocks and other assets. High and low real interest rates are driven of course by monetary policy and are crucial parameters to be considered when developing an investment strategy. The trend in stock prices and the currency reflects all these forces.

Many of these forces are driven by the Fed, whose actions impact trends in commodities and inflation, as well as growth, liquidity, and the level of interest rates. It is to this subject that we will turn in the next chapter.

Chapter
7

THE CENTRAL BANK AND YOUR INVESTMENTS

There is no doubt that trends in levels of interest rates are one of the most crucial variables in driving an investment strategy (Figure 7-1). They determine the kind of environment that impacts the stock market, the U.S. economy, inflation, and the U.S. dollar vis à vis other currencies. For these reasons it is important to understand how, and by whom, short-term interest rates are driven.

INTEREST RATES

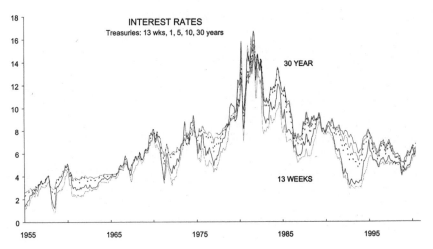

Figure 7-1. Interest rates are the fever chart of any economy. The higher they go above 5 to 6 percent, the more a country suffers major imbalances and rising inflation. The lower interest rates go below 5 to 6 percent, the more pronounced the imbalances become as deflation raises its ugly head.

The central bank of any country—the Federal Reserve for the United States is the institution that has the power and the authority to impact trends and levels of short-term interest rates. Consequently, the central bank has a huge impact on the financial markets, and savvy U.S. investors understand how the Federal Reserve shapes the economy.

In an effort to understand the workings of the Federal Reserve, let's look at how it is organized, how it conducts monetary policy, what monetary policy is, how monetary policy impacts the growth of the money supply, and what the instruments of monetary policy are.

Another important variable that is controlled by the Federal Reserve is the level of real interest rates, and we have seen in the previous chapter how this is a crucial variable in determining the kind of financial markets we should expect.

It is important to recognize that at a time of crisis, central banks intervene to cushion the blow, as in the 1970s when several banks failed. There are two main reasons for bank failures. The first one is rising interest rates, which represent rising costs for banks, since banks have to borrow money to relend at a higher interest rate. As short-term interest rates rise, because of the Fed's tightening and strong economic conditions accompanied by inflationary pressures, bank profit margins are squeezed.

The second reason for bank failure is that some banks have a loan portfolio that has been extended to marginal clients. During times of rising interest rates, these clients find it difficult to repay the loans. As a result, because of rising short-term rates, the raw material for banks, and problems with loan portfolios, bank failures are more likely. This occurred in 1992–1993 when there were real estate problems in the United States that led to the savings and loan debacle. It happened again during the global financial crisis that began in 1997 in Asia and expanded throughout the world, particularly to Brazil and Russia in 1998.

During a financial crisis, a central bank has the crucial role of providing liquidity to the banking system in order to keep it viable and to make sure the crisis does not spread to other sectors of the economy and other economies around the world. The central bank recognizes the difficulties the banking system faces due to rising short-term interest rates and issues related to the loan portfolio of the banks. These are typical problems the central bank follows very closely. The failure of a major bank, however, or a major global region, like Asia in 1997, forces the central bank to provide extra liquidity to the banking system, trying to make sure that the problems of the banking system do not spill over to the rest of the economy.

It is clear that the Federal Reserve has huge impact. It has an enormous effect on the U.S. economy, inflation, and the money supply. It also provides assistance to institutions and countries that have difficulties so that the economy continues to expand in an orderly fashion. The Fed makes use of several tools when handling crises. From tools to monetary policy, the Fed's actions have many implications for investors. Let's take a look at the Fed, how it works, and what it means to investors.

The Federal Reserve System

Just prior to the founding of the Federal Reserve in 1913, the nation was plagued with financial crises. At times these crises led to panic, where people raced to their bank to withdraw their money. A particularly severe panic in 1907 resulted in bank runs that wreaked havoc on the fragile banking system and ultimately led Congress to write the Federal Reserve Act. Initially created to address banking panics, the Federal Reserve System is now charged with a number of broader responsibilities, including fostering a sound banking system and a healthy economy.

Establishing the nation's first central bank was no simple task. Although the need for a central bank was generally undisputed, for decades early supporters debated the delicate balance between national and regional interests. On a national front, the central bank had to be structured to facilitate the exchange of payments among regions to strengthen the standing of the United States in the world economy. On a regional front, it had to be responsive to local liquidity needs, which varied across regions of the United States.

Another critical balancing act was between the private interest of banks and the centralized responsibility of government. What emerged with the Federal Reserve System was a central bank under public control with countless checks and balances. Congress oversees the entire Federal Reserve System, and the Fed must work within the objectives established by Congress. Yet Congress gave the Federal Reserve the autonomy to carry out its responsibilities insulated from political pressure.

Each of the Fed's three parts: the Board of Governors, the regional Reserve banks, and the Federal Open Market Committee, operates cooperatively, yet independent of the federal government to carry out the Fed's core responsibilities. What makes the Federal Reserve independent? Three structural features: the appointment procedure for governors, the appointment procedure for Federal Reserve bank presidents, and the funding of the Federal Reserve.

There are seven governors on the Federal Reserve Board, and they are appointed by the President of the United States and confirmed by the Senate. Independence is derived from several factors. First, appointments are staggered to reduce the chance that a single U.S. President could load the Board with appointees. Second, terms of office are 14 years, much longer than elected officials' terms.

The appointment procedure for Federal Reserve bank presidents is also an element that provides independence to the Federal Reserve. Each Reserve bank president is appointed to a five-year term by the bank's board of directors, subject to final approval by the board of Governors. This procedure ensures independence because the directors of each Reserve bank are not chosen by politicians, but are selected to provide a cross-section of interests within the region, including those of depository institutions, known financial businesses, labor, and the public.

Last, but not least, what provides independence of our central bank is funding. The Fed is structured to be self-sufficient in the sense that it meets its operating expenses primarily from the interest earnings on its portfolio of securities. Therefore, it is independent of congressional decisions about appropriations. Even though the Fed is independent of congressional appropriations and administrative control, it is ultimately accountable to Congress and comes under government audit and review.

The chairman, other governors, and Reserve bank presidents report regularly to Congress on monetary policy, regulatory policy, and a variety of other issues, and meet with senior administration officials to discuss the Federal Reserve's and the Federal government's economic programs.

At the core of the Federal Reserve System is the Board of Governors, or Federal Reserve Board. The Board of Governors is located in Washington, D.C., and is a federal government agency—that is the Fed's centralized component.

The Board consists of seven members, called governors. These governors guide the Federal Reserve's policy action. The seven governors, along with a host of economists and support staff, help write the policies that help make our banks financially sound, and help formulate the policies that make our nation economically strong.

A considerable amount of information concerning the activities of the Board of Governors and its economists, as well as specialized surveys that are conducted by the Federal Reserve System is available on the Internet by accessing the website of the Federal Reserve System.

Investors are urged to carefully read the many reports and studies released by the Fed free of charge through the Internet. For instance, governors actively lead committees to study prevailing economic issues, ranging from affordable housing and consumer banking laws to interstate banking and electronic commerce. The Board also exercises broad supervisory controls over member banks ensuring that commercial banks operate responsibly and comply with federal regulations.

Probably their most important responsibility, however, is participating in the Federal Open Market Committee (FOMC), the committee that directs the nation's monetary policy. Heading the Board are a chairman and vice chairman, who are appointed by the U.S. President to serve four-year terms.

The chairman reports twice a year to Congress on the Fed's monetary policy objectives, testifies before Congress on numerous other issues, and meets periodically with the secretary of the treasury.

The FOMC is the Fed's chief monetary policymaking body. The role of the FOMC is to manage the nation's money supply. The FOMC meets typically eight times a year in Washington, D.C.

At each meeting the FOMC discusses the outlook of the U.S. economy and the best way to promote the economy's sustainable growth. The FOMC then discusses how the Fed will use its various policy tools to put the policy in place. Finally, the policy is used as a directive that drives one of three outcomes: easing, tightening, or maintaining the growth of the nation's money supply—whichever is conducive to fostering a healthy economy at the time.

The FOMC has nineteen members, twelve of whom are voting members—the seven members of the Board of Governors, the president of the Federal Reserve bank of New York, and four other Reserve bank presidents who serve one term on a rotating basis. At every meeting, however, all twelve Reserve bank presidents participate in FOMC policy discussions, whether or not they are voting members.

The minutes of the Federal Open Market Committee also are available on the Internet. These minutes are very valuable reading for those investors who want to learn how to analyze economic and financial data, how the Fed interprets these data, and how the Fed uses these data to impact the interest rates and the economic environment. This is definitely recommended reading for investors to establish a sound and informed investment strategy. Even if these minutes are available with some delay, they still provide valuable clues about monetary policy, and about the direction in which the Federal Reserve is leaning. It is better for investors to analyze data themselves. It helps to gain insights that otherwise would be impossible to acquire by relying on analysis offered by the media.

The third part of the Federal Reserve System consists of the twelve Federal Reserve banks. The operations of the Federal Reserve System are conducted through a nationwide network of twelve Federal Reserve banks with branches around the country. Each branch of a Federal Reserve bank has its own board of directors, composed of five or seven members. A majority of three or four, as the case may be, is appointed by the head office directors and the others by the Board of Governors.

The directors of each Federal Reserve bank oversee the operations of their bank under the overall supervision of the Board of Governors. They establish, subject to approval by the Board, the interest rates the banks charge on short-term collateral loans to member banks and on any loans that may be extended to nonmember institutions. National banks are required by law to be members of the system. Commercial banks chartered by any of the 50 states may elect to become members if they meet the requirements established by the Board of Governors. The member banks own all the stock of the Reserve banks. Nonmember institutions, that is, institutions that elect not to be part of the Federal Reserve System, include savings banks, savings and loan associations, and credit unions. The directors appoint the bank president and first vice president, and recommend their salaries, all of which is subject to final approval by the Board.

Earnings of the Federal Reserve banks are derived primarily from interest received on their holdings of securities acquired through open market operations and on their loans to member banks. More than 80 percent of Reserve banks' earnings have been paid into the Treasury since the Federal Reserve System was established. Should a Reserve bank be liquidated, its surplus, after all obligations have been met, would become the property of the U.S. government.

What Guides Monetary Policy?

The main function of the Federal Reserve is to control the growth of money and credit. Monetary policy is the set of actions that lead to the expansion of money and credit in such a way as to produce a stable, growing economy at reasonable stable prices.

What this means is that the objective of the Fed is to achieve growth in the money supply to create an environment characterized by low inflation, usually expected to be below 2 percent, with as little volatility as possible in the business cycle. We have learned that historical evidence suggests that inflation below 2 percent is close to price stability and is usually accompanied by stable economic growth, which does not show, for instance, the type of instability and volatility of the 1970s. The risk of following a low inflation policy is that it may lead to deflation under some conditions. Since deflation is the outright decline in consumer prices, it would create economic conditions that would not be beneficial for the country. Establishing an inflation target of 2 percent, therefore, creates a safety cushion in case of unexpected events.

The issue from the Federal Reserve's standpoint is to determine the information needed to guide monetary policy to meet its ultimate objective. There has been a continuing debate about this for a number of years both inside and outside the Federal Reserve. Some have argued that interest rates are the principal guide for monetary policy, in the belief that interest rate guidelines can be related more dependably to current and prospective expenditures by key sectors of the economy and therefore to the ultimate economic objectives of full employment, reasonable price stability, and international competitiveness.

However, others have advocated the idea that growth in one or more measures of the money supply should be the main focus of the Federal Reserve. Since they believe that the control of the money stock will more surely and predictably lead to the overall economic effects that are desired, they argue that the focus of the Fed should be the money supply. Still others have taken an eclectic position. They believe that no one financial variable can or should be taken as a unique guide for monetary policy in view of the complexity of the economy, the wide variety of financial influences on spending, and the changing attitudes of businesspeople, investors, and consumers toward spending and liquidity.

Clearly the issues are serious, broad, and difficult to tackle. It is important to recognize what the issues of concern are for the Federal Reserve System and what their response to these issues is. We will see how investors can assess the actions of the Fed, assess their own issues and concerns, and then derive a proper investment strategy.

Another important issue the Fed has to consider is the monetary problems that develop around the world, and their impact on the U.S. economy. Judgments have to be made continually on what should be done and what kind of monetary policy should be followed. Whatever processes the FOMC goes through to reach a consensus and whatever the resulting action the FOMC takes, there are two main results of monetary policy. One is the growth of the money supply, and the second is the trend and level of real short-term interest rates.

Let's talk about the money supply and how it is defined. There are several measures of money supply. It is important to recognize the difference between them. From an investor's viewpoint, they provide the same information. But sometimes some measures are better than others, so it is always important to understand these definitions. There are times when, because of technological innovation or changes in the structure of the banking system, some measures of the money supply become distorted. For this reason, it is always appropriate to follow many measures and recognize that some may be distorted because of temporary factors. Money supply data are available from the Fed every week through the Internet, and the historical data are also available on the websites of the Fed and the Federal Reserve Bank of St. Louis.

There are three main measures of the money supply. The first one is called M1 and consists of currency, traveler's checks of nonbank issuers, and demand deposits at all commercial banks. The second measure of the money supply is M2, and is made up of M1 plus savings deposits including money-market savings accounts, small-denomination time deposits, and balances in retail money-market funds. The third measure of the money supply is M3, which consists of M2 plus large-denomination time deposits in the amount of $100,000 or more, balances in institutional money funds, and Eurodollars held by U.S. residents in foreign banks.

The money supply is a measure of how much money is in the economy—M1 is a narrow definition of the money supply, M2 is a broader definition of the money supply, and M3 is an even broader definition of the money supply. There is also a fourth definition, which is called MZM— that is, money with zero maturity (Figure 7-2). It is defined as M2 plus institutional money funds, minus total small-denomination time deposits.

Many assets are closely related to cash, and the public can readily switch between cash and these other liquid assets. Much of the time, switches are in response to changing interest rate differentials between these assets. At other times though, the switches may reflect a growing awareness of a way to increase income, or they may simply reflect shifting attitudes of the public. All these factors impact in different ways the various measures of the money supply.

From an investor's viewpoint, following the money supply is crucial because the growth of the money supply is a very important leading indicator of the economy. It predicts turning points in the economy both at troughs and at peaks with a lead of more than one year. The typical measure that is used is the rate of change in the money supply over 12 months. For instance, the growth of the money supply bottomed in 1984 and increased sharply in 1985 and 1986. The bottom in the growth of the

FINANCIAL CYCLES

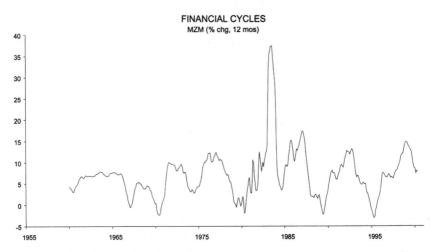

FINANCIAL CYCLES
MZM (% chg, 12 mos)

Figure 7-2. Growth in the money supply is one of the major driving forces of the business and financial cycles. There have been seven cycles in the growth of MZM since 1960. In 1995 the eighth financial cycle began unleashing the same forces experienced in the previous seven cycles.

money supply was followed in 1986 by a strong pickup in the growth of industrial production. In 1992 the growth of the money supply peaked and then declined sharply until 1995. The growth in industrial production peaked two years afterward in late 1994 and early 1995 and declined for a year.

Strong growth in the money supply suggests there is a lot of liquidity being injected into the economy and there is a lot of credit available to businesses, investors, and consumers. As this liquidity moves through the economy, more and more people take advantage of it. Eventually spending increases, the economy strengthens, and economic growth increases. However, when the money supply starts to slow down, credit is made available at a lesser pace to business, investors, and consumers. Therefore, the economy gradually slows down as less money is available and less money is spent. Historical data show that financial cycles, defined as the fluctuation in the growth of the money supply, have a length of approximately five to seven years from trough to trough.

Of course, one should expect that as liquidity increases, the stock market performs well, and as liquidity decreases—that is, the rate of growth of the money supply declines—there is less reason for stock prices to rise.

Tools of Monetary Policy

The Fed obviously cannot directly control inflation, or the growth of the economy, or employment, or trends in the stock market. What it can do is indirectly affect these by changing the growth of the money supply or by changing the levels of real short-term interest rates. The Fed can do this by buying and selling government securities through open market operations and by regulating the discount rate. Both of these methods work through the market of bank reserves known as the federal funds market.

The third tool of monetary policy is the ability to make changes in reserve requirement of the banks. Banks and other depository institutions are legally required to hold a specific amount of funds in reserve. These funds, which can be used to meet unexpected outflows, are called *reserves*, and banks keep them as cash in their vaults or as deposits with the Fed. There has to be a fixed ratio between funds loaned and reserves held by the banks. The Fed has an impact on interest rates and the money supply by changing the amount of reserves it requires banks to hold. By increasing reserve requirements, the Federal Reserve is telling banks to lend less, and of course as banks lend less, the money supply slows down and interest rates rise in the near term. If instead the Federal Reserve tells banks that they can decrease their reserves, banks can lend more money, injecting more liquidity into the system. With this action, the money supply accelerates as people borrow more money. Because of the increased amount of money, interest rates tend to decline in the near term.

At reporting time, banks need to show to the Federal Reserve that they have the appropriate level of reserves. In order to meet this need, banks often have to borrow for very short periods of time, sometimes just a few hours, from banks that have plenty of reserves. The rate that is charged when banks lend reserves to each other is called the *federal funds rate*. This is an important rate because corporations also have to borrow for very short periods of time to maintain the required balance in their bank accounts, and the interest rate charged is closely related to the federal funds rate.

A way of controlling the money supply and interest rates is through open market operations. This is the major tool the Fed uses to affect the supply of reserves in the banking system. The Fed achieves its objective by buying and selling government securities on the open market. These operations are conducted by the Federal Reserve Bank of New York.

Suppose the Fed wants the funds rate to fall in the near term. To do this it buys government securities from a bank. (Government obligations are called *bills* if their maturity is less than a year; they are called *notes* if their maturity is less than 10 years; and they are called *bonds* if their maturity is greater than 10 years.) The Fed then pays the bank for the securities it purchased, thus increasing the bank's reserves. As a result the bank has more reserves than it is required to hold. The bank can now increase its lending activity to consumers, investors, and business-people. This increase in liquidity is what makes the federal funds rate and other short-term interest rates fall in the near term and the money supply accelerate. The federal funds rate is the interest rate charged on reserves traded among commercial banks for overnight use in amounts of 1 million dollars or more.

When the Fed wants the federal funds rate to rise, it reverses the process—that is, it sells government securities. The Fed receives payment in reserves from banks, and this payment lowers the supply of reserves in the banking system. Since there is now less money to lend, interest rates rise and the money supply starts slowing down.

Another way of controlling interest rates and the money supply is through the discount rate. Banks can borrow reserves among themselves and from the Federal Reserve banks at their discount windows. The interest rate they must pay on this borrowing is called the *discount rate*. Discount window borrowing tends to be small because the Fed discourages such borrowing except to meet occasional short-term reserve deficiencies. The discount rate plays a role in monetary policy because, traditionally, changes in this rate have an announcement effect; that is, they sometimes signal to markets a significant change in monetary policy. A lower discount rate may signal a more expansionary policy to the banks, while a higher rate can be used to indicate a more restrictive policy. This higher rate is a signal to the banks that the Federal Reserve is discouraging borrowing and lending through the discount window. Therefore, banks have to become more cautious and careful about how they manage their reserves.

The times characterized by rising short-term interest rates and discount rates are critical for the banking system and the stock market. A negative configuration of interest rates for the stock market is a rising Treasury bills rate and a rising discount rate. During these times, it is not unusual to see the Treasury bills rate well above the discount rate. This is a clear indication of an aggressive tightening of monetary policy by the Federal Reserve, attempting to slow down the economy and keep inflationary forces under control. An example of such periods can be seen from 1987 to the end of 1988, throughout 1994, and beginning in 1999. All these periods have signaled a high-risk area for the stock market, and they have determined conditions that dictated extreme caution for investors. Sector and stock selectivity is crucial during these times because the bond market tends to perform very poorly during such times, and therefore does not offer a safe alternative to stocks.

Because the discount rate establishes the cost that members will have to pay to borrow reserves from Federal Reserve banks, it plays a significant role in the decision a bank makes about whether to borrow at the Federal Reserve discount window. For example, if the rate on short-term Treasury bills is high in relation to the discount rate, a member bank may prefer to borrow from the Federal Reserve rather than sell Treasury bills in its portfolios. Similarly, if the rate charged for reserves obtained through the Federal Reserve funds market is high, a bank has an incentive to use the discount window.

If monetary policy is tightening, it is understood that the Federal Reserve is using open market operations, reserve requirements, or the discount rate to slow down the growth of the money supply by letting short-term interest rates rise. When instead the Federal Reserve eases its monetary policy, it is understood that the Fed is using open market operations, reserve requirements, or the discount rate in order to favor an acceleration of the money supply by letting short-term interest rates decline.

Financial Cycles

The amount of money made available by the Fed is the main driver of the economy and the financial markets. Changes in the growth of money create huge waves, lasting about five to seven years, that have a big impact on our lives and on the price of most assets.

From 1960 to 1995 there have been seven major financial cycles, and each cycle started with the money supply accelerating rapidly from a low level close to 0 to 3 percent in a weak economic environment. Growth in monetary aggregates in a typical financial cycle has risen to 10 to 15 percent, to decline again to about 0 to 3 percent. A complete cycle includes two consecutive troughs, and this period of time usually spans about five to seven years (look back at Figure 7-2).

The stock market performs well during the first half of the financial cycle, when growth in liquidity increases. However, stocks perform poorly in the second half of a financial cycle, when liquidity slows down.

The stock market closely follows changes in liquidity because its strength or weakness depends on how much money there is in the system. If money grows rapidly, some of it is invested in the economy by businesses and consumers, and some is invested in stocks, and stocks rise. However, when liquidity slows down, stocks decline as investors sell stocks to raise money to be used for other purposes.

The eighth financial cycle since 1960 began early in 1995, with the growth in MZM close to 0 percent. The first half of the cycle ended in March 1999 when the growth of most monetary aggregates peaked and MZM was expanding at a rate of about 15 percent. Most measures of the money supply slowed down in 1999, and not surprisingly, the overall market became much more erratic, with a very large number of stocks forming major peaks. Broad market averages, such as the S&P 500, showed no change from March 1999 to March 2000.

The growth in monetary aggregates, which is a measure of liquidity provided by the Fed to the system, can be used to assess what is happening and what is likely to happen to the business cycle and the financial markets (Figure 7-3). A financial cycle goes through four distinctive phases.

- In phase one of a financial cycle, liquidity accelerates, accompanied by a strong stock market. In the meantime the economy grows slowly, commodities are weak, and short-term and long-term interest rates

INTEREST RATES–THE FEVER CHART OF AN ECONOMY

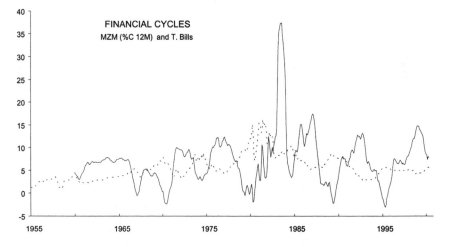

Figure 7-3. An increase in the growth of MZM is followed by a stronger economy, which is followed by rising short-term interest rates. The rise in short-term interest rates reduces the demand for money (negative feedback), inducing a decline in the growth of MZM and the economy and eventually causing short-term interest rates to decline. Lower short-term interest rates cause an increase (positive feedback) in the demand for money and rising growth in MZM.

decline. It is quite typical for the dollar to strengthen during this phase in anticipation of a strong economy and lower inflation.

- In phase two, the economy begins to pick up its pace and grows more rapidly. Commodities and short-term and long-term interest rates bottom and then rise. The stock market continues to rise. The dollar remains strong.

- In phase three, the growth in monetary aggregates declines while the economy remains strong. Interest rates and commodity prices keep rising as the dollar sputters. Stocks begin to perform poorly. This is a critical phase for the stock market because it becomes much more selective. Investors should recognize that risk is at the highest level, and their investment strategy should become much more defensive. Short-term interest rates typically rise at least 2 percentage points (200 basis points) during phase three of a financial cycle.

- In phase four, the protracted decline in liquidity and the sharp rise in interest rates that occurred in phase three cause the economy to slow down quite visibly. As the economy begins to grow slowly, interest rates and commodity prices peak and then decline. By this time the growth in monetary aggregates is very slow, close to 0 to 3 percent. The stock market bottoms as the dollar rises. The decline in interest rates stimulates new borrowing, and a new phase one of the financial cycle is under way again.

Financial cycles are closely related to major crises, which provide excellent investment opportunities for investors. The real estate crisis of 1992–1993, the Asian crisis in 1997, and the Latin American and Russian crises in 1998 were all accompanied by aggressive easing by the Federal Reserve and by the strong growth in the money supply. The main reason, of course, is the concern of the Federal Reserve that a financial crisis of major proportions would affect in a negative way the banking system, and as a result, the rest of the country or the global economy. For this reason, it becomes a priority to provide liquidity to the banking system in the United States and to global banks, in conjunction with central banks of other countries, so that a smooth operation of the economy can be maintained. Because of the strong relationship that exists between growth in the money supply and growth in stock prices, it is not unusual to see financial crises accompanied by a strong stock market. The main reason is that the aggressive injection of liquidity in the banking system spills over in the financial markets, thus placing upward pressure on stock prices. It is exactly what happened in 1992–1993 and in 1997 and 1998.

Assessing Monetary Policy

From the Federal Reserve's viewpoint, the objective is to solve the problems of the domestic and sometimes international economy through the use of real interest rates and growth in monetary aggregates. As it was discussed in detail in a previous chapter, the Fed uses the level of real interest rates to control inflationary pressures. Which indicators, then, should an investor use to follow and assess the Fed's monetary policy?

The growth in the economy and inflationary trends, such as an acceleration in wages, rising commodity prices, or significantly lower real short-term interest rates, are the most useful indicators to follow to determine the direction of interest rates. Other indicators include the indexes published by the National Association of Purchasing Managers. It is useful to follow the indexes for both the manufacturing and nonmanufacturing reports. An important indicator released by the National Association of Purchasing Managers is the percentage of purchasing agents showing slower deliveries. When the indexes of the purchasing managers rise well above 50, they suggest that the economy is very strong and that the odds favor higher short-term interest rates. When these indicators fall below 50, it is an indication that the economy is slowing down, and therefore, the odds favor short-term interest rates to decline.

Another indicator to assess monetary policy is the dollar. A strong dollar suggests that monetary policy is conducive to lower inflation and, therefore, to solid economic growth. If the dollar is weak, then there are two possibilities. Either the Federal Reserve is too easy and so the money supply is growing too rapidly, or real interest rates are too low and so monetary policy is inflationary.

A weak dollar usually reflects a monetary policy that is too easy and is conducive to periods of higher inflation. These are periods when the money supply grows rapidly and real short-term interest rates are kept below 1.4. However, sometimes a currency can be weak because of an excessively tight monetary policy in a country. For instance, in the 1990s, the tight monetary policy of the Japanese central bank induced very weak economic conditions, and the yen reflected such conditions by weakening against the dollar. On the other hand, in the 1970s monetary policy in the United States was too easy and the dollar slumped.

Other important indicators to assess monetary policy are the price of gold and the price of commodities. If the price of gold or commodities is weak, the odds are that the Federal Reserve is following a fairly tight monetary policy. During such times it is not unusual to see real interest rates reaching fairly high levels and the money supply growing slowly.

However, as we will discuss in more detail later, weak commodity prices signal low inflationary pressures; therefore, they indicate that monetary policy is tight. If the level of real interest rates is above their long-term average, monetary policy is noninflationary. On the other hand, if interest rates are close to inflation, making real short-term interest rates low, monetary policy is easy and one should expect strong growth in the money supply, higher prices for commodities, and most likely a weak dollar.

The stock market itself can be used to assess the direction of monetary policy. If the stock market grows rapidly, it is because there is ample liquidity supplied by the Federal Reserve to drive stock prices higher. Its trend, therefore, suggests the Federal Reserve favors a stimulative monetary policy leading to a stronger economy. However, stock prices trading in a range or declining are a reliable signal that the Fed policy is tight and that the Fed is trying to reduce the amount of liquidity available in the economic system and let market forces slow down the economy to a nonnflationary pace.

The money supply itself is another important measure that should be used to assess monetary policy. Monetary aggregates growing less than 4 percent over 12 months reflect a fairly tight monetary policy. This type of growth is conducive to very slow economic growth and poor stock market performance. On the other hand, monetary aggregates growing at a rate above 10 percent are an indication that monetary policy is easing. Of course, rising growth in the money supply means liquidity is rising, and therefore, the Fed is easy and it favors a stronger economy and rising stock prices. A slowdown in the money supply is a sign the Fed is tightening and there is less liquidity in the system, suggesting the Fed favors slower economic growth.

One of the indicators that we will discuss in more detail later, but we mention here to keep the list complete, is the yield curve. The yield curve reflects the difference between long-term interest rates and short-term interest rates. When short-term interest rates are low, relative to long-term interest rates, it is a signal that banks are encouraged to lend; and it is an indication of an easy monetary policy. As the yield curve flattens, in other words the difference between long-term and short-term interest rates decreases, the Fed is in the process of tightening; and therefore, the economy is likely to grow more slowly because lenders do not have an incentive to meet borrowers' demands for money.

The spread between BAA bond yields and 10-year Treasury bond yields is also an excellent gauge to assess monetary policy. This spread is closely correlated to the growth of the money supply. A rise in this spread is typically associated with a period of easing monetary policy.

However, a decline in the spread is associated with periods of tightening monetary policy.

The signs providing clues to the direction of monetary policy can be recognized by how the markets react to the actions of the Fed. The most important indicators for this purpose can be summarized as follows:

- The level of real short-term interest rates

- Growth in the money supply

- The trend in commodity prices and in gold and crude oil prices

- The dollar

- The price index of the National Association of Purchasing Managers

- The index of economic activity of the National Association of Purchasing Managers and the delivery index

- The stock market

- The yield curve

- The spread between BAA and 10-year Treasury bond yields

Investment Implications

A tightening of monetary policy implies a decrease in liquidity in the system. During such times, financial assets tend to perform poorly. Because of the lack of liquidity, businesses and consumers tend to sell financial assets and use the proceeds to invest in their businesses and to raise cash balances.

On the other hand, when the Federal Reserve is following an easy monetary policy, injecting liquidity in the system, this increased liquidity cannot be used right away by the real economy. It is placed temporarily in the financial markets waiting to be used. This is the main reason why stocks and bonds usually rise during these times of expansion in monetary aggregates.

Monetary policy impacts two main crucial economic variables: the growth of the money supply and the level of real interest rates. It is important to recognize the impact of these two variables on the economy, because as mentioned in a previous chapter, strong growth in the money supply eventually causes the economy to expand rapidly, creating a high-risk environment for the stock and bond markets. The reason for this high risk is that strong growth in the economy is followed by an increase in short-term interest rates, and an increase in short-term inter-est rates has always had a negative impact on stock prices. It is also true that a strong economy creates great business opportunities, and there-fore, business tends to borrow aggressively, thus placing upward pres-sure on long-term interest rates, thus having a negative impact on bond prices. This is also a time when inflation increases, raising the inflation premium embedded in bond yields. On the other hand, a slow econo-my creates investment opportunities. As the economy slows below its long-term average growth rate, upward pressure on interest rates declines, thus allowing short-term interest rates to decline and provide a very favorable environment for the stock market. Also, weak economic conditions convince business to borrow less, therefore creating down-ward pressure on long-term interest rates. Of course, these are times when inflationary pressures subside, reducing the inflation pressure embedded in bond yields. This situation typically creates a favorable environment for the stock and bond markets.

In order to keep abreast of the trends and position of financial cycles, investors need to follow the money supply, and for that matter, all the measures of money: M1, M2, M3, and MZM, because their growth tells you what will happen to the economy. If the money supply begins to accelerate, and this is typically favored by the Federal Reserve during a period of slow economic growth, the investor should look for a stronger economy—one to two years into the future. If the money supply grows very rapidly, let's say close to 15 percent, the economy should be expected to be very strong. The good news for investors is that stocks will be strong because liquidity is growing rapidly.

However, one should be aware that strong monetary growth is the seed that eventually will bring higher short-term interest rates and a weak stock market, usually after 2 to 2 1/2 years. The money supply is therefore a crucial leading indicator for investors. Strong growth in the money supply is followed by strong growth in the economy and in industrial production, income, sales, and employment, which are the typical coincident indicators. Broad measures of the money supply should be growing anywhere between 5 and 7 percent. Much higher growth rates than 5 to 7 percent create the conditions for very strong economic activity. If the money supply grows too rapidly for too long, it will cause the lagging indicators—inflation, business costs, commodities, and interest rates—to rise.

As the price of money increases, it becomes more and more expen-sive to borrow. An increase in interest rates would gradually discourage businesses from making investments and expanding capacity, thus reducing the demand for money. As a result, the money supply slows down. Only substantial weakness in the economy and lower interest rates will encourage businesses to start borrowing again. This is the time that costs (raw materials, wages, and interest rates) decline, thus improving margins. For this reason, following a decline in interest rates, the money supply starts accelerating again and a new financial cycle is under way.

The point being emphasized here is the important interplay between the money supply and interest rates. Their relationship is a typical relationship that exists between leading and lagging indicators. A trough in the growth of the money supply is followed, after about two years, by a trough in the growth of the economy. A trough in the growth of the economy is followed, after about two years, by rising short-term and long-term interest rates. An increase in short-term and long-term interest rates is followed almost immediately by a decline in the growth of the money supply. A decline in the growth of the money supply is followed, after about 2 to 3 years, by a decline in interest rates. The decline in interest rates is followed almost immediately, by more rapid growth in the money supply.

From the investor's viewpoint, there cannot be a decline in interest rates without a substantial deceleration in the growth of the money supply. The reason is that a prolonged decline in the money supply is followed, after about 2 years, by a decline in the growth of the economy. Because of the slow growth in the economy, the demand for money subsides, thus allowing interest rates and the price of commodities such as crude oil to decline (Figure 7-4). On the other hand, strong acceleration of the money supply will eventually lead to higher interest rates. Strong growth in the money supply is followed by a strong economy, and because of the strong economy, businesses and consumers increase their borrowing activity, thus placing upward pressure on interest rates.

This process can also be formalized in terms of leading, coincident, and lagging indicators. We have seen that the money supply is a leading indicator. What we call the economy, which is reflected by what happens to employment, production, income, and sales, is a coincident indicator. Interest rates are a lagging indicator. The interaction between these parameters can be visualized as follows:

- A trough in the growth of the money supply is followed by a trough in the growth of the economy.

- The trough in the growth of the economy is followed by a trough in interest rates.

OIL PRICES AND TREASURY BILLS

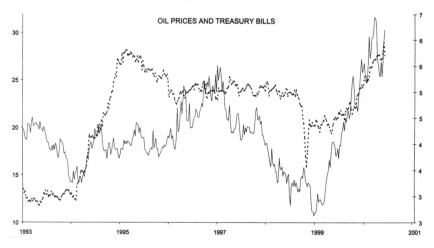

Figure 7-4. The cyclical turning points in short-term interest rates (rates on 13-week Treasury bills) coincide with important turning points in the price of commodities, such as crude oil. They are both dependent on the strength of the economy and on previous expansion of monetary aggregates. This implies the Fed has a limited amount of control on interest rate trends.

- Troughs in interest rates are followed by a peak in the growth of the money supply.

- A peak in the growth of the money supply is followed by a peak in the growth of the economy.

- A peak in the growth of the economy is followed by a peak in interest rates.

- And a peak in interest rates is almost immediately followed by an increase in the growth of the money supply.

And the cycle starts all over again.

How does the Fed fit in this process? The Fed cannot substantially change the trend in interest rates because they have been determined by how fast the money supply expanded, by the strength of the economy, and by borrowing activity. The Fed can have an impact on the growth of the money supply through the level of interest rates relative to inflation. That is the other variable of monetary policy, real interest rates. They are impacted in a profound way by the Federal Reserve, because the Federal Reserve manages the rise in interest rates so that their increase or decrease does not become disruptive for the economy and the financial markets. What is important and is crucial for investors to remember, is that the growth of the money supply, the amplitude and length of its cycle, determines business cycle conditions and trends in the financial markets.

Real interest rates, as we have seen in a previous chapter, have a fundamental impact on inflation expectations and overall inflation. Changes in real interest rates affect the demand for goods and services because they impact borrowing costs, the availability of bank loans, and foreign exchange rates. For this reason, real interest rates are an important tool of monetary policy. While real interest rates represent the difference between short-term interest rates and inflation, nominal interest rates are the level shown without adjustments for inflation.

In 1978, nominal short-term interest rates averaged about 8 percent, and the rate of inflation was 9 percent. Even though nominal interest rates were high, monetary policy was stimulating demand, with negative real short-term interest rates of -1 percent. Real short-term interest rates were very low. Money, as a result, was very cheap, and monetary policy was very easy. That was the main reason inflation soared in those years.

In contrast, in 1998, nominal short-term interest rates were close to 5 percent. The inflation rate was about 2 percent and the positive 3 percent in real short-term interest rates reflected a fairly tight monetary policy. The point is that nominal interest rates don't provide, per se, a true indication of monetary policy. The nominal funds rate of 8 percent in 1978 was much more stimulative than the 5 percent rate in early 1998. The reason is that in 1978 inflation was above 8 percent, thus making real interest rates very low and very stimulative because the price of money in real terms was actually negative. On the other hand, in 1998 when interest rates were 5 percent and inflation was close to 2 percent, real interest rates were much higher, in relative terms, than in 1978, with nominal interest rates about twice the level of inflation. Thus, the high level of real interest rates in 1998 was one of the main reasons inflation was low.

A decrease in real interest rates lowers the cost of borrowing and leads to increases in business investments, consumer spending, and household purchases of durable goods, such as autos and new homes. This has inflationary implications because demand for goods and services increases considerably when the cost of money in real terms, that is, after inflation, is low. This extra demand is what produces inflationary pressures.

When real interest rates rise at high levels, the reverse is true. The cost of borrowing increases, and only those businesses that have projects with a very high return can make the investment, due to the high real cost of borrowing.

What is the impact of real interest rates on the economy? Declining real interest rates are a sign that money is becoming less expensive, and therefore, consumers and businesses tend to borrow aggressively during such times, causing the economy to grow rapidly, stimulating inflationary forces.

How do real interest rates and the money supply impact the financial markets? High real interest rates help to keep inflation under control. This is a long-term determining factor for the stock and bond markets. From a business cycle viewpoint, the money supply has a more immediate impact for investors. When interest rates decline due to slow growth in the economy, credit expands because businesses and consumers borrow more aggressively due to the lower cost of money. As a result, the money supply grows more rapidly, positively affecting stock prices. An example of this situation occurred in 1995 when the money supply accelerated sharply as interest rates declined. This configuration was followed by strong economic conditions in 1997–2000, accompanied by sharply rising stock prices in the years from 1995 to 1999.

After a protracted period of strong growth in the money supply, the economy strengthens and the demand for money increases, placing upward pressure on interest rates. This is the time when investors have to be more cautious about the outlook of stock prices. When interest rates rise, the demand for money eventually declines, and the money supply slows down. The stock market, which reflects trends in liquidity, cannot perform well under conditions of slower growth in the money supply. A good rule of thumb is to expect slow growth in the money supply and, therefore, poor market conditions after approximately two months of rising interest rates.

The investor has to keep in mind that only a slowdown of the money supply of one to two years, followed by slower growth in the economy and lower interest rates, creates the conditions for the next bull market. From an investor's viewpoint, it is important to be convinced that there is a close relationship between the money supply and stock prices. And since the level and trend of interest rates affect the growth of the money supply, they do have an impact on the stock market. The stock market is affected indirectly by the rise in interest rates, contrary to what is generally believed. It is quite typical for headlines to say interest rates are rising, and therefore, the stock market is in a high-risk territory. That is indirectly true. The real impact on stock prices is actually due to the decline in the growth of the money supply, which is caused by the increase in the cost of money, which discourages borrowing and therefore reduces the amount of liquidity in the system.

An increase in short-term interest rates is followed by a decline in the growth of the money supply almost immediately and in stock prices after about two months. A decline in stock prices and in the growth of the money supply is followed by a decline in interest rates after about one year after the economy begins to slow down. A decline in short-term interest rates is followed by an increase in the growth of the money supply and in stock prices almost immediately.

These relationships are very important in determining the dynamics of risk, as far as investing in the stock market. In order to formalize this relationship, it is important to recognize that growth in the money supply and stock prices are leading indicators, the economy is a coincident indicator, and interest rates are a lagging indicator. Because of the relationship between leading, coincident, and lagging indicators, the following occurs:

- A trough in the growth of the money supply or stock prices is followed by
- A trough in the growth of the economy, which is followed by
- A trough in interest rates, which is followed by
- A peak in the growth of money supply and stock prices, which is followed by
- A peak in the growth of the economy, which is followed by
- A peak in interest rates, which is followed by
- A trough in the growth of the money supply and stock prices.

The relationship between financial markets and the money supply can also be formalized in terms of phases of the financial cycles. In phase one of a financial cycle:

- Liquidity or growth of the money supply increases.
- The stock market rises.
- The economy is still slowing down.
- Commodities are declining.
- Interest rates are declining.
- Inflation is declining.
- The dollar is strengthening.

In phase two of the financial cycle, it is quite common to see that:

- Liquidity is increasing.
- The stock market is increasing.

- The growth of the economy is bottoming and then rising.
- Commodity price are bottoming and then rising.
- Interest rates are bottoming and then rising.
- Inflation is bottoming and then rising.
- The dollar continues to strengthen.

In phase three of the financial cycle:

- Liquidity begins to decline.
- The stock market declines.
- The economy remains strong.
- Commodities continue to rise.
- Interest rates continue to rise.
- Inflation remains in an upward trend.
- The dollar weakens.

In phase four of the financial cycle, it is typical to have the following:

- Liquidity, or growth in the money supply, declines.
- The stock market declines.
- The economy weakens.
- Commodities decline.
- Interest rates decline.
- Inflation declines.
- The dollar continues to weaken.

The decline in interest rates in phase four triggers the series of events that characterizes phase one.

It should be noted that the level of real short-term interest rates in phase 2 impacts the size of the increase in commodity prices and interest rates occurring in phase 3. When real short-term interest rates in phase 2 are low, as they were in 1992 and 1993, investors should expect a strong rise in commodity prices and interest rates in phase 3, as was the case in 1994. However, if real short-term interest rates in phase 2 are high, as they were from 1996 to 1998, investors should expect a below average increase in overall commodity prices and interest rates, as it happened in 1999 and in 2000.

Chapter
8

INFLATION AND YOUR INVESTMENTS

As we expand our analysis of the behavior of economic and financial indicators, it should become increasingly clear that all these gauges are closely related to each other. They all help in understanding how business and financial cycles go through their different stages. It is also helpful if readers remind themselves that all these indicators discussed belong to one of three categories.

As we have learned, the overwhelming majority of economic and financial indicators are either leading indicators, coincident indicators, or lagging indicators of the business cycle. It is also important to be aware of the relationship between these three groups of indicators. Once one knows what group an indicator belongs to, it is easy to understand it and use it as a tool for forecasting and assessing the risks presented by the financial markets.

In the previous chapter we saw that important financial variables, such as growth in the money supply and short-term interest rates, belong to a specific classification. The growth of the money supply is a leading indicator of the business cycle. Short-term interest rates are lagging indicators. We also found that stock prices, since they reflect the amount of liquidity in the banking system, are also leading indicators of the business cycle, whereas inflation is a lagging indicator.

We already have a powerful model tying together these crucial variables. This model allows us to tie together the behavior of the economy, the money supply, and short-term interest rates. A rise in the growth of the money supply is followed, after one to two years, by a stronger economy. A stronger economy, characterized by business growth rising above its long-term average, is eventually followed by higher short-term interest rates. The reason, as discussed earlier, is that these are times when there is considerable pressure on resources, such as productive capacity, employment, and commodities. As a result, strong demand for credit places upward pressure on short-term interest rates.

After a few months of rising short-term interest rates, the growth of the money supply declines due to the increased cost of credit. This development is followed, after about one to two years, by a slowdown in the economy and eventually by lower short-term interest rates. Lower short-term interest rates are followed, after a few months, by rising growth in monetary aggregates, and the cycle starts all over again.

These relationships can best be followed by using the concepts relating peaks and troughs of leading, coincident, and lagging indicators. Since the growth of the money supply is a leading indicator, the growth of industrial production is a proxy for economic trends, and the level of short-term interest rates is a lagging indicator, the following lead-lag relationships tie these indicators together.

• A trough in the growth of the money supply is followed by

• A trough in the growth of industrial production, which is followed by

• A trough in short-term interest rates, which is followed by

• A peak in the growth of the money supply, which is followed by

• A peak in the growth of industrial production, which is followed by

• A peak in interest rates, which is followed by

• A trough in the growth of the money supply.

And the cycle starts all over again.

In this chapter we will examine the process of inflation in more detail than in Chapters 2 and 3. We will look at how inflation is related to the business cycle, how and when it becomes a problem, and what the conditions are that will bring it under control again.

Commodities are important indicators of business cycle development. Their behavior can provide unique information. We will explore when one should expect a rise or decline in the price of commodities and how this change in commodity levels is related to the business cycle and to inflation.

Because of the impact that wages have on inflation, we will devote a section to their impact and to the conditions that cause wages to be inflationary. This issue is important because a tight labor market and rising wages are not necessarily inflationary. The level and trend of inflation also plays a major role in the value of the dollar against other currencies.

Of course, this is an important subject because changes in the dollar have a major impact on returns of foreign investments.

Finally, in the last section we will recap the main points of the chapter and examine how they should be used to develop an investment strategy.

Inflation and the Business Cycle

Inflation is mainly a monetary phenomenon. This means that inflation is caused primarily by the actions and the policies of the central bank. The actions of the Fed are crucial in determining the growth of the money supply and the level and trend of interest rates relative to inflation—that is, real interest rates (look back at Figure 6-2).

Sometimes an international or domestic crisis, like the savings and loans and real estate debacle in the early 1990s, forces the Fed to ease its monetary policy and provide liquidity to cushion the crisis. The careful investor recognizes what is happening if he or she can observe a sharp increase in the growth of the money supply, accompanied by lower real interest rates. Such conditions happened seven times since 1960, most recently in 1984, in 1989, and in 1995. In all these instances the money supply accelerated from growth levels below 3 percent to close to 15 percent as short-term interest rates gradually declined.

It is not unusual under circumstances of crisis that the level of real short-term rates falls to or below the level of inflation. When this happens, it should be interpreted as a sign that the Fed has decided to solve the crisis using an easy monetary policy. A similar situation happened in 1997 during the financial crisis in Asia. The Fed at that time aggressively eased its monetary policy by increasing the growth of the money supply and lowering real short-term interest rates. Those were the years when Thailand, South Korea, Malaysia, and Indonesia attracted capital to their countries by offering cheap labor and guaranteeing fixed exchange rates to the dollar. By doing so, they were eliminating the foreign exchange risk from the hands of foreign investors. The problem was created by the fact that the capital that entered the country was not used to improve the overall conditions of the economies, but was squandered on unproductive projects. Eventually, loans could not be repaid and a financial crisis occurred. Currencies had to be sharply devalued, creating huge losses for the original investors, mainly banks. Because of these crises, the Federal Reserve was compelled to stabilize the international banking system by allowing the money supply to grow more rapidly.

There are times when the economic cycle slows down and the Fed is
forced to increase liquidity to raise the growth of the money supply to
more normal levels. The ideal growth of the money supply in a noninflationary environment is close to 5 to 6 percent. A protracted period
when the growth of the money supply is below this range is likely to
cause the economy to grow too slowly and the unemployment rate to
rise. On the other hand, a protracted period of growth in the money supply well above 5 to 6 percent is likely to stimulate too much economic
growth and place pressure on productive resources, creating pronounced inflationary risks. The strong growth in the money supply is
an important signal that the business cycle will soon turn around, and
economic conditions will improve. Inflationary pressures increase when
the growth of the money supply rises to around 10 percent, the economy is growing at well above potential, and real short-term interest rates
are low or below their historical average of about 1.4.

In the second half of the 1990s the United States experienced high
growth in the money supply and robust economic growth with low inflation. The main reason was the high level of real short-term interest rates.
High real short-term interest rates above 1.4 suggest the real cost of
money was high and provided discipline in the way it was spent or
invested. However, the strong growth in the money supply and the
strong economy in the late 1990s suggested that inflationary pressures
were strong, thus creating a high-risk environment for the financial markets. Because of rising inflationary forces, interest rates moved higher,
causing lower growth in the demand for money in 1999 and 2000 as
business postponed new investments due to higher interest rates. Lower
demand for money slows down the expansion of the money supply,
which has a negative impact on stock prices. The point is that inflationary pressures eventually have a negative impact on monetary aggregates
and stock prices.

In Chapter 2, we examined two measures of inflation—the growth in
consumer prices and the growth in producer prices. Consumer prices
measure the increase in prices at the consumer level, while producer
prices measure changes in prices at the producer level.

The cyclical timing of consumer and producer prices is that of a lagging indicator. The difference between producer and consumer prices is
that producer prices are more volatile than consumer prices, meaning
that they rise faster and decline faster. The main reason producer prices
are more volatile than consumer prices is that their change is affected
mainly by changes in commodity prices. They are more sensitive than,
say, changes in medical costs or changes in housing costs, which are

included in consumer prices. But the cyclical turning points of the two inflationary measures are the same. This means that when the economy is too strong and there are inflationary pressures, one should see growth in consumer prices rise, accompanied by higher growth in producer prices. When growth of consumer prices declines, one also should see a decline in the growth of producer prices.

Producer prices do not add additional information to the inflation process. They only confirm that inflation is on the way up or on the way down. It is important to recognize that all the goods at the consumer level and at the producer level—from food to apparel to medical services—tend to accelerate and decelerate together. Their growth rate may be different, but the cyclical timing is that of the lagging indicators.

Let's see how the process of inflation evolves during a typical business cycle. The risk of inflation arises when the economy is growing very rapidly or real interest rates are low. A strong economy is characterized by intense use of resources and a strong demand for money. For instance, during such times it's quite typical to experience a sharply declining unemployment rate. The reduction of available skilled labor places upward pressure on wages, which tend to grow faster. In these cases, GDP is found to grow well above 2 1/2 to 3 percent.

Declining or low unemployment rates suggest the labor market is becoming tight. Under these conditions wages rise faster. Initially, businesses can absorb these increases in wages by increasing productivity. This can be achieved as long as new capacity can be added and skilled labor is plentiful. But when capacity is close to being fully utilized and labor is difficult to find, productivity begins to slow down. This development places upward pressure on unit labor cost—that is, wages adjusted by productivity.

Another development caused by a strong economy is the increase in demand for raw materials. Their prices are the first to rise as an economy grows more rapidly (Figure 8-1). The increase in these prices can be initially absorbed through process efficiency.

The third factor that has an important impact on inflation when the economy is strong is the demand for money. Short-term interest rates are very sensitive to credit demands as raw materials are sensitive to production requirement demands (Figure 8-2). However, there is a point when increases in raw material costs impact the profitability of businesses.

The process can be better visualized by using the logical model tying together leading, coincident, and lagging indicators. By using the growth of the money supply as a leading indicator, the growth of the economy as a coincident indicator, and commodity prices and the change in the

COMMODITY PRICES

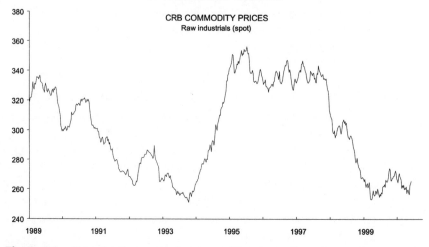

Figure 8-1. Major turning points in commodity prices reflect changes in economic conditions caused by fluctuations in the growth of monetary aggregates.

RAW MATERIALS AND T BILLS

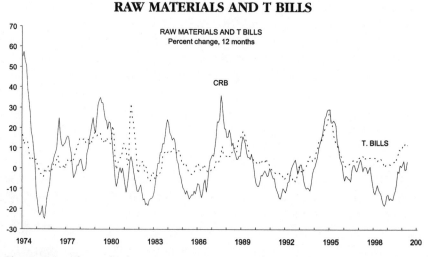

Figure 8-2. The cyclical turning points in commodity and short-term interest rates coincide. The amplitude of the move depends on the level of real short-term interest rates that has preceded them.

producer and consumer prices as lagging indicators, the relationship between these forces can be summarized as follows:

• A peak in the growth of the money supply is followed by

• A peak in the growth of the economy, which is followed by

- A peak in commodity prices and, in the growth of producer and consumer prices, which is followed by

- A trough in the growth of the money supply, which is followed by

- A trough in the growth of the economy, which is followed by

- A trough in commodities commodity prices and in the growth of producer and consumer prices, which is followed by

- A peak in the growth of the money supply.

And the cycle starts all over again.

A strong economy, therefore, causes prices of resources such as labor, raw materials, and money to increase. Initially, businesses try, to absorb these increases in cost, but eventually profit margins start decreasing. This is the time when corporations need to pass these cost increases on to the consumer. The costs of labor, raw materials, and money represent the cost of running a business, and therefore, their upward trends have a negative impact on profitability. Because of the negative effect of inflation on profitability, businesses attempt to cut costs as profitability declines. The implications are (1) less borrowing by delaying the implementation of planned projects; (2) lower inventories to cut raw material costs; and (3) layoff of employees to reduce labor costs.

From the consumers' viewpoint, rising inflation reduces real income and decreases their purchasing power. Therefore, the reaction of consumers to rising inflation is to decrease the level of spending, causing the economy to slow down.

The outcome of the actions of businesses and consumers is to slow down the economy. This slowdown will continue until the causes that initiated it—that is, rising commodity prices, rising labor costs, and rising interest rates—decline. Only then will lower inflation improve consumers' income and induce them to buy more. On the other hand, lower costs improve business margins, encouraging businesses to implement those projects that were shelved because of rising costs and lower profitability.

The Federal Reserve has an impact on the inflationary spiral if they keep real short-term interest rates too low and the money supply growing too rapidly for too long. In the typical financial cycle, the growth of the money supply rises from a level below 3 percent to above 10 percent, well above the average growth rate of about 5 to 6 percent. The fluctuations of the business cycle arise because of the sharp accelerations and decelerations in the money supply. The challenge for the Fed is to keep the growth of the money supply as close as possible to 5 to 6 percent and to try to avoid the sharp fluctuations in liquidity which cause the volatility of the business cycle. It is very important for the investor to follow these two parameters of monetary policy to determine what type of inflationary cycle to expect.

Commodities and the Business Cycle

The price action of commodities such as copper, natural rubber, crude oil, aluminum, and steel provides very useful information to investors. Commodities are very sensitive to demand. Since demand for commodities depends on how strong the economy is, they provide very timely information on the direction of the business cycle. Their importance comes from their price sensitivity to demand. As demand increases because of stronger business conditions, commodities provide immediate, unbiased information to the investor on what is happening in the economy. If commodities decline in price, they tell the investor that the economy is not as strong as it used to be. Their action, therefore, provides an objective measure of how the markets are responding to economic conditions. The importance of commodities is that they provide prompt feedback to the investor on what is happening to the economy. It is an objective and unbiased measure as reflected by the markets.

Economic indicators assembled by the government are available with at least one-month lag after the fact. They come in too late. Commodities are available every day and are not subject to revision. For this reason every financial newspaper around the world has many, many pages devoted to the price of commodities. They provide the sophisticated businessperson and investor crucial input to make important decisions based on their understanding of the behavior of commodity prices. Trends in the prices of commodities such as copper, aluminum, natural rubber, crude oil, gold, silver, palladium, platinum, and steel give the investor important clues to what is happening in the economy. The CRB commodity indexes are also very useful in assessing trends in business conditions because they represent the action of a basket of the most commonly used commodities. The rise in the price of these indexes suggests the economy is strengthening considerably. On the other hand, a weakness in price suggests business is slowing down in a visible way.

Another important feature of commodities is that they all tend to move in the same direction. It is very unusual to see one commodity strong and all the other commodities weak. Eventually, the commodity that has risen in price too fast will decline and display a rate of growth similar to the rate of growth of other commodities. For instance, in the 1999–2000 period, although crude oil soared from $10 to about $32 a barrel, gold prices remained stable at around $300 an ounce while other commodities displayed small changes. This was a sign that commodity price increases were not widespread.

Commodities are a lagging indicator, but they do not lag changes in economic growth by much. As such, the increase in commodity prices is a sign the economy is strengthening. A weakening or slowdown in the growth of commodity prices signals the economy is slowing down.

Another important element is that commodity prices rise only when the economy is strong, but we saw that the economy is strong only when the Fed has eased monetary policy aggressively and real interest rates are low. If real interest rates are high, it is rare to see firm commodity prices for an extended period of time. The odds are that commodity prices will either stay stable or decline when real interest rates are high.

In the 1970s all commodity prices rose due to easy monetary policy: strong growth in the money supply and low real short-term interest rates. The prices commodities are more volatile than producer or consumer prices. As a result, their change provides clues about the future direction of inflation. If commodity prices accelerate across the board, this is a signal that inflation will eventually start rising. Sharply rising commodity prices are the outcome of too much growth in the money supply, low real short-term interest rates, and a strong economy. This is the perfect combination of ingredients driving up inflation in a major way. If the economy slows down and commodity prices decline or slow down, this is a signal that the forces of inflation are subsiding. This is particularly so if the slowdown in the economy and in commodities has been preceded by a slowdown in the growth of the money supply and by high real short-term interest rates.

Wages and Inflation

Growth in wages is closely related to the behavior of the business cycle. As the economy strengthens, the growth in wages tends to increase as unemployment declines. As unemployment declines, confirming a strong economy, the tighter the labor market becomes and the more pressure there is on wages to rise. A slowdown in the economy close to or below the long-term average of 2 1/2 to 3 percent creates an increase in the unemployment rate; and with more availability of workers, growth in wages is likely to stabilize or decline.

The growth in wages has the same turning points as inflation because its behavior is that of a lagging indicator. The outcome is that turning points in wages follow turning points in coincident indicators both at troughs and at peaks of the business cycle.

The process can also be visualized as follows:

- A peak in the growth of the money supply is followed by
- A peak in the growth of the economy and employment, which is followed by
- A peak in the growth of wages, which is followed by
- A trough in the growth of the money supply, which is followed by
- A trough in the growth of the economy and employment, which is followed by
- A trough in the growth of wages, which is followed by
- A peak in the growth of the money supply.

And the cycle starts over again.

Because of the cyclical relationship between wages and inflation, it is generally believed that a tight labor market, a strong economy, and rising wages are inflationary. There is not necessarily a relationship between wages and inflation. In other words, growth in wages may not be inflationary.

In the 1960s and the 1980s the U.S. economy experienced strong growth in wages but very low inflation. In fact, in the 1990s wages were growing at 3 to 4 percent, while inflation was close to 2 percent. In spite of this evidence, policymakers, including some members of the Federal Reserve System, believed in the Phillips curve. The Phillips curve relates the simple fact that a higher unemployment rate is associated with lower inflation and a lower unemployment rate is associated with higher inflation. The policymakers' conclusion is, let's not let the unemployment rate fall too far down; otherwise that could be a signal that inflation will start rising due to higher wages. Again, this is a fallacy because the facts have shown quite clearly that wages in the 1960s and the 1990s were rising faster than inflation and inflation remained under control. The only thing that the Phillips curve shows is the obvious truth that as employment growth declines, wages accelerate. However, the experience of the 1960s and the 1990s shows quite clearly that an increase in the growth in wages is not necessarily inflationary.

So how is this dilemma solved? The dilemma is solved by looking again at real short-term interest rates. High real short-term interest rates increase the cost of borrowing, and businesses are forced to invest in higher-rate-of-return projects. Consumers, on the other hand, are also discouraged from overspending due to the higher cost of borrowing.

Let's look at it from a business viewpoint. The higher cost of borrowing forces businesspeople to invest in projects that have a higher rate of return. But projects with a higher rate of return are usually projects with a high-technology content and higher productivity. This is the missing link—productivity growth. High real short-term interest rates force businesses to be efficient and therefore increase their productivity. As productivity increases, the higher growth of productivity allows businesses to absorb the higher increase in wages. For instance, if wages are increasing at 4 percent and productivity is also increasing at 4 percent, the unit labor cost to business is zero.

Wages are not the elements that create inflation. The element that creates inflation is low productivity growth. However, with high real short-term interest rates, by keeping prices down and the inflationary process low, it forces businesses to improve productivity. Since businesses cannot raise prices in a period of low inflation, they have to improve productivity to improve efficiency and improve margins. Wages are not inflationary unless productivity slows down dramatically. But this can only happen in an environment of relaxed monetary policy with very low real short-term interest rates at or below the inflation rate. For instance, although in 1999 workers' compensation was rising at a very strong 5.2 percent pace because of a very strong manufacturing sector, unit labor costs, that is, labor cost adjusted for productivity, were actually down 1.7 percent because of strong productivity growth of 6.9 percent in the manufacturing sector.

Investors should look at the trend of unit labor costs which is a quarterly release by the Bureau of Labor Statistics that ties productivity to workers' compensation and also shows the unit labor cost index. Unit labor costs also are lagging indicators. Unit labor costs typically tend to rise after the economy is growing very rapidly and slow down following a slowdown in the economy. However, if—and this is a very important point—real short-term interest rates remain high, one should not expect a strong rise in unit labor costs, if any at all. The main reason is that high real short-term interest rates keep inflation low. As a result, businesses cannot raise prices. In order to improve profitability, corporations have to increase productivity, which keeps labor costs down. We will see later how this information regarding trends in commodities, trends in unit labor costs, and trends in inflationary pressures impact decisions concerning investments in bonds.

Currencies, Inflation, and Foreign Investments

Inflation is the cancer of the economy. Rising inflation is a sign that the economy is operating less efficiently. It means that businesses are allowed to raise prices rather than improve productivity to improve their profitability. Rising inflation has a negative impact on productivity as businesses find it easier to raise prices rather than investing to improve productivity in order to increase margins. Rising inflation means that people who rely on fixed incomes have their source of their livelihood depleted by external forces and they are forced to live with smaller resources.

Rising inflation creates discontent in the economy and in the population as people see their money decline in worth. The quality of goods goes down as businesses cut costs to improve profitability. The whole economic process becomes distorted.

The financial markets, as inflation rises, reflects this uncertain state of affairs, and they act very poorly, as they did in the 1970s. Rising inflation rattles the economy and the financial markets. That's why the Federal Reserve and central banks around the world are committed, at least on paper, to keeping inflation under control and to achieving price stability. Price stability really means that with prices growing slowly, businesses are forced to improve margins by increasing productivity, and this increased productivity creates a stable business cycle, sound growth, and high real income as wages rise above the inflation rate.

Rising inflation also usually is associated with an overwhelming role of the government in the workings of the economic process. A definitive example is what happened in the 1970s in the United States. Inflation soared from 3 percent to 15 percent as the federal government aggressively expanded social programs and at the same time was fighting the war in Vietnam without raising taxes. Spending was funded by keeping very low interest rates relative to inflation, causing inflation to soar, thus indirectly raising tax revenues as income was artificially raised by inflation. Circumstances like these force the economy to operate at inefficient levels. Look at Europe, for example, where the more socialistic governments have been associated with an economy growing more slowly. This is the reason why the economies in Europe grew slowly in the 1990s. Japan also was in a long recession in the 1990s due to the close control by government and cartels over the way its economy operates.

As we have seen in Chapter 6, rising inflation is eventually associated with high unemployment rates as businesses cut employment, and recessions are usually the rule, not the exception. The United States has proved that by maintaining some freedom in the marketplace, a country can achieve solid economic growth and a low unemployment rate.

Of course as inflation rises, interest rates also rise. Lenders ask for a higher return for the money they lend to keep into account the inflation risk. When inflation rises, everything seems to be going wrong. On the other hand, the 1960s and the period following the 1980s showed quite clearly that low inflation is accompanied by stable economic growth.

The currency of a country reflects this state of affairs and is a delicate mechanism measuring the imbalances of one country relative to the others. A strong dollar reflects the fact that the U.S. economy is performing well, with stability and low inflation. A weak currency reflects a country that has economic problems, inflation problems, and productivity problems—a country that lacks stability and the conviction to solve the issues.

Currencies, over the long term, reflect the inflation differential between two countries. The inflation differential measures the relative efficiencies between two countries. A country with low inflation is more efficient and more stable than a country with higher inflation. Therefore, a country with a weak currency reflects a country that is relatively worse off than a country with lower inflation. This is an important fact to recognize because when investing in foreign stock markets or in foreign assets, one has to assess the impact that the currency has on the performance of the investment.

For instance, let's say a U.S. investor invests in Japan, and the Japanese market rises 20 percent, providing the investor with a 20 percent capital gain. However, if the Japanese yen declines 20 percent, the total gain for the U.S. investor is zero. Although the investor has a 20 percent profit from stocks, it takes 20 percent more yen to buy dollars to repatriate his investment: therefore, the net gain is zero.

Foreign investments should be made in countries that have a strong currency to avoid the currency risk, because a currency loss takes away from the gain from the investment in that foreign country. Since the long-term trend of a country's currency is determined by the trends of inflation in that country, before investing, an investor should do a cursory check of the level of real interest rates for that country. It will provide the investor with a very simple way to recognize what the currency risk is in that investment. Inflation in a country depends mostly on the level of real interest rates.

For instance, in 2000, South Korea had short-term interest rates of close to 6 percent and inflation of 1 percent. Clearly, South Korean monetary authorities were following a sound monetary policy. Short-term interest rates were low, close to the norm of 5 to 6 percent, real interest rates were high with short-term rates higher than inflation, and inflation was low by many standards. Clearly, all this information suggests that South Korea is a country that has a firm or strong currency.

However, let's say the United States has short-term interest rates of 5 percent and inflation of 2 percent, and, for example, Venezuela and Mexico have short-term interest rates close to 35 percent and inflation of 30 percent. In this example, the currencies of Venezuela and Mexico offer a currency risk. The first reason is because high short-term interest rates well above the 5 percent norm tell the investor that a country has serious structural problems. The second reason is that real interest rates are extremely low relative to those of the United States. In this example, interest rates in the United States are more than two times inflation. However, in Venezuela and Mexico real interest rates are only 1.2 times the inflation rate. This means that monetary policy in Venezuela and Mexico is conducive to a weak currency relative to the U.S. dollar since monetary policy in these two countries is likely to produce higher inflation than in the United States. Therefore, these two countries offer a high currency risk and should be avoided. These global numbers are available on the Internet or in any weekly edition of the *Financial Times* or the *Economist*.

Investment Implications

The trend in inflation provides very useful information on the long-term trend of the financial markets. Stable, low inflation reflects a sound economy. Inflation, as with all lagging indicators, needs to be stable to provide a favorable economic environment for the financial markets. Low inflation implies a stable economic environment, which is what is required to have stable short-term and long-term interest rates, and therefore favorable trends in stocks and bonds.

However, rising inflation, rapidly rising commodity prices, accelerating labor costs, and rising interest rates represent serious warning signals for investors, suggesting that risk is rising rapidly for the stock and bond markets. As the lagging indicators rise, one should expect the leading indicators to perform poorly. Therefore, as inflation, labor costs, and interest rates are rising (they are all lagging indicators), they have a negative impact on the stock market, which is a leading indicator. If inflation rises, the risk of investing in the stock market increases because of rising interest rates even if earnings per share rise sharply during most of these periods (Figure 8-3). Therefore, one should move away from investing in stocks. During periods of rising inflation, investors should concentrate on investments such as precious metals, real estate, and energy stocks—that is invest hard assets, as in the 1970s.

Inflation and investment in hard assets are connected to the business and financial cycle through the following model. In this model the growth of the money supply is a leading indicator, the economy is a coincident indicator, and commodities and inflation are lagging indicators:

• A peak in the growth of the money supply is followed by

• A peak in the growth of the economy, which is followed by

• A peak in inflation, in the price of copper, aluminum, and the CRB commodity index, and in real estate prices, which is followed by

• A trough in the growth of the money supply, which is followed by

• A trough in the growth of the economy, which is followed by

EARNINGS PER SHARE AND COMMODITIES

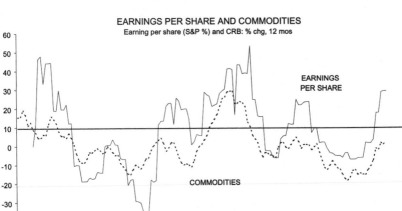

Figure 8-3. Cyclical turning points in the growth of earnings per share of the S&P 500 and commodity prices coincide. The main driving force behind them is the growth of the economy. A strong economy causes earnings per share, commodity prices, and interest rates to rise, thus creating a negative environment for stocks. However, over the long term, the growth in earnings per share is closely related to the nominal growth of the GDP, the money supply, and stock prices.

- A trough in inflation, in the price of copper, aluminum, and the CRB commodity index, and in real estate prices, which is followed by

- A peak in the growth of the money supply.

And the cycle starts all over again.

When inflation is rising, short-term interest rates are also likely to rise and follow the upward trend of inflation. During such times, as stocks become riskier, returns from short-term money-market instruments, which provide a safer alternative to stocks, are going to increase. Money-market instruments, therefore, provide a safe harbor for capital that would be at risk if invested in equities.

When inflation, commodity prices, interest rates, and labor costs are declining, it is a sign that the economy will soon grow at a sound pace. In such a favorable economic environment, one should expect stocks and bonds to perform considerably better than hard assets such as real estate, precious metals, or energy stocks.

The signs favorable to stocks and bonds are the following:

- Slow growth in the economy, below the long-term average growth rate

- Rising growth in the money supply

- Real short-term interest rates above the long-term average of about 1.4 percent

- Stable or declining inflation

- Stable or declining commodities

- Stable or declining interest rates

The risk of high inflation can be recognized when:

- The money supply has been growing at well above the 6 percent pace.

- The economy is very strong, growing at well above its long-term average of 2 1/2 to 3 percent.

- Real short-term interest rates have been close to or below their long-term average of 1.4 percent for more than a year.

- Commodities are rising sharply.

- Interest rates are rising.

These conditions will be examined in more detail in the chapters that follow.

Chapter
9

BONDS AND BUSINESS CYCLES

The subject of bond investment is very complex. Everything that we have reviewed thus far has an impact on the behavior of bond prices. Bond prices, and the interest derived from bonds, are very important economic indicators for investors because they provide crucial information on the risk of the financial markets. Furthermore, bonds can also be an excellent investment vehicle at specific points in the business cycle.

Bonds and bond investments have been the subject of many, many books and cannot be done justice in just a few pages. Although not an exhaustive treatment, we will try to capture the basic elements of bond investing. We will first define what a bond is, look at how to invest in bonds, and see what the difference is between investing in bonds and investing in bond mutual funds.

We will then deal with the behavior of bond yields and the business cycle and examine how the forces affecting bond yields change as the economy moves from periods of slow growth to strong growth to slow growth again. As a bond investor, one needs to recognize the properties of bonds—which bonds are riskier, which bonds are safer, and which bonds provide the greatest profit potential or the greatest loss potential at different phases of the business cycle.

We also will discuss the yield curve, an important indicator relating long-term and short-term interest rates. A simple way to visualize the yield curve is to take the difference between long-term Treasury bond yields and the rate on 13-week Treasury bills. This measure provides information on the strength of the economy and on how risky it is to invest in the stock market.

The credit cycle, which is the action of the spread of yields of bonds of different quality, is another development that has important implications for Fed policy. By examining the differences between yields of corporate bonds and yields of Treasury bonds, investors can recognize important trends with crucial implications for the economy, stock prices, and overall investment strategies.

We will review all this information and determine how to find investment opportunities in bonds and what indicators are useful to predict the direction of bond yields. In the final section we will look at the investment implications of the material presented in this chapter.

Bond Features

When a company needs capital to finance large investments, it sells bonds to investors. These bonds represent an obligation of the borrower to repay the lender in a certain number of years. An important borrower is the U.S. government. The government needs to issue bonds to investors to raise money to finance day-to-day operations or major government programs.

The obligation of repaying the lender rests on several parameters. The first one is interest. This is the obligation of the borrower to pay the lender a certain value, which the lender knows ahead of time. This is called the *coupon* of the bond. The coupon has the property of not changing during the life of the bond. If the lender commits itself to repay $100 per bond per year, that commitment would be in force throughout the life of the bond.

The second feature of a bond is its *maturity*. The borrower borrows the money for a specified period of time, which is stated at the time of issuance of the bond. The typical maturity can reach thirty years. Once the maturity has been established, generally it cannot be changed. Some bonds, however, do have a "call" feature, giving the issuer of the bonds the right to call back the bond under certain conditions. This *call feature* is disclosed at the time the bond is issued. The borrower might use the call feature, for instance, if interest rates decline. The borrower could reduce interest rate costs by buying back the bonds it issued at a higher interest rate and reissue the same quantity of bonds at a lower interest rate. From the investor's viewpoint, a bond with this call feature has negative implications because long-term returns are not known, due to the possibility that the bonds may be bought back by the original borrower. For this reason, bonds with a call feature have a yield higher than bonds with the same characteristics of coupon and maturity but without the call feature.

Another feature of a bond is the *price*. At the time a bond is issued, the price is at par and is shown in the newspaper as 100. The price of most fixed income securities is quoted in percentages of the par value, which is usually set at $1,000. For example, a price of 80 for a $1,000 par value bond means 80 percent of $1,000, or $800. Similarly, a price of 110 1/2 means 110.5 percent of $1,000, or $1,105. When the security sells at a price above par, it is said to be selling at a premium. If it is below par, it is trading at a discount.

Another element identifying a bond is its yield. The yield is computed by dividing the coupon of the bond—we must remember that the coupon cannot be changed—by the price of the bond. If a coupon is $100 and the price of the bond is $1,000, then the yield of the bond is 10 percent. This is also called the *current yield*.

Another yield, which is very important when buying bonds, is the *yield to maturity*. The yield to maturity is a measure of the annual return on the investment until the security comes due. This figure takes into account the amount paid for the bond, the interest rate, and the length of time to maturity. The yield to maturity on a security is different from the current yield whenever the price paid for the security is different from the security's par value.

Another important concept to remember when buying bonds is that the price of the bond changes. The reason an investor might pay more or less than $1,000—assuming $1,000 is the par value—is because the general level of interest rates changes depending on what is happening in the economy. Therefore, as long-term interest rates change, investors require a higher or lower rate of interest from the bonds they buy.

Let's assume the coupon of a bond is $100 and the general level of long-term interest rates is 10 percent. Therefore, the price of the bond will be set by the market at $1,000, and so the current yield is 10 percent.

Let's assume—for reasons that will be explained later—interest rates rise to 15 percent. Because of the rise in interest rates, investors will start selling bonds to buy securities until they yield 15 percent. In other words, market participants will continue to sell bonds to buy higher-yielding bonds. The price of the bonds will have to decline to a level so that the $100 coupon will yield 15 percent. The price of the bonds, there-fore, will have to decline to $667. Only at this price, in fact, is the cur-rent yield 15 percent. This is obtained by dividing $100 (which is the coupon) by $667 (which is the price of the bond). What is important is that a rise in interest rates caused a decline in the price of the bonds; or to put it in a different way, bond prices decline when long-term interest rates rise.

Let's assume that, instead, interest rates decline from 10 to 5 percent. The price of the bonds will have to rise to $2,000. At this price, the $100 coupon divided by $2,000 yields a 5 percent current yield. What has happened is that a decline in long-term interest rates has caused the price of the bond to rise. In this case, investors will aggressively buy bonds to lock in a higher rate of return as they recognize that yields are declining. Buying by the investors has, therefore, the effect of placing upward pressure on the bond price. The important concept to remember is that because the coupon is contractually fixed by the borrower, a rise in long-term interest rates causes bond prices to decline, and a decline in long-term interest rates causes bond prices to rise. As the price of bonds and the resulting change in long-term interest rates move, the investor will be able to profit from the situation. We will first see how the business cycle impacts the trend of long-term interest rates, and then we will discuss investment strategies to take advantage of the cyclical movement in bond prices.

Another feature of bonds is their *quality*. This is important because the price action of bonds depends on the quality of the borrower. The quality of the bond reflects the credit rating of the borrower. U.S. government bonds have the highest quality.

Rating agencies provide information on the quality of corporate borrowers. For instance, AAA bonds are the highest-rated-quality corporate bonds. BAA-rated bonds have lower quality. BBB bonds are the lowest rated of the investment-grade bonds. Different rating agencies use different rating symbols, and investors should inquire about them before purchasing bonds.

Another important element to consider when buying or selling bonds is *liquidity*. This is also an important factor, as we will see, in determining the price of the bonds. The liquidity of the bonds reflects the quantity of the bonds that have been issued, and the U.S. government bond market is extremely liquid. Investors can buy and sell U.S. government bonds at any time during the business day.

However, sometimes a small company will issue only a small quantity of bonds, and it may become difficult to find either a buyer or a seller of those particular bonds. This lack of liquidity has an impact on the bond's price. This is one of the reasons why lower-liquidity bonds demand a higher yield. In other words, if an institution issues a small quantity of bonds, only a few investors can buy them. As a result, if investors need to sell some of the bonds purchased, they will find it difficult to place them, since the market is limited. Sometimes an investor may need to sell his or her bonds immediately. The outcome is that the seller will have to make price concessions in order to liquidate his or her position. Because of this risk, low liquidity bonds carry a premium to protect investors from the lack of liquidity.

The main features of a bond can be summarized as follows:

- *Coupon.* Represents the fixed amount of dollars the investor will receive every year

- *Maturity.* Represents the period of time at the end of which the lender will be repaid the principal

- *Price.* Represents the value of the bond as set by the market

- *Current yield.* Is obtained by dividing the coupon by the price of the bond

- *Yield to maturity.* Measures the annual return of the bond until it matures

- *Quality.* Reflects the credit rating of the borrower

- *Liquidity.* Represents the number of bonds issued by the borrower

- *Call feature.* Gives the borrower the right to call back the bond

Bond Yields and the Business Cycle

In order to place long-term interest rates or bond yields into a business cycle context, it is important to recognize that bond yields behave like a lagging indicator. Let's see why. As business begins to grow faster after a prolonged slowdown, leading indicators are already rising, and the money supply has been accelerating for several months. Real short-term interest rates tend to be low when the economy is growing slowly as the Fed eases its monetary policy in order to provide the necessary liquidity to the system. Businesses are beginning to see signs of recovery, with profit margins improving due to declining costs. Companies are placing new orders now to replenish inventories; production starts improving; consumer confidence begins to rise as employment increases. The slow growth of the economy is accompanied by lower inflation, weak commodity prices, and declining bond yields due to the sluggish demand for money since business is not aggressive with its investment plans.

As the economy begins to strengthen, borrowing activity is not yet strong, but business does start to increase its borrowing as new business opportunities arise. One of the first signs the economy is beginning to accelerate from a period of slow growth is that short-term and long-term interest rates stabilize because of the gradual increase in borrowing. Businesses are encouraged by the prospect of increased sales and by low interest rates. The unemployment rate also declines, and growth in wages stabilize. With improving production, commodity prices also stabilize and then begin to go up. Inflation stops declining and stabilizes.

As the economy continues to strengthen, growth goes above its long-term average and strains in the business cycle begin to appear. Orders are growing very strongly, consumer confidence is at very high levels, levels of spending and income are high, and production and employment continue to reach new peaks. Commodities are now rising sharply.

Businesses try to meet the strong demand by expanding output more aggressively. Borrowing increases to expand capacity, wages accelerate, and commodities continue to rise. Inflationary pressures are now quite visible, placing upward pressures on long-term interest rates. An increasing demand for money, and the fact that lenders are now trying to protect their capital against the risk of higher inflation by raising the inflation premium embedded in bond yields, makes bond yields rise (Figure 9-1). Bond prices now begin their cyclical decline as yields rise. All the lagging indicators are now rising. The increase in the lagging indicators, which reflect trends in business costs, is now placing downward pressure on profitability. This, in due time, causes businesses to be more defensive and cut costs. The result is that orders for raw materials decline, hiring decreases, layoffs increases, businesses undergo restructuring to improve margins, inventories are pared down, and investments are reduced because of rising and high long-term interest rates.

The slowdown phase of the business cycle is now beginning, with all the lagging indicators, including long-term interest rates, at high levels.

INFLATION AND BOND YIELDS

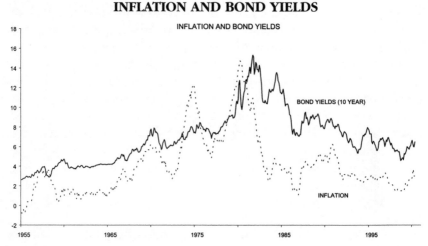

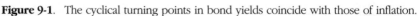

Figure 9-1. The cyclical turning points in bond yields coincide with those of inflation.

This situation will last until the economy slows down to the point where its growth is below its long-term average of 2 1/2 to 3 percent. When growth finally declines and is slow because of reduced investment plans, hiring, and inventory accumulation, inflation declines. As inflation subsides, bond yields decline along with overall business costs, and bond prices bottom. Lower demand for money, and the fact that lenders are now reducing the inflation premium embedded in bond yields, makes bond yields decline. As these costs keep declining, eventually profitability improves, businesses again see opportunities, they start borrowing again, and a new business cycle is under way again.

Long-term interest rates rise, as all lagging indicators do, when the economy is overheating, wages and overall inflation are accelerating, and commodity prices are increasing. Bond yields decline, as all lagging indicators do, when businesses slow down, and the economy, wages, borrowing, and overall inflation begin to decline.

The question is, when is the appropriate time to buy bonds? The answer—when the economy begins to slow down and all indications are that it will continue to slow down because of a continued decline in the growth of the money supply and in most leading indicators. Bond prices rise when the economy grows at or below its long-term average growth rate and inflation is stable or declining. Bonds are not a good investment when yields are rising due to strong economic conditions and rising inflation caused by rapid growth in money supplies and inflationary pressure.

The basic process tying bond yields or long-term interest rates to the business and financial cycles can be summarized as follows. The model used is the same as the one used to tie together the leading, coincident, and lagging indicators. In this case, the growth of the money supply is a leading indicator, the growth in industrial production is a coincident indicator, and bond yields and inflation are lagging indicators. The following model brings these variables together:

- A peak in the growth of the money supply is followed by

- A peak in the growth of industrial production, which is followed by

- A peak in inflation and bond yields, which is followed by

- A trough in the growth of the money supply, which is followed by

- A trough in the growth of industrial production, which is followed by

- A trough in inflation and bond yields, which is followed by

- A peak in the growth of the money supply.

And the cycle starts all over again.

Factors Influencing Bond Price Fluctuations

Three primary factors determine the degree of price fluctuations of fixed-income securities. The first one is the maturity of the bond, the second is the coupon rate, and the third is the actual level of interest rates from which the fluctuations begin. Each of these factors can influence the degree of price fluctuations of a bond on its own or in combination with one or both of the other factors. In order to understand how each factor works, we will consider each separately. They are all useful in guiding the investor in an investment strategy for bonds.

We can begin by examining maturity. The longer the maturity, the greater the price change and the price volatility of the bond. Let's assume yields increase from 7.11 percent to 9.48 percent, or by one-third. The price decline of an 8 percent coupon bond maturing in 5 years will be approximately 9 percent. An 8 percent coupon bond maturing instead in 20 years will decline by close to 21 percent. An 8 percent coupon bond maturing in 30 years will lose 23 percent of its value. In other words, the longer the maturity of the bond, the more pronounced the decline of the price of the bond, assuming the same quality, the same yield, and the same change in long-term interest rates.

The implications of this behavior provide an important rule in investing in bonds. If interest rates are expected to rise, the investor should own short-term maturities in order to minimize capital losses. In fact, when long-term interest rates rise because of a strong economy and rising inflation, the ideal strategy is to own money-market instruments, which are the instruments with the shortest maturity. Money-market instruments, maturing in the near term, are not vulnerable to capital losses. These short-term IOUs have little or no price sensitivity to changes in interest rates, because the principal will be repaid to the lender within a very short time, usually just a few weeks.

If interest rates decline, investors can expect the longest-maturity bonds to appreciate the most. Therefore, if interest rates are expected to decline, investors should own bonds with the longest maturity for any type of bonds, in order to maximize capital gains. For instance, government bonds are available with a 30-year maturity.

The second element driving price volatility of a bond is the coupon rate, or the yield of the coupon bond at par when the bond is issued. The lower the coupon rate, the greater the price volatility. Let's assume that yields increase by one-third from 7.11 percent to 9.48 percent. The price decline of an 8 percent coupon bond maturing in 20 years is close to 21 percent. The price decline of a 4 percent coupon bond maturing in the same number of years is close to 24 percent. Clearly, the lower-coupon bond offers the greater price volatility. If interest rates are expected to decline, the bonds that offer the greatest profit opportunities are those with the lowest coupon rate, because of the higher volatility or sensitivity to changes in market interest rates.

This characteristic of bonds leads to another important element to be considered when implementing an investment strategy based on bonds. If interest rates are expected to rise, it is better to own high-coupon-rate bonds. Actually, in this case, the best strategy is not to own bonds at all in order to avoid capital losses. However, if interest rates are expected to decline, capital gains are maximized by investing in low-coupon-rate bonds.

The third element determining price volatility of bonds is the yield level from which a yield fluctuation starts. The higher the yield level, the greater the price volatility. For instance, if one buys bonds when interest rates are 15 percent, price volatility is higher than that of bonds purchased when interest rates are at 8 or 6 percent. That's why in 1982, when yields on 10-year Treasury bonds peaked at about 15 percent, it was a great time to buy bonds, because it provided the highest level in the last century from which to buy bonds. In fact, the total return (interest plus capital gains) of bonds outperformed stocks during the first years of their decline because of the capital gains they provided since interest rates started to decline from very high levels.

Another element used in determining the price fluctuations of a bond is the quality of the bond. A bond with a higher quality will have a lower yield than a bond with the same maturity and a lower quality. The reason bonds with a lower quality have a higher yield is that investors require a premium for lending money to a lower-quality borrower. As a result, lower-quality bonds tend to sell at a lower price for the same maturity, thus offering a higher yield because of the risk premium embedded in that bond. Because of the higher risk of lower-quality bonds, one should expect that the fluctuations of these bonds are more pronounced than the fluctuations of higher-quality bonds.

As noted earlier, the highest-quality bonds are U.S. government bonds, and it is against these which all the other bonds are measured. Many criteria go into the formulation of the ratings of the quality of a bond, including (1) the amount and composition of any other existing debt of the issuer, (2) the stability of the issuer's cash flow, (3) the ability of the issuer to meet scheduled payments of interest and principal on their debt obligations, (4) asset protection, and (5) management ability.

Another element that determines price fluctuations is liquidity. The liquidity, or the marketability, of a bond influences the rate of interest it pays and the yield spread between it and other securities. Marketability is made up of two elements: (1) the number of bonds which can be bought or sold at one time without significantly affecting the price of the bonds, and (2) the amount of time needed to complete the desired transactions. All factors being equal, the securities that are less marketable and less easy to trade have a higher yield relative to other, more liquid securities. A highly liquid security can be purchased and sold in large amounts over a very short time period, while an illiquid issue is one that takes time or price concessions or both to effect a trade of even moderate size. It is reasonable to expect a highly liquid bond to have much lower price volatility than a less liquid bond. In a way, the lack of liquidity can be perceived as a higher risk for that bond because of the promptness with which that bond can be bought or sold.

Another feature that should be considered when buying and selling bonds is call protection. Certain long-term securities can be redeemed or called by the borrower prior to their regularly scheduled maturity. Investors normally do not like this callability feature because bonds are most often called after interest rates have fallen so new bonds can be issued at the lower rate of interest. Calling an issue merely for the purpose of reissuing new bonds at the lower rate of interest is known as *refunding*.

The main factors influencing bond price volatility, as a function of changes of market interest rates, can be summarized as follows:

- *Maturity.* The longer the maturity, the greater the price change.

- *Coupon rate.* The lower the coupon rate, the greater the price change.

- *Yield level.* The higher the yield level, the greater the price volatility.

- *Quality.* The bonds with lower quality may be expected to have higher price volatility.

- *Liquidity.* Lack of liquidity increases the price volatility of the bond.

The Yield Curve

The subject of interest rates and their relationship to the business cycle is one of the most complex subjects to investigate. Few analysts have surpassed Mr. Sidney Homer in the understanding of such a delicate, complex subject. When we talk about interest rates, we have to distinguish between trends in short-term interest rates and long-term interest rates.

The relationship between short-term and long-term interest rates provides very important information on the economy, including both the risk the relationship represents for the financial markets and the outlook of the economy itself. Since short-term interest rates are much more volatile than long-term interest rates, short-term interest rates tend to rise faster and decline faster than long-term interest rates.

The relationship between yields of different maturities is called the *term structure of interest rates*. The curve that represents this relationship is called the *yield curve*. Yields are measured on the vertical axis, and years to maturity are represented on the horizontal axis. Often the yield curve is upward-sloping, with short-term interest rates lower than long-term interest rates. There are times when the yield curve is flat, with short-term rates approximately equal to long-term interest rates. And there are very rare times, as in the 1970s and in 2000, when short-term interest rates rise above long-term interest rates. During such times the yield curve is downward-sloping. The daily shape of the yield curve can be found on the Bloomberg website.

From a business cycle viewpoint, the slope of the yield curve provides important clues to the future trend of the business cycle. One can measure the slope of the yield curve as the difference, or ratio, between long-term interest rates and the rate on the three-month Treasury bill. As this spread declines, the yield curve is flattening, and as the spread widens, the yield curve is steepening (Figure 9-2).

The analysis of yield curves at various points in the business cycle suggests that an upward-sloping yield curve, a yield curve whereby long-term interest rates are higher than short-term interest rates, is usually associated with good future economic growth and orderly financial markets.

A flattening of the yield curve, that is, when the spread between long-term interest rates and short-term interest rates decreases, is experienced when interest rates are rising. Flattening of the yield curve is usually associated with business beginning to slow down from the rapid pace typical of the initial phase of an expansion. The transition from a flattening position to a downward-sloping position of the yield curve, when short-term interest rates go above long-term interest rates, reflects an economy likely to enter a recession, with extremely tight credit conditions and a very high risk for the financial markets. Periods of a downward-sloping yield curve always have been associated with credit crunch, issues of financial viability of institutions, deep recessions, and rising inflation. There have been few periods like this; they were mostly experienced in the 1970s.

The reason these events are unlikely is because the experience of the 1970s was unique. In those years inflation was created by rising regulations, strong growth in monetary aggregates, and real short-term interest

YIELD CURVE AND INDUSTRIAL OUTPUT

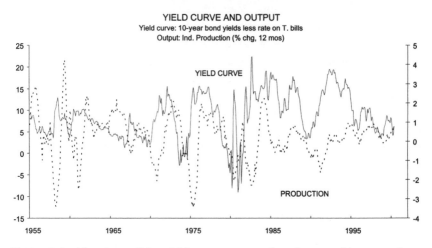

Figure 9-2. The slope of the yield curve, measured as the spread between short-term and long-term interest rates, is a leading indicator of the business cycle. A decline in the spread leads a decline in economic growth. A widening of the spread leads rising growth in economic activity.

rates well below their historical average for many years. Unless these conditions repeat themselves, which is highly unlikely, financial stability rather than financial instability should be expected.

The historical evidence suggests that the yield curve is a very important leading indicator of economic growth. The lead is often several months at major turning points of the business cycle.

One reason the spread between short-term and long-term interest rates is a leading indicator is because the difference between long-term and short-term interest rates represents an incentive for lenders to lend money and provide credit to borrowers.

Banks collect money from consumers and pay consumers an interest rate on their deposit tied to the 90-day Treasury bill rate. The banks then lend the money to consumers or businesses to be invested in long-term projects, charging long-term interest rates. When long-term interest rates are much higher than short-term interest rates, the margins derived from the transactions are high. In other words, when the yield curve is steep, lenders are encouraged to lend, thus stimulating the economy with increased liquidity. As the yield curve flattens and the spread between short-term and long-term interest rates declines, there is less profit margin for lenders. As the yield curve flattens because of this smaller incentive, lenders do not provide credit to businesses or consumers as aggressively as when the yield curve was much steeper. As the yield curve flattens, lack of credit availability to businesses or consumers eventually causes the economy to slow down.

When the yield curve is inverted or downward-sloping, with short-term interest rates higher than long-term interest rates, there is little or no incentive for lenders to lend money. They can take their profits and invest in Treasury bills and make more money than they would by lending to business. This is why during such times it is said there is a credit crunch. The reason is that lenders do not have an incentive to lend long-term money. However, as the yield curve steepens, this incentive to lend more money increases, and gradually the economy picks up.

The relationship between changes in the yield curve (a leading indicator), the growth in industrial production (a coincident indicator), and short-term interest rates (a lagging indicator) can be summarized by using the relationship existing between leading, coincident, and lagging indicators:

- A flattening of the yield curve is followed by
- Slower growth in industrial production, which is followed by
- A peak in short-term interest rates, which is followed by
- A steepening of the yield curve, which is followed by
- Rising growth in industrial production, which is followed by
- Rising short-term interest rates, which is followed by
- A flattening of the yield curve.

And the cycle repeats itself.

The Credit Cycle

We have seen in the previous section that yields on corporate bonds with the same maturity may be different because of quality. The yield on a bond of lower quality is higher because lenders attach a risk premium to that particular bond; therefore, they require a higher rate of interest. There are two basic ways to compute the spread between the yield of two securities. One is computed by taking the difference between the two yields. A second way is to compute the ratio between the two yields. For instance, if the interest rate on BAA-rated bonds is 8.0 percent and the yield on 10-year Treasury bonds is 7 percent, the spread between the two interest rates can be represented as 1 percent (by taking the difference between the two yields) or 1.4, computed as the ratio between 8 and 7 percent.

The driving force behind changes in spreads is the demand for credit and the strength of the business cycle. Corporate bond yields will always be higher than Treasury bond yields with the same maturity because Treasury bonds are the safest and most liquid instruments. The backing of the U.S. government is a formidable clause behind the safety of such bonds. For this reason, the spread between corporate bonds and Treasury bonds, computed using the ratio between the two yields, will always be greater than 1.

The behavior of this spread, which is a leading indicator of the business cycle, provides further information on the soundness of the economy and the financial markets. Spreads rise because business sees opportunities ahead and begins to borrow to make the new investments. The increased demand for money is reflected in higher spreads and in the acceleration of the money supply. Because of the expansion of liquidity, the economy begins to strengthen, thus reinforcing the need for credit. Spreads and growth in the money supply continue to rise as interest rates decline or remain stable. Spreads increase as the economy strengthens because an increasing number of marginal borrowers are drawn to the market to borrow and make new investments. The market, of course, requires higher spreads for these marginal borrowers due to the higher credit risk. Therefore, a combination of strong credit demand and the increased number of borrowers with lower credit standing raises the spreads between low-grade and high-grade bonds. Eventually the increase in interest rates caused by a strong economy discourages further increase in the demand for credit. The money supply slows down, spreads decrease as demand for money decreases, and eventually the economy slows down due to the slowdown in liquidity and in investment (Figure 9-3). For instance, in 1995 the demand for credit began to expand again, due to lower interest rates.

At that time, the money supply was growing very slowly, and the spread between the yield on BAA bonds and 10-year Treasury bonds was at a cyclical low of about 1.2 (using the ratio between the two yields). The eighth financial cycle since 1960 was under way again, with the growth of the money supply rising to 15 percent in 1999 and the spread between BAA bond yields and 10-year Treasury bond yields soaring to 1.6. As interest rates began to rise in 1998–1999, the demand for credit declined, resulting in a peak in the growth of the money supply and in spreads.

When the economy is weak, interest rates decline until business finds their level attractive again to justify new investments. At that particular

MZM AND BOND SPREADS

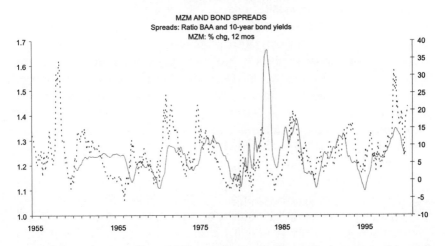

MZM AND BOND SPREADS
Spreads: Ratio BAA and 10-year bond yields
MZM: % chg, 12 mos

Figure 9-3. The growth in MZM coincides with the cyclical pattern of spreads between the yields on BAA and 10-year Treasury bonds. Investors can therefore use bond yield spreads as a way of confirming the implication of the trend in the growth of the money supply.

point, the spreads stop declining and the demand for money increases, resulting in an increase in growth in the money supply. A new credit cycle is under way again.

The important point to remember is that the growth in stock prices coincides with the growth of the money supply and yield spreads. Yield spreads are therefore, a leading indicator of the economy, and their turning points coincide with the turning points of the growth of the money supply and stock prices. One way to rationalize this is to think that high spreads represent great demand for money that eventually will cause interest rates to rise. Therefore, high yield spreads represent an extreme that will force the money supply to grow at a slower pace, thus affecting the growth of the economy.

Forecasting Bond Yields

In order to forecast bond yields, it is useful to remember that long-term interest rates are a lagging indicator of the economy, and as such, they rise only after a protracted period of strength in business activity. Furthermore, since yields reflect the inflationary expectations of the lender, their trend also coincides with the trend of inflation. As for all lagging indicators, the forecasting process begins with examining the trend of the leading indicators such as the growth of the money supply, the yield curve, quality spreads between BAA bond yields and 10-year Treasury bond yields, or consumer sentiment.

A period of several months of growth in the leading indicators is followed by an increase in the coincident indicators such as employment, income, sales, or production. Several months of strong growth in these indicators is followed by a bottoming of the lagging indicators. Bond yields stop declining and trade in a narrow range as commodities, inflation, and labor costs begin to slowly accelerate.

Bond yields rise too, together with all the lagging indicators, and they will peak only after a protracted decline of several months in the leading indicators and in the coincident indicators. In other words, bond yields cannot show a cyclical peak unless the growth of the money supply declines for at least 12 months and the coincident indicators show visible weakness.

Strong growth in the money supply, strong growth in the economy, rising commodities, and rising inflation form a very bearish configuration for bonds. During such times, bonds should be sold. On the other hand, a protracted slowdown in the money supply, followed by a weaker economy, declining commodities, and lower inflation, represents a very bullish environment for bonds. During such times, bonds should be bought.

An indicator useful to predict the direction of bond yields is real bond yields. Real bond yields are measured as the difference between yields on Treasury bonds less inflation. Real bond yields below their historical average are inflationary, because during such times money is inexpensive relative to inflation and therefore stimulates excessive demand for credit, strong economic conditions, and rising inflation. This is bearish for bonds. When real bond yields are well above their historical average, bond yields tend to decline or stay stable. High real bond yields, above 4.0 percent, are bullish for bonds, and low real bond yields, below 2.8 percent, are usually bearish for bonds. In measuring real bond yields, it is recommended to take the yield on 10-year Treasury bonds and subtract inflation—that is, the growth over 12 months in the consumer price index.

Another indicator that is useful in assessing the direction of bond yields is the price index of the National Association of Purchasing Managers. This price index shows the percentage of managers reporting that they have paid higher prices. When this percentage increases above 50 percent, inflationary pressures are quite strong, and of course, this is bearish for bonds. On the other hand, when this price index is declining and falls below 50 percent, inflationary pressures are decreasing and the economic environment becomes bullish for bonds.

The National Association of Purchasing Managers publishes in its monthly report, available on the Internet, the purchasing managers index. This index oscillates around 50 percent. When this index rises above 50 percent, it indicates the economy is growing rapidly and is very strong. Bond yields tend to rise during these times. When the index falls close to or below 50 percent, bond yields tend to decline, making bonds a good investment.

The relationship between the growth in the money supply and the growth in nominal GDP also provides clues to the direction of bond yields. Growth in monetary aggregates (e.g., MZM) above the growth in nominal GDP suggests that credit is expanding faster than the economy. This situation is inflationary and therefore is conducive to higher bond yields. During such times, bonds should be sold. On the other hand, when the growth in the money supply falls below the growth in nominal GDP, the economy should be expected to slow down and inflationary pressures to decrease. These developments are conducive eventually to lower yields. During such times, bonds should be bought. The yield on five-year Treasury bonds follows GDP growth quite closely (Figure 9-4).

Another indicator useful in assessing the direction of bond yields is commodity prices, which tend to move ahead of long-term interest rates. Following the price of gold and crude oil, and the price of raw materials such as copper and aluminum, will give a good indication if the economy, and in particular the manufacturing sector, is strengthening. Bond yields should be expected to rise when the prices of commodities rise. On the other hand, when the economy is weak and commodity prices decline, the odds favor stable or lower bond yields and therefore a strong bond market.

Bond investors are also advised to keep in mind that bond yields are highly seasonal. They tend to rise from the end of November to the end of May. They remain stable or decline from June to the end of November. This is a statistical curiosity proved by many years of historical evidence. One reason for this seasonality may be that in the summer months business slows down and there is less need for financing. The outcome is lower demand for money and more stable bond yields.

Since bond yields and inflation are lagging indicators, the relationship between leading, coincident, and lagging indicators can be used to forecast the outlook for bond yields. For this purpose, we will consider the growth of the money supply, yield spreads, and the yield curve as lead-

GDP AND BOND YIELD

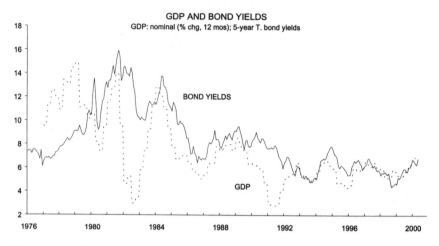

Figure 9–4. The level of bond yields depends on the growth in nominal GDP (before inflation).

ing indicators. The growth in industrial production is a coincident indicator, and inflation and bond yields are lagging indicators:

- A peak in the growth of the money supply, in yield spreads, and in the yield curve is followed by

- A decline in the growth of industrial production, which is followed by

- A decline in inflation and bond yields, which is followed by

- A trough in the growth of the money supply, in yield spreads, and in the yield curve, which is followed by

- A trough in the growth of industrial production, which is followed by

- A trough in bond yields and inflation, which is followed by

- A peak in the growth of the money supply, in yield spreads, and in the yield curve.

And the cycle starts again.

Investors also should use the information provided by real bond yields to determine the extent of the rise or decline in yields. A low real bond yield rate is likely to be followed by a sharp rise in bond yields. On the other hand, a high real bond yield rate may signal that the peak in bond yields is imminent. Of course, the implication of real short-term interest rates on overall inflation trends should also be part of the forecasting process.

Investment Implications

Bonds are an attractive investment when the economy is growing slowly, the money supply is slowing down, real yields are high, the purchasing managers index declines below 50 percent, and commodity prices are weak. Under these conditions one should buy long-term bonds or mutual funds investing in long-term bonds.

However, as soon as there is some evidence that the economy is strengthening, such as a protracted increase in the money supply, rising commodity prices, accelerating industrial production, high consumer confidence, low real bond yields, or a sharp rise above 50 percent in the purchasing managers index, investors should recognize that bond yields are likely to have reached a bottom for that particular cycle. At this point it is important to start reducing the maturity of the portfolio by transferring money into shorter-term maturities in order to protect the portfolio from losses, since short-term maturity bonds have lower price volatility.

When there are signs that the economy is in the process of gaining strength, it is time to become defensive and shorten the maturity of the bonds even further. An alternative would be to reduce the amount invested in bonds and increase the investment in money-market instruments or money-market mutual funds.

It is crucial for a successful investment program in bonds to use a flexible investment strategy. Investors need to gradually increase the maturity of the portfolio when yields are declining or remain stable. However, maturity should be decreased as yields rise in order to minimize capital losses.

When a credit cycle is at its worst with spreads increasing, it is appropriate to buy short-term, lower-grade bonds because lower-grade bonds have a very high yield relative to Treasury bonds. This provides a good way to lock in high interest rates. The best strategy at these times is to buy short-term bonds for income purposes. This is a safe, prudent strategy to take advantage of the credit cycle.

It is also important to remember that bond prices change, and the investor in bonds will suffer capital losses when yields rise. On the other hand, there are excellent opportunities when the economy slows down. Investment in bonds can produce very attractive returns coming from capital gains and interest at these times.

If bond yields are expected to rise, bond investments should be gradually sold, and the proceeds should be placed in short-term bonds, Treasury bills, or money-market mutual funds. If investors have used bond mutual funds to take advantage of the cyclical price change of bonds, investments in bond mutual funds should be sold at this time and the proceeds placed in Treasury bills or money-market mutual funds.

There are two ways to invest in bonds. The first alternative is to buy the actual bond, a procedure similar to buying stocks. The second choice is to invest money in a mutual fund investing in bonds.

The decision of choosing between the two investment vehicles is important because they have different risk and return characteristics. When investors buy bonds, they are assured they will receive the value of the bond at par when the bond matures. This is the reason it is generally believed that investing in bonds is safer. No capital losses are incurred if the bond is held to maturity, provided the bond is of high quality.

However, the buy-and-hold strategy has a cost that impacts the total return of the bond portfolio. If interest rates rise, investors could have achieved a higher return by investing their capital in short-term instruments and reinvesting their money in bonds when interest rates decline. A buy-and-hold strategy is a safe strategy, but provides lower returns than the one based on business and financial cycle considerations.

The second alternative is to buy bonds through mutual funds that invest in bonds. In this case, there is no par value, and the net asset value of the mutual fund will change as interest rates rise and decline. The net asset value will decline in a period of rising interest rates and rise when interest rates decline. Clearly, investing in bond mutual funds is much riskier than buying the physical bond because the value of the capital will fluctuate, with no guarantee of receiving a preestablished dollar amount at a future time. The reason is that bond mutual funds do not have a maturity date.

Investing in bonds provides a cushion of safety for the investment portfolio by reducing its volatility. However, by doing so, investors do not take advantage of the great opportunities offered by other forms of investment when interest rates decline. Furthermore, the buy-and-hold strategy would cause you to miss the superior returns offered by choosing bonds at major cyclical turning points in interest rates, as discussed in this book. Reducing volatility of the value of your portfolio is not as much dependent on the amount of bonds you own, but above all, on how you adapt your strategy to financial cycle fluctuations.

Chapter
10

THE STOCK MARKET AND BUSINESS CYCLES

In the previous chapters, we learned how risk changes and how economic and financial indicators help in assessing the direction of risk. To understand risk, we had to understand how the economic indicators were interrelated. For this purpose we used simple business cycles to illustrate their relationships. Eventually, at the end of the analysis of business and financial cycles, we concluded that most indicators can be subdivided into three categories: leading, lagging, and coincident indicators.

The model relating these three sets of indicators can be summarized as follows:

- A peak in the growth of the leading indicators is followed by

- A peak in the growth of the coincident indicators, which is followed by

- A peak in the growth of the lagging indicators, which is followed by

- A trough in the growth of the leading indicators, which is followed by

- A trough in the growth of the coincident indicators, which is followed by

- A trough in the growth of the lagging indicators, which is followed by

- A peak in the growth of the leading indicators.

And the cycle starts all over again.

Some of the most important leading indicators mentioned in previous chapters are:

- Growth in the money supply

- Stock prices

- Quality spreads between the yields of BAA corporate bonds and Treasury bonds

- The yield curve

- The dollar

The most important coincident indicators include:

- Industrial production

- Income

- Retail sales

- Employment

Among the most relevant lagging indicators to consider are:

- Short-term and long-term interest rates

- Changes in unit labor costs

- Changes in consumer prices

- Changes in producer prices

- Changes in commody prices

- Changes in inventory

- Changes in consumer installment credit

We have learned that strong growth in the leading indicators is a warning that the economy is going to be robust, and this will be reflected eventually by rising coincident indicators. The issue of risk for the financial markets appears when the lagging indicators start rising rapidly, preceded by strong growth in the leading and coincident indicators. Since stocks are a leading indicator, a rise in the lagging indicators, such as inflation, bond yields, short-term interest rates, and growth in unit labor costs, should be taken as a warning that stocks are likely to encounter some turbulence. A rise in the lagging indicators should be taken, therefore, as a warning that risk is increasing for equities, and so a defensive strategy becomes appropriate. On the other hand, a decline in the lagging indicators points to lower risk and higher stock prices.

We also looked at the long-term trends in the economy and how they have been impacted by the level of real short-term interest rates. The point was made that low real short-term interest rates create inflationary pressures, and high real short-term interest rates have been accompanied by stable or declining inflation. Because of the importance of real short-term interest rates, we reviewed the role of the Federal Reserve in controlling the level of interest rates and in affecting the growth of the money supply. Because of their crucial impact on the economy and the financial markets, we have discussed the role of commodities, the process of inflation, and its impact on the dollar.

The trend of inflation is a crucial determinant of the direction of long-term interest rates or bond yields. We used this information to establish guidelines on how to profit from changes in bond yields caused by rising or declining inflation. We showed how a bond investment strategy is closely related to changes in the business cycle. A strong economy is associated with higher long-term interest rates and a weakening economy with lower long-term interest rates due to a softening in the demand for long-term capital.

All these developments are related and have a crucial impact on the stock market. The next two chapters will be devoted to this important issue. This chapter will deal with how the forces released by the business cycle impact the risk of owning stocks. The crucial questions to be answered, are these: Should an investor increase or decrease his exposure to equities? Is now the time to be 100 percent in stocks?

We will attempt to answer these questions in the pages that follow by using the information developed in the previous chapters.

Long-Term Stock Returns and Strategies

In this section we will analyze in detail what is really meant by investing over the long term and what the implications of doing so are. What is widely known and accepted is that the long-term investor will do well because the trend of the market is up and has provided a return of close to 7 percent in capital appreciation and about 3 percent in dividends, with a total return of about 10 to 11 percent. (Incidentally, 7 percent is close to the average long-term growth in the money supply.)

The essence of the argument is that investors should not try to time the market because over the long term the market has provided a very attractive return. However, this is true only if the world works in an ideal way and events are predictable. Let's see why.

It is important to have an understanding of the meaning of *long term*. In fact, *long term* has a meaning only in hindsight. To recognize why this is so, let's take some periods of history as an example. For instance, in 1900 the Dow Jones Industrial Average was 77.60. In 1922 the Dow Jones Industrial Average was 63.90. In 1932, that is, after 32 years, the Dow Jones Industrial Average was 50.16. Clearly, for an investor in 1900, long-term investing held little comfort for him because he would have seen the average stock price decline for 32 years. If he were planning to retire within those 32 years, the outcome of his investment would have been very poor.

Another example is 1928 when the S&P 500 was 17.66. In 1949 the S&P 500 was standing at 16.76. Investors of the time who were thinking long term would not have seen their capital grow at all for 21 years if they had invested their money in 1928. Another more recent example is what happened after 1968. In 1968 the S&P 500 was standing at 100.53. At that time short-term interest rates were 5 percent. In 1982, the S&P 500 was 109.65 when short-term interest rates were yielding a return of close to 20 percent. Clearly, a buy and hold for these 14 years would have provided little return, and stocks would have been a poor choice when short-term interest rates would have provided returns close to 10 percent on average for that period and close to 20 percent toward the end of the 1970s.

The point is that the long term is an ideal world because there have been extremely long periods of 20 to 25 years when the market did not provide any return. There were periods between 1945 and 1968 and between 1982 and 1999 when stocks provided returns of close to 20 percent. The average long-term return you read about is an average of returns of periods when stocks appreciated 20 percent and long periods when they did not grow at all. Almost 50 percent of the time, the stock market did not provide any return at all in the last century.

The purpose of this analysis is to say that nothing is easy in the investment world and investors have to be aware of the kind of investment environment they are facing. If the future is anything like the first 45 years of the twentieth century and investors are planning to retire in 15 years, they could be hurt because of the poor returns. There is no easy formula for making money, and investors have to be aware of the overall financial and economic climate to make informed investment decisions. The concept of risk and the concept of what kind of investment to utilize are of paramount importance. For instance, in the 1970s cash and hard assets were the investments of choice. The reason was that inflation was rampant as the Fed followed an easy monetary policy. Because of rising inflation, the price of any tangible asset, such as real estate, art, coins, gold, and other commodities, soared. At the same time, the value of stocks and bonds declined sharply as interest rates reached historical highs.

The objective of this chapter is therefore to provide a sense of the investment times. What can you expect? What should you look for? What is the risk you are facing? The two questions investors should ask as they watch the financial markets are "Should I be more aggressive or should

I be more defensive in my investment approach?" and " What kinds of times are we living in?" We will try to answer these questions in the pages that follow.

Stock Prices and Business Cycles

In order to have a better appreciation of how the stock market relates to the business cycle, one can think about the stock market as a reservoir of liquidity—a huge pond with a lot of money that people can access when they need it. When investors don't need money for their own consumtion, they put it in this reservoir known as the stock market, and so the level of the reservoir increases. The level of the reservoir declines when people need the money for other investments, for purchases, or for other endeavors.

You can think of trends in economic conditions as regulators of the level of the stock market, or this reservoir. When the economy is improving and becomes strong, investment opportunities arise when businesses need money to expand production capacity, or to buy a new process that will increase productivity, and therefore improve the profitability of the business. Returns from these investments could be as high as 40 or 50 percent. These types of returns overpower the returns from the stock market. Therefore, when the economy is strong and the outlook for business improves considerably, investors take the money from the reservoir—that is, the stock market—and invest it in the real economy.

When the economy slows down and the opportunities are not as numerous, businesspeople, investors, and consumers take their money and put it in the stock market. They "park" the money until the next opportunity arises. This framework is one way to rationalize why the stock market performs poorly during periods of strong economic growth and instead provides above-average returns when the economy slows down and grows very slowly. When the economy starts growing at a rate of above 3 or 4 percent, investors are close to periods of high risk. This is when the market becomes more volatile and only a few sectors maintain an upward trend. On the other hand, when the economy is sluggish and growth is below its long-term average, money goes into the stock market and stocks show a broad advance and become an attractive investment. Later, we will review in more detail how to measure risks and opportunities.

Some analysts suggest that the market is forward-looking. Conventional wisdom believes the market is strong during periods of

weak economic growth because the market anticipates a stronger economy in the future and higher earnings. This may be misleading, because
the market is a collection of investors and it has been proved that the
overwhelming majority of investors have a very poor track record in
anticipating either the strength of the economy or the strength of the
stock market. How can the market then be forward-looking when market participants are not?

It seems more reasonable to believe that the stock market adjusts itself
automatically to changing economic conditions and reflects capital flows
from the real economy to the stock market when the real economy does
not offer opportunities. Capital flows reverse themselves by going back
to the real economy when higher returns can be expected from investments in a particular business.

Earnings grow at the same rate as nominal GDP—that is, at the same
rate as the economy. Yearly growth in nominal GDP has been close to
7.5 percent since 1946. Stock prices rose at the same pace as GDP,
reflecting growth in the overall wealth of the economy in the same period. Earnings are just part of a bigger and more important picture.

The approximate 8 percent long-term growth in stock prices reflects
the overall growth of the economy of about 8 percent. The fact that corporate earnings are also increasing at about the same rate is just a con-
firmation of the overall rising trend of the wealth created by business
activity. The point is that there is no causality between earnings and
overall stock market performance. The trend in earnings and stock prices
reflects and is driven by the overall trend in the growth of liquidity and
overall business conditions.

But, then, do earnings have a short-term impact on the trend of stock
prices? Strong earnings growth over one or two years is the outcome of
very strong economic conditions when sales rise rapidly and costs are
still relatively well behaved. For instance, let's take 1994. The economy
was robust, and earnings per share of the S&P 500 index grew strongly,
a whopping 34 percent. According to the general consensus, the market
should have been very strong. But do not jump to conclusions. In the
same year, commodities soared, bond yields jumped, and Treasury bills
grew very rapidly. In spite of strong earnings growth or because of
sharply higher commodities or interest rates due to the robust business
activity, the market actually declined 4 percent.

Let's take another example and look at what happened in 1998. This
was a year when earnings per share actually declined 6 percent. Because
of the weakness induced by the Asian debacle, commodities and interest rates declined. The stock market was not disappointed at all by poor

earnings performance because of the weak economy. In fact, the stock market soared 31 percent.

The point is that strong earnings are usually associated with a strong economy, and—keep in mind the concept of reservoir—people draw from the stock market to invest in the real economy during such times. And therefore the market is weak during a strong economy and strong when the economy is weak, independently from earnings performance (see Chapter 8, Figure 8-3).

Does that mean that earnings do not matter? Of course they matter. They are particularly important when one has to choose a stock, and we will review this concept in the next chapter in more detail. However, the idea that investors can use earnings to justify that the market is rising because of anticipated stronger overall earnings in the economy is a fallacy and does not lead to correct strategic decisions. The main point to remember is that stronger earnings are associated with a strong economy and therefore a less exuberant stock market.

The stock market, which represents a measure of liquidity, is a very important leading indicator of the economy. A strong stock market says that the economy also will be strong because there is a lot of liquidity ready to be used eventually in the real economy. A weak stock market is an indication that the economy will slow down and liquidity in the economic system is drying up. The time to worry about the stock market is when the lagging indicators start rising. This is an indication that a very strong economy is overheating, and one should expect liquidity to be taken out of the stock market to be invested in the real economy.

On the other hand, as long as the lagging indicators are declining or stable, then the economy is growing with no excesses, its growth is stable and is within acceptable bounds; and therefore the stock market is on a solid foundation.

Assessing Stock Market Risk

The most crucial aspect in assessing stock market risk is not a lack of timely information about economic and financial developments. The real issue is an emotional one. The data discussed in this section will give you proven guidelines on how to assess the risk of the market. The difficult thing will be to believe what the data tell you. This is a common problem, caused mostly by greed. "The market has gone up so much, why should I start selling? Why don't I let things go? After all, over the long term I will make it up anyway." (which we have seen is not the case). The main problem is to be able to objectively recognize what the information is telling you to do. Trying to be sensible and professional in what you reasonably expect is crucial in managing risk.

What follows are some basic guidelines for measuring risk. They will help you answer the question; Is now the time to be 100 percent in stocks? The more the indicators tell you that you should not be invested in stocks, the more money you should have in money-market instruments, such as 13-week Treasury bills or money-market mutual funds.

1. The Economy

A strong economy with low unemployment, preceded by strong growth in the money supply, is usually a serious and reliable warning sign that the risk for the market is rising (Figure 10-1). Above-average growth in the coincident (the economy) and leading (growth in the money supply) indicators points to continued solid growth, which is likely to create excesses. Low risk occurs when the economy is slowing down below its growth potential, the unemployment rate is rising, and there is a sense of discomfort in the population. Newspapers are full of stories about "soft landings" and risk of recession. These are times that have been preceded by protracted declines in leading indicators.

STOCK PRICES AND BUSINESS CYCLES

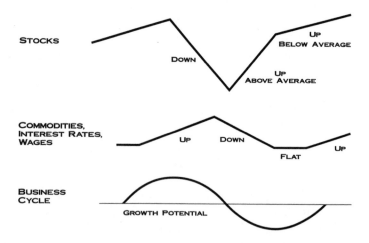

Figure 10-1. The stock market is related to the business cycle and trends in commodities and interest rates. A strong economy is associated with rising commodities, rising interest rates, and weak stock prices. The stock market shows the best performance during periods of weakening economic activity and declining commodities and interest rates.

2. Financial cycles

Charting the growth of various measures of the money supply (M1, M2, M3, MZM) over 12 months and of the adjusted monetary base over several decades provides the best way to see periodicity of a financial cycle. By charting one measure of money supply together with all the leading, coincident, and lagging indicators, you will be able to see the business and financial cycles come alive.

The relationship between stock prices and the money supply can best be seen by comparing the rate of change of the S&P 500 with the rate of change of the money supply over 12 months (Figure 10-2).

Another important relationship is obtained by comparing on the same chart the growth of the money supply over 12 months and short-term interest rates. This relationship shows that declining short-term interest rates are followed by rising growth in the money supply, which is favorable to stocks. However, rising short-term interest rates are followed by declining growth in the money supply, which is a negative development for stocks.

From a strategic viewpoint, periods of rising growth in the money supply are less risky for stock investors than periods of declining growth in the money supply, as we illustrated in the discussion on financial cycles in Chapter 7. The data needed to perform this analysis are easily acces-

MZM AND S&P 500

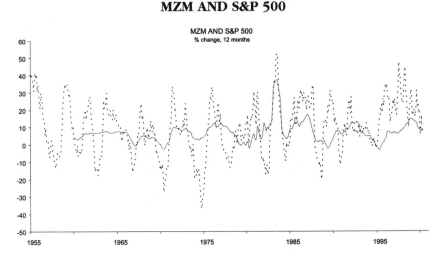

Figure 10-2. The growth in the money supply is closely related to the growth in stock prices. Declining growth in the money supply is associated with poor market performance.

sible at the website of the Federal Reserve Bank of St. Louis. Their FRED database provides all the information required.

3. Short-Term Interest Rates

Declining or stable short-term interest rates are an indication the economy is slowing down or is growing at a pace close to or below $2^1/_2$ to 3 percent. This is the time the stock market offers little risk, and so investors should be in stocks aggressively. The rise of the stock market is broad, and it is not difficult to find stocks to buy. The time to worry is when, in response to a more spirited economy, short-term interest rates start rising. During such times the market becomes more selective, and it becomes increasingly difficult to buy attractive stocks. During such times it is prudent to raise cash. A sound rule of thumb is to start aggressively reducing your exposure to stocks after two to three months of rising short-term interest rates. Also, during such times it is not unusual to derive higher returns from cash than from stocks. Conservative investors will find that an investment of 100 percent in money-market instruments is likely to perform on average like, or better than, the overall stock market. This strategy provides considerably more safety and peace of mind than going through the volatility the market displays during times of rising short-term interest rates.

Since interest rates are a lagging indicator, their trough leads a peak in stock prices (a leading indicator). By inverting the level of interest rates, therefore, one finds that the inverted level of interest rates leads peaks and troughs in stock prices. This lead time is maintained when the rate of change of interest rates (inverted) is compared with the rate of change of stock prices.

4. Commodities

The trend in commodity prices, and by commodity prices we mean the CRB raw industrial index (spot), confirms the trend in short-term interest rates. Therefore, if one sees short-term interest rates rising and at the same time commodity prices also rising, this is confirmation that the economy is very strong, and will have a negative impact on the stock market (see Figure 10-1).

If, on the other hand, short-term interest rates decline and commodity prices decline, this is confirmation that the economy is slowing down and weakening. This configuration suggests stocks are becoming attractive again. If commodities stabilize after a period of decline, the economy is improving and gaining more strength. Under these conditions, one should see short-term rates also stabilize. Trends in the prices of commodities should be used to confirm the message given by trends in interest rates. It is also important to remember that if real short-term interest rates are high, neither the increase in commodity prices nor the threat that the incresed prices pose to inflation is going to be pronounced.

5. Inflation and Bond Yields

Inflation has an important impact on stocks. The 1970s have clearly proved this point, both over the long term and over the short term. If one sees unit labor costs or inflation rising more rapidly, this is a bad sign for the economy. It shows that the economy is overheating and creating the type of environment that has always had a negative impact on the stock market. The reason is that rising inflation causes bond yields to move higher, reflecting a higher inflationary premium. Rising bond yields, as is the case for short-term interest rates, are followed quite closely by a peak in stock prices.

On the other hand, declining inflation and declining bond yields are a sign that the economy has weakened and that the inflationary problems are being solved, thus creating an environment more favorable to stocks. These relationships can be viewed in the context of business and financial cycles as follows:

- A peak in the growth of the money supply and stock prices, both leading indicators, is followed by

- A peak in the growth of the economy (coincident indicator), which is followed by

- A peak in inflation and bond yields (both lagging indicators), which is followed by

- A trough in the growth of the money supply and stock prices, which is followed by

- A trough in the growth of the economy, which is followed by

- A trough in inflation and bond yields, which is followed by

- A peak in the growth of the money supply and stock prices.

And the financial cycle starts all over again.

The trend in bond yields is an excellent leading indicator of the stock market. A bottom in bond yields leads a peak in stock prices; and a peak in bond yields and inflation leads a bottom in stock prices. This is the typical relationship between leading indicators—that is, the stock market—and lagging indicators—that is, bond yields and inflation.

6. Bond Yields and Price Earnings Ratios

The trend in bond yields, as we have seen above, has an important impact on stock prices. So it is important to closely follow the level of bond yields in order to determine the level of overvaluation or under-valuation of the stock market.

The historical relationship between bond yields and price-earnings (PE) ratios provides very useful guidelines on the proper level of valuation. In order to measure this relationship, one needs to construct a diagram showing on the x-axis the level of 10-year Treasury bond yields and on the y-axis the PE ratio of the S&P 500. If one goes back 20 years and plots for every month the corresponding PE ratio of the S&P 500 for every level of 10-year bond yields, the outcome is a scatter diagram showing the historical relationship between the PE ratio and the level of 10-year Treasury bond yields. The graph shows how the PE ratio has changed in time with the changing level of bond yields (Figure 10-3).

This relationship shows that the higher the bond yields, the lower the price-earnings ratio of the market. On the other hand, the lower the level of the bond yields, the higher the PE ratio of the market. The main point of this relationship is that the higher the bond yields go, the lower the fair value of the market becomes. On the other hand, the lower the bond yields go, the higher the fair value of the market becomes.

BOND YIELDS AND PE RATIO

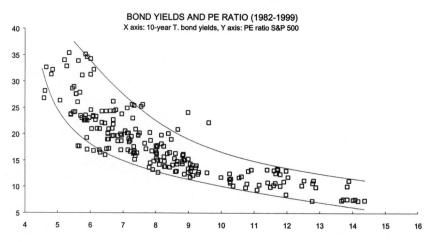

Figure 10-3.   The PE ratio of the S&P 500 is related to the level of 10-year Treasury bond yields. For any level of yields, investors can assess whether the market is over-valued or undervalued.

The reasons for the inverse relationship between bond yields and the PE ratio are the following: When bond yields are very high, they reflect economic conditions characterized by high inflation and uncertain economic times, as we experienced in the 1970s. During such periods the PE ratio declines because market participants are not willing to pay a high price for 1 dollar of earnings. They see a lot of risk in the marketplace, and therefore, they do not attach much value to the level of earnings due to the high economic uncertainties. On the other hand, declining yields anticipate more robust and stable economic conditions, and so market participants are willing to pay a higher PE ratio because of the perceived lower risk.

The scatter diagram relating 10-year high-yield bonds and PE ratios shows that when bond yields are close to 12 percent, the historical range for the PE ratio has been between 9 and 14. In this case, when the PE ratio is close to 9, the market is undervalued. This is the time when an aggressive investment in stocks is justified. On the other hand, when the PE ratio is at 14, the market is overvalued. The reason the market is overvalued is because, historically, the market was never priced with a PE ratio above 14 when bond yields were at 12 percent. Caution should be exercised when the PE ratio is close to 14.

There have been periods when bond yields have been 10 percent, and the scatter diagram shows that acceptable PE ratios during such times are between 11 and 20. In other words, with bond yields at 10 percent and a PE ratio at 11, the market is undervalued; the closer the PE ratio goes to 20, the more that the market becomes overvalued and therefore the more that risk increases.

When yields are close to 8 percent, the PE ratio has moved between 13 and 25. This means that when yields are 8 percent, an aggressive investment in stocks is justified when the PE ratio is close to 13 because the market is undervalued. When the PE ratio goes higher and gets close to 25, the market becomes very expensive and risk is high. Therefore, by looking at the historical relationship between yields and PE ratios, one can determine a measure of the overvaluation and undervaluation of the market and derive, as a result, a sense of risk.

In the late 1990s the PE ratio was close to 33, with yields at 6 percent. The market was overvalued and the risk was high, thus representing a high-risk investment. The reason the market was overvalued was because the market had never before been priced with a PE ratio above 33 when yields were at 6 percent. The point is that exposure to stocks should be decreased as the market becomes overvalued relative to the 10-year bond yield. On the other hand, stocks should be accumulated gradually as the market becomes undervalued relative to the 10-year bond yield.

7. The Yield Curve

The relative movement of short-term and long-term interest rates provides very important clues and information about the risk and opportunities offered by stocks. The yield curve can be measured, as mentioned above, by the difference between short-term and long-term interest rates. When this difference increases, the yield curve steepens. As the difference decreases, the yield curve flattens. The shape of the yield curve should be used in conjunction with the conclusions derived from the analysis of the growth of the money supply.

A steepening in the yield curve is an important leading indicator, pointing to a much stronger economy. As a result, a steep yield curve in a strong economy represents a high-risk environment for the stock market.

On the other hand, when the yield curve flattens—that is, when the difference between short-term and long-term interest rates decreases—and the economy grows slowly, it suggests the market risk is low. Therefore, a flattening yield curve provides clues that there is an environment more conducive to higher stock prices because of lower risk. For instance, the yield curve measured as the difference between the 10-year bond yields and Treasury bills flattened considerably between 1994 and the end of 1995. This flattening of the yield curve was followed by a slowdown of the economy in 1995, which was followed by a period of stable and lower short-term interest rates. This environment was conducive to a strong stock market in 1995.

On the other hand, the yield curve steepened sharply between the end of 1998 and mid-1999, and the steepening of the yield curve was followed almost immediately by considerable strength in the economy and eventually by rising short-term interest rates, thus creating a negative environment for the stock market for most of 1999 and into 2000.

8. The Dollar

As we have learned, the currency of a country provides important clues about the health of its economy. A strong currency reflects a country with solid economic conditions characterized by low inflation, a stable economic environment, and high real interest rates. This is the kind of environment in which stock prices thrive. On the other hand, a weak currency reflects a country with economic instability, with structural problems, and with rising inflation—definitely not an environment conducive to a strong stock market. For these reasons, when establishing an investment program in stocks, it is important to remember to look at the trend of the dollar.

If the dollar is strong, relative to the major currencies such as the Euro and the yen, it is an indication the U.S. economy is stable and conducive to higher stock prices. However, a weak dollar, which is usually accompanied by rising inflation and overheating economic conditions, reflects an economic environment not favorable to stocks. When the dollar is weak against a currency, it means that it takes an increasing number of dollars to buy a unit of a foreign currency. Another way of expressing the same idea is to say that it will take fewer units of a foreign currency to buy 1 dollar. For instance, if the yen moves from 120 to 110 yen to the dollar, it means that the dollar has weakened because it takes only 110 yen to buy 1 dollar. The only way to protect a U.S. dollar investor against a devaluation of the dollar is to invest in countries with stronger currencies, or to buy commodities and inflation hedges, such as hard assets.

The trend of the dollar is therefore an important indicator for establishing an investment program in stocks. For instance, if investors are worried about serious problems with the stock market and are forecasting a sharp decline but the dollar is very strong and rising to higher levels, the odds are that whatever weakness in stock prices investors are experiencing, it is probably temporary and the market will likely soon resume its upward momentum.

On the other hand, if there is bullish sentiment and people are expecting stocks to move higher but the dollar is weak against the major currencies, the odds are that the market will soon enter a period of consolidation and correction. During such times, investors may want to reduce their exposure to stocks.

9. Utilities

Utility stocks, because of their heavy investment in equipment and infrastructures, are very sensitive to directions in interest rates. If economic and monetary conditions point to a likely rise in interest rates, utility stocks anticipate these developments by declining ahead of the overall market. If, on the other hand, interest rates are likely to decline, utility stocks anticipate this trend by rising ahead of most stocks.

The trend of utility stocks provides an important indication of the risk of the market. If utilities are weaker than the overall market, the odds are that stocks are close to a high-risk point and caution should be exercised. If, however, utilities are strong and in a firm rising trend, the odds are that the market is on sound footing and an aggressive investment strategy is justified.

10. Trading Volume

Trading volume is a very important and reliable indicator of stock market trends. It provides information on the soundness of the market from an internal market perspective. Trading volume is important because the market rises when volume expands. Volume represents buying power, and stocks rise only if volume expands and rises to new highs.

When trading volume declines, it means there is less market participation and less buying power, and therefore, it is a sign the market is headed for a period of consolidation or correction. If volume declines and the market continues to rise, this is an indication that the market will soon reach a peak. The sharper the decline in volume, the sharper the decline in stock prices.

There is a point after a protracted decline in stocks when volume suddenly explodes. These selling climaxes, as they are usually called, actually identify buying opportunities, because this is the time when weak investors panic and sell and when strong, savvy investors buy. A major rise in volume is an opportunity to buy, because it is a signal that a support level for the market has been reached. The important point is that any new buying should be made when the market is in a period of expanding volume. Stocks should not be bought when volume declines, because lower trading volume suggests stocks are more likely to decline than rise.

11. Volatility

Market volatility provides an important measure to assess the psychology of market participants. An increase in market volatility suggests market participants don't feel comfortable with the financial markets, and therefore, they tend to trade very actively, creating higher volatility in the marketplace. On the other hand, low volatility suggests market participants feel comfortable with the economic environment and the financial market, and as a result the odds favor higher stock prices. Declining or low volatility is a sign of confidence in the appreciation of equities. On the other hand, a rise in volatility is an indication of higher risk in the marketplace.

The VIX index is published weekly in *Barron's* and is an index representing market volatility. The market has low volatility when this volatility index is between 15 and 22. On the other hand, as volatility rises to 40–45, the market risk becomes high.

The Technology Dimension

Since the mid-1980s, technology stocks have soared. The strong move is best represented by the 10-fold rise in the NASDAQ index from the mid-1980s through the end of 1999. The meteoric rise of the NASDAQ index, which is heavily weighted by technology stocks, confounded the experts, who continued to be skeptical of the lasting strength of this sector of the market. There are two ways of explaining the strong performance of technology stocks.

The first one is that technology stocks strengthened when inflation declined from 15 percent to about 3 percent. Corporations found that they could not raise prices in this environment, in order to improve margins, contrary to what happened in the 1970s. Declining and low inflation forced businesses to maintain stable prices. The alternative to raising prices to improve profitability was, therefore, to restructure, to cut costs, and to rely heavily on technology to improve the efficiency and profitability of the enterprise. This shift in technology requirement created a boom in computers, software, telecommunications, and electronics. Because of the strong demand from businesses, technology companies experienced consistent earnings and sales growth of 40 to 50 percent per year. This spectacular financial performance attracted investors, who caused technology stocks to rocket. The proponents of this theory suggest that the technology boom occurred because inflation declined, and the boom will continue as long as inflation remains below 3 percent. For instance, while the technology-biased NASDAQ index rose 10-fold from 1990 to 2000, the more diversified Dow Jones Industrial Average and S&P 500 index increased just four times.

In the 1970s the technology boom was nonexistent because companies found it much easier and much less expensive to raise prices to improve profitability, rather than make heavy and expensive commitments in technology investments.

A second view of the technology boom is based on the life cycle development of a new invention. In order to explain the strength of the technology and Internet stocks, it might be useful to compare their outlook with the development of any new invention. Let's take, for example, what happened to the railroad industry. After all, the steam engine and the railroad network could be closely related to the digital network.

At the beginning the railroad had serious problems because businesses and people found it difficult to accept the need to build complex infrastructures to support the railroad's growth. As a result, its acceptance was very limited. Although the steam engine was invented in 1826, the rapid growth phase of the railroad took place 80 years later. This was the time when consumers and businesses realized the advantage of moving large quantities of goods for long distances at a reasonable cost. The infrastructure was finally in place to make the invention of the steam engine a success. By that time the railroad penetrated new territories, the population close to the network, grew more rapidly, and commerce sprouted everywhere, swiftly blooming.

As it happened to other products and inventions, the rapid growth phase ended, and the railroad business reached its mature phase. This is the time when businesses grow at the same rate as the population, and competition from other businesses becomes intense. The same life cycle can be found in electricity and light bulbs, cars and tires, and many more products.

There is no doubt the digital network is in its infancy. The computer and the Internet really have just been invented, and there is still a large segment of the global population that does not even know what the system is all about. The Internet was introduced before the personal computer and in the beginning was used only by the military. The PC was only introduced in the 1980s with primitive software. Software is still primitive, considering the money that users still need to spend to constantly "maintain" their system.

The PC is still far from being easy to use, and there is no doubt the Internet is in a developmental phase, with most businesses not knowing exactly how to take advantage of it. It is not even clear what type of communication infrastructure will eventually prevail. Is it a system to make faster decisions? A system to deliver entertainment? News? Is it a system to manage a business in a different way? Is it an advertising medium? All of the above? What is it anyway?

The digital network has not yet reached the fast growth phase on a global basis; new communication standards have not yet been fully developed. An investor can be sure that even this innovation soon will reach its fast growth phase. This will be the time when new markets and new products we cannot even envision will be in place to support the Internet's fast growth phase of its life cycle.

With this type of scenario in mind, it is difficult to speak about overvaluation of technology stocks, because we have not even entered the fast growth phase. This phase should last about 20 years, which is the typical fast growth period of major innovations.

Between the current state of development and the time when the Internet finally will be an accepted product, growth will be phenomenal. How do you take advantage of this scenario? Which companies will be the winners? No one knows who will be the dominant players. Maybe the dominant players are not born yet. Even Microsoft, a major software innovator, seems to have already reached the mature phase of its life cycle. Will General Motors reinvent itself and become the new leader in this new age?

What should an investor do? The best approach is to keep a very diversified portfolio of technology stocks. Since this is unrealistic for the average investor, the solution that makes sense is to buy a wide variety of the best-performing technology mutual funds. Let the managers of these portfolios figure out who the ultimate winners will be in the Internet landscape.

How much money should you invest? It is always a good idea to start a new investment program with a small amount of money and then slowly increase your investment. Technology stocks, according to these views, are simply not going to go up in a straight line, but they will continue to outperform the broad market.

Investment Implications

The importance of identifying the degree of market risk is that it guides investors to minimize losses and reduce volatility of returns. In order to assess risk, it is crucial to recognize the stage of the business cycle and the financial markets in general.

We have seen that rising growth in the money supply represents an expansion in credit demand accompanied by a strong stock market (look back at Figure 10-2), which leads to stronger economic activity. Stronger economic activity is confirmed by rising commodity prices and eventually by rising short-term and long-term interest rates. The rise in commodity prices and in short-term and long-term interest rates is an indication that risk is increasing rapidly and stock prices are becoming likely to decrease.

A decline in stock prices is accompanied by declining growth in the money supply, an indication that the economy will weaken because of lack of credit demand and therefore lack of investments. The economy will continue to slow down until commodity prices decline and short-term and long-term interest rates decline. A decline in short-term interest rates and bond yields is an indication that the economy has weakened significantly, that credit demand will soon expand due to lower interest rates, that the money supply will grow faster, and that stocks are headed higher. A new financial cycle is under way again.

In investing, there is no easy formula, but recognizing the current stage of the business and financial cycle is a crucial first step in minimizing risk and in managing your portfolio.

One way to look at this issue is to ask the question, is now the time to be 100 percent in stocks? From what we have discussed in this book so far, an investor should be 100 percent in stocks when:

- The economy is weakening.

- The money supply is growing more rapidly.

- Short-term interest rates are declining or are stable.

- Commodity prices are declining or are stable.

- Inflation and bond yields are declining or are stable.

- The relationship between bond yields and the price-earnings ratio shows the price-earnings ratio is much closer to the undervalued level than the overvalued level.

- The yield curve is steepening.

- The dollar is strong.

- Utilities are rising.

- Trading volume is expanding.

- Volatility is declining or low.

On the other hand the investor should have a very low exposure to stocks when:

- The economy is strong.

- The money supply is slowing down.

- Short-term interest rates have been heading higher for two or three months.

- Commodity prices have been heading higher.

- Inflation is rising due to higher unit labor costs, higher commodity prices, and higher oil prices.

- Bond yields are rising.

- The PE ratio is much closer to the overvalued level than the undervalued level using the relationship between bond yields and the PE ratio.

- The yield curve is flattening.

- The dollar is weak.

- Utilities are weak.

- Trading volume is declining and low.

- Volatility is high or rising.

These are the two extremes between low risk and high risk. As the indicators show that risk is increasing, investors should decrease their exposure to stocks and adopt a more defensive strategy by investing more of their capital in money-market instruments. The amount invested depends on the level of acceptable risk, the investor's tax situation, and his or her age; and it could range from 100 percent to 50 percent or less. As the indicators show that risk is decreasing, investors should increase their exposure to equities remembering that the portfolio management issue is not an issue of buying or selling, but rather an issue of gradually changing the profile of the portfolio to the changing risk of the investment environment.

Chapter
11

TECHNICAL ANALYSIS OF STOCK MARKET TRENDS

The approach followed in this book is to consider the stock market as an integral part of the economic and financial system. As economic growth changes from very slow to rapid and then slow again, many forces are released by businesses and consumers. These forces act on the financial markets and also on the stock market. We have also seen that declines in financial measures, like declines in the growth in the money supply or stock market, have a negative impact on business activity. The view, therefore, has been that one cannot look at the stock market in isolation, because it is part of a system. The stock market impacts the system, and on the other hand, the system impacts the stock market. The framework provided in this book helps you analyze this interrelationship.

The approach followed by those investors who use technical analysis of stock market trends is completely different. Technical analysis begins with a very crucial assumption, which is that all the information about the market is embedded in the market itself. It may seem like a narrow way of looking at the action of stock prices; however, technical analysis provides some very useful tools for investors. There is no single answer to the dilemma of when to increase investments in stocks or when to decrease investments in the markets. Technical analysis provides further information, and the serious investor cannot disregard this important analytical arena.

In the following sections the most important and commonly used technical indicators are reviewed together with their use and pitfalls. There is no system that provides the final answer to success. As in any endeavor, investing requires a lot of information, work, analysis, and understanding of what is happening in the marketplace and in the economy. It requires focus, and above all, concentration. The information in this chapter will provide some tools to further increase your inventory of techniques, so that you can more precisely measure the amount of risk in the marketplace.

The major objective of technical analysis is to provide information about the market using internal market data. The idea is that the action of the market itself is powerful enough to provide a sense for timing an investment decision. The analysis of the internal data of the market can be done by using many indicators. In the following sections they will be introduced, explained, and defined.

What Do We Mean by "the Market"?

When reporters talk about what the market did at the end of the day, they always report three leading market indexes: the Dow Jones Industrial Average, the Standard and Poor's 500 index, and the NASDAQ composite index. The Dow Jones Industrial Average was created more than 100 years ago when it was difficult to make complex computations of stock prices. For this reason, it consists of only 30 blue-chip stocks that represent the best companies of American big business. People refer to the Dow Jones Industrial Average as the market. Initially it was concentrated in industrial stocks. However, with time, and as technology companies grew very rapidly, the Dow average has gradually lost its "smokestack" bias. Because it was created before computers were invented, the Dow index is computed very simply. Originally, Charles Dow created this index by adding the prices of 30 stocks and dividing the result by 30. Over the years, the divisor, which originally was 30, became smaller because of stock splits and the changing components in the average. However, the Dow Jones Industrial Average is still computed the same way it was more than 100 years ago. Because of the way it is computed, the index is a price-weighted average. As a result, the largest companies have the largest influence on the index. General Electric is one of the most influential stocks in the Dow, and therefore, changes in General Electric stock have a large impact on the size of the change in the Dow Jones Industrial Average.

Another popular index is the S&P 500, and it's computed by weighting the market capitalization of the stocks used in the index. As a result, companies with large market values, such as General Electric, Cisco, and Microsoft, have the biggest influence. The S&P 500 contains 500 stocks chosen by Standard and Poor, which is a unit of the McGraw-Hill Companies. The stocks included in this index are the leading companies in all U.S. industries. The S&P 500 has a heavy representation of large international, steady-growth companies. Because of the features of the S&P 500, it tends to mirror the action of the stocks of large companies.

The NASDAQ composite index contains close to 5,000 stocks. All these stocks are traded on the NASDAQ stock market. This index is dominated by computer, telecommunication, and biotechnology companies, which represent close to 75 percent of the market value of the index. The NASDAQ, like the S&P 500, is also weighted by the capitalization of the stocks included in its index and contains big technology stocks, such as Cisco, Microsoft, and Intel, that have a huge influence on its movement.

There are other more specialized indexes that measure sectors of the market. You can find these subindexes on any financial page of a daily newspaper. Although these three indexes do not represent "the market," they are a good proxy of what is happening in the marketplace. The purpose of technical analysis is to understand their action and have a sense of the likely direction of the market. In order to do so, other information is necessary.

At the end of each day, several statistics are made available to investors about the action that took place on the New York Stock Exchange and on the NASDAQ. The first item is the number of stocks that have advanced during the day, the number of stocks that have declined, and the number of stocks that were unchanged (meaning there was no price change from the closing of the previous day to the closing of the following day). Other important data are the trading volume of advancing stocks, the trading volume of declining stocks, and the total trading volume that took place on a particular stock exchange.

In the following sections some of the most important technical indicators will be discussed. For the sake of simplicity, the Standard and Poor's index will be used to show how these measures can be used to derive more information about the action of the market, and also to show whether the market is at a high or low risk level.

Moving Averages

When one looks at the price action of the market, it is very difficult to establish its trend because of the jagged pattern of the price during a week or month. One of the most often used techniques to smooth the price action of stocks is moving averages. A moving average is a way of averaging the price, and as an outcome the smooth line that is derived provides information on the direction of the market. There are two types of moving averages. A *simple moving average* obtained over a period of, say, 20 days is calculated by adding the market value of 20 days and dividing the outcome by 20. The following week the new week is added and the first week is dropped from the average. The total obtained is once again divided by 20. The formula to compute a moving average over a period of n days is the following.

Simple moving average = $(P1+P2+ \ldots + Pn)/n$

where P equals the price.

If $n=10$, then on the 10th day, the price of the previous 10 days is added, and the outcome is divided by 10. On the 11th day, the sum of the price of the previous 10 days is added, and the outcome is divided by 10. The computation is repeated each day or week, if a 10-week moving average is computed.

The problem with a simple moving average is that it sometimes can be erratic. The reason it can be erratic is that it responds twice to each piece of information: once when the new information is added and again when it's dropped off. The problem is that when a high price is dropped, the moving average is likely to tick down. On the other hand, when a low price is dropped, the moving average is likely to move up, even if the price went up that day, but by an amount smaller than the value that was dropped. The solution to this unreliability is to use a second type of moving average, which is called an *exponential moving average.*

An exponential moving average gives more weight to the latest data and responds faster to changes than a simple moving average. At the same time, the exponential moving average does not jump in response to all data being dropped off. The reason it does not respond erratically is because of the way it is computed. It gives more weight to the most recent data and less weight to the old data. The formula to compute an exponential moving average (EMA) is the following.

EMA=price today* K+EMA yesterday* $(1-K)$

where K equals $2/(N+1)$ and N is the period of the EMA.

Just like the formula for the simple moving average, the formula for the exponential moving average is a continuous formula, which means that each day the latest price is factored in and old data are taken out of the average. On the other hand, because of the way the exponential moving average is computed, the older data have less importance.

Moving averages tend to lag the action of the market. This is the price that investors have to pay because of the smoothing effect of the moving average. The use of moving averages is twofold. The first important use is to provide a visual aid for determining the trend of the market.

The second important use of a moving average comes into play when the actual value of the market falls below the value of the moving average. This is an important signal that should not be taken lightly—especially if the moving average is close to 40 weeks. In fact, a rule of thumb is that the longer the periods used for the moving average, the more important the signal when the market either falls below or rises above the moving average. For instance, if we use a 40-week moving average and the market falls below it, the signal should be taken as a serious warning that the trend in the market is changing in a significant way. On the other hand, the violation of the downside or the upside of a 10-day moving average is not as important as a violation of a 40-week moving average.

The risk with these kinds of timing techniques is that investors could be whipsawed. This occurs when, for instance, the market falls below the moving average, thus giving a sell signal. Then it suddenly reverses itself and, after a few days or a few weeks, moves above the moving average again, providing a buy signal. As you know by now, there are no simple or totally reliable rules in the investment arena. Each signal may or may not be important. It has to be put in context with all the rest of the information the investor is following.

Several websites on the Internet provide stock market charts and stock charts with moving averages where the user can choose the moving average span. The most frequently used moving average is over 40 or 50 weeks, and when using daily charts, the 10- or 25-day moving averages are also widely used.

Moving Averages Crossovers

When one computes a 20-week moving average and then computes a 40-week moving average, the 20-week moving average moves more rapidly with the market than the 40-week moving average. The use of a fast and a slow moving average can provide further information on the action of the market. The investor can obtain an oscillator, which is an indicator that moves around zero, by taking the difference of the two moving averages. This indicator provides a buy signal when the oscillator rises above zero and a sell signal when it falls below zero. This methodology has been called a moving average convergence-divergence (MACD) indicator. The difference between the two moving averages can be smoothed further by using a moving average.

The indicator obtained using the moving average crossover technique is called the MACD oscillator. A different way to compute the oscillator is by using two exponential moving averages: one short term and one long term. The MACD indicators are available free from almost all charting services, such as ClearStation.com and BigCharts.com.

Momentum Indicators Using Moving Averages

By taking the ratio of the price of a stock or of a stock market index and its moving average, one obtains an oscillator that moves around the value of 1 (Figure 11-1). This indicator has important characteristics, because after examining a period of several months, it can be seen that this ratio oscillates between two extreme values: an upper value and a lower value. This indicator reflects the momentum of the market or a stock. When it moves close to the upper value, the market momentum is very strong and the market is rising very rapidly. On the other hand, when the momentum indicator falls close to the lower range, then the market is very weak and the momentum is negative.

When the momentum is very strong and the indicator is close to the upper range, then the odds are that the market has passed its largest rise and will start rising more slowly or will decline. Momentum can remain strong, of course, and the oscillator can remain at the upper range for a long time. However, it is a signal that the market rise has been very sharp

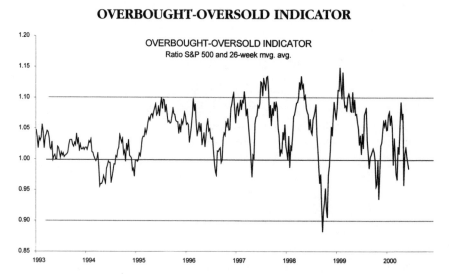

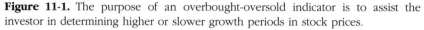

Figure 11-1. The purpose of an overbought-oversold indicator is to assist the investor in determining higher or slower growth periods in stock prices.

and the odds that the market is likely to grow more slowly or decline have increased. The decline of the momentum indicator from high levels represents a strong signal that the market may be entering a correction phase.

The same can be said when the momentum indicator falls to the lower range. This is a sign the market has declined substantially, and for investors what is important is that a decline to very low levels in the momentum indicator suggests that the market may be close to a turning point. Of course, in major bear markets, caution should be used because the market could stay oversold for a long time.

Another momentum indicator can be obtained using two moving averages: a fast moving average and a slow moving average. The ratio between the fast moving average and the slow moving average is a momentum indicator that is much smoother than the previous one and can be used in the same way.

Market Breadth Indicators

Market breadth provides information on the overall strength of the market. Especially at major market peaks, the situation arises when the widely known stock market indexes, like the Dow Jones Industrial Average or the S&P 500, rise to new highs when most of the stocks decline. The reason is that the market rises because of the action of just a few stocks, but the majority are already in their own bear market. In order to measure this case of divergence that provides important clues about the strength and the health of the market itself, market breadth indicators are very useful.

Market breadth indicators are computed using the number of issues that advance and the number of issues that decline during the day or during the week. The data can be easily found on the financial page of any newspaper.

One of the most popular breadth indicators is the advance-decline line. The advance-decline line is calculated by subtracting the number of stocks that decline in price each week from the number that advance. This difference is then accumulated. When more stocks are advancing than declining, the advance-decline line rises.

On the other hand, when the majority of issues fall in price, the advance-decline line heads down. This line peaks ahead of the market, because as the market gets closer and closer to the top, it also becomes more selective. This means investors tend to focus only on the most widely known and liquid issues and ignore the rest of the list. The advance-decline line is not as crucial at market bottoms, because it usually turns up when the overall market bottoms. The advance-decline line is an important indicator, especially at market tops.

Another way of measuring market breadth, and at the same time computing a momentum indicator, is by taking the ratio between advancing and declining issues. If the market is very strong and there are more advances than declines, the ratio increases rapidly and reaches an upper range.

If, on the other hand, the market declines and there are more declining stocks than advancing stocks, the indicator declines and falls to a lower range. This ratio could be volatile, so a 13-week moving average may be appropriate to smooth out its volatility. When this measure rises too fast and goes to an upper range, clearly the market went up very rapidly and it needs to rest. This is a time to expect slower growth in stock prices and possibly a decline.

On the other hand, when this momentum indicator falls to the lower range, and there are considerably more declining than advancing issues, momentum is negative, and its extreme position suggests that the odds favor a market bottom in the near future. Caution again should be exercised, because the advance-decline ratio, as all the other momentum indicators, could stay in overbought territory (close to the upper range) or in oversold territory (close to the lower range) for a protracted period of time during the strong market moves on the upside or the downside.

Other important momentum indicators are obtained using the data released by Investors Intelligence. This organization makes available by subscription the data concerning the percentage of stocks on the New York Stock Exchange above their 30-week moving average and the percentage of stocks above their 10-week moving averages. These two indicators are important, because when there are many stocks above their 30- and 10-week moving averages, the market is strong and is rising. The upper limits of these indicators are around 65 to 70 percent. This is usually a time when the market has been through a very strong rally for several months, with most of the stocks participating. It indicates that the move is probably close to entering a mature phase characterized by slower growth in stock prices.

On the other hand, when these gauges fall below 30 percent, that is, there are 30 percent or less stocks above their 30- and 10-week moving averages, it signifies that the market has been declining quite sharply and very few stocks are in a rising trend. This signals that the market is very oversold, and any rise in these indicators signals that the market is likely to have reached an important and significant bottom.

Rate of Change as Momentum Indicators

One of the most important tenets of technical analysis is that all the information about what is happening in the market is in the market itself. One way of determining what the market is saying is to compute the rate of change of market indexes. The most common rate of change is that over 13 weeks. This is a rolling percentage change of, for instance, the S&P 500 over a 13-week period. When the change in the market rises to an upper range, investors take profits and the rate of change declines. The same holds true when the market declines and the rate of change falls so low that new buyers come in and the rate of change rises.

The rate of change over 13 weeks oscillates between –10 percent and + 10 percent. In other words, when the market declines 10 percent over a 13-week period, then the market is deeply oversold and the odds favor new buyers coming in. On the other hand, when the market rises sharply over a 13-week period and stocks rise above 10 percent, sellers come in to take profits, suggesting the market is overbought.

The same computation can be used on other indexes, such as the NASDAQ. By computing the rate of change over 13 weeks in the NAS-DAQ index, one recognizes that this index has been more volatile than the S&P 500, and the rate of change is anywhere between 25 percent and –25 percent. These are extreme levels. When the NASDAQ appreciates 25 percent over a 13-week period, the odds favor strong selling pressures. On the other hand, when the market falls 25 percent over a 13-week period, then one can expect buyers to come in because the market is very oversold. These ranges are subjective and depend on the investment horizon of a particular investor. For this reason, all these indicators have to be analyzed very carefully to determine the personal requirements and confidence in using them.

Chart Patterns

The analysis of a graph showing the action of an index or the price of a stock provides very useful information about its profit potential. The first step in looking at a chart is to determine what the trend is. Is the stock or the index in a rising trend, is it in a declining trend, or is it consolidating? The pattern of a stock in a rising trend is that the following high is always above the previous high and the following low is always above the previous low. Usually the following low is somewhere close to 50 percent of the distance between the previous bottom and the previous high.

A declining trend is characterized by the following low below the previous low and the following high below the previous high of a stock. A stock in a phase of consolidation is a stock that trades within a range, so the bottoms and the tops are always within a well-determined range. (This pattern, as we will discuss later, has great profit potential. But we need to know how to use volume to take full advantage of these patterns.)

In a stock that is consolidating, the higher range is called the *resistance level* and the lower range is considered as *support*. The reason is that as the stock rises and reaches the higher range, sellers come in because they believe the stock or the market is overpriced at that level and they sell. In this case the market or the stock has reached a resistance level. On the other hand, when the stock falls to the lower range, buyers come in because they are convinced that at that level the stock offers value. In this case the market or the stock has reached a support level. This duel between buyers and sellers is what creates a trading range for a particular stock.

It is always useful to draw two lines, one touching the upper range of the stock price and one touching the lower range. By doing so, the investor can better visualize the channel that identifies the trend of the stock. The channel of a rising stock is upward-sloped, while the channel of a declining stock is downward-sloped. When the price of the stock touches the upper or lower channel line, it is an indication that the stock has reached an overbought or oversold level. When the price of the stock in a rising trend falls below the lower channel line, it is a possible indication that the trend has changed and a new channel should be drawn. On the other hand, if the stock is on a downtrend and at some point it moves above the upper channel line, then the possibility should be investigated that the trend of the stock has changed from down to up.

An important pattern that develops when the stock changes trends is called double top or double bottom. Let's tlook at an example of a double bottom. This occurs when a stock is in a downtrend; the channel slopes downward, and the stock reaches a new low. Suddenly the stock has strong rebound, often piercing and moving above the upper channel line. Has the trend changed? In order to draw this conclusion, one has to expect the next correction. If the next bottom doesn't fall below the previous bottom, then the odds are that the stock has reached a temporary bottom and is retesting the previous low.

A double top occurs after a strong rise in the stock. The top is reached, followed by a sharp decline. Then buyers come in and the price of the stock rises sharply, but it doesn't move above the previous high. The pattern formation is a double top. The odds are that the stock is in the process of changing trend from the upside into the downside.

In order to make a final decision about the possible change in the trend of the stock, however, we need to talk about volume, which is the subject of the next section.

Trading Volume

The level and the trend of trading volume on the New York Stock Exchange or the NASDAQ constitute one of the most important and sometimes overlooked and misunderstood indicators to assess stock market trends. When investors and analysts talk about trading volume, they refer to all the shares traded during the day or week on one of the major stock exchanges. Trading volume represents the amount of shares bought and sold for any stock.

In order to gain an appreciation of the meaning and importance of trading volume, one has to think of trading volume as buying power. With this interpretation, rising trading volume reflects increased buying from investors. It means that investors see opportunities and are increasing their buying activities of stocks. On the other hand, declining trading volume suggests that buying power is drying up. Investors do not feel as aggressive as before. Therefore, they are scaling down their buying activity.

The reason trading volume is important as a technical indicator is because it provides very useful information to investors. Volume leads the stock market by several weeks (when weekly volume is used) or several days (when daily volume is used). Weekly trading volume needs to be smoothed using a 13-week or 17-week moving average. The graphs showing the smoothed weekly trading volume and the S&P 500 illustrate quite clearly the important property of trading volume, which is to lead the stock market at important turning points. A decline in trading volume precedes a decline in the stock market, and an increase in trading volume anticipates a bottom in stock prices.

If, during a major market decline, volume remains low and stays below previous highs, it is realistic to expect that the market will continue to decline because there is no buying power coming into the market. A bottom can be anticipated when volume starts increasing as the market declines. It is true that people refer to these types of patterns as selling climaxes, but another way to look at these patterns is as buying climaxes. In other words, stocks during the final phase of the market decline are transferred from weak hands to strong hands—that is, to the savvy investors who have the courage and the foresight to increase their purchasing of stocks, as they recognize that stocks have declined enough and are attractive again.

As the market rises and volume begins shrinking, investors have to be concerned because buying power is decreasing. So the market cannot go much farther ahead. So, declining trading volume should be a warning for investors that the market is set for a period of consolidation. On the other hand, sharply increasing trading volume, especially after a protracted market decline of 10 to 15 percent, is a strong indication that an important bottom is at hand.

Volume is a very useful indicator in conjunction with the consolidation pattern of a stock—that is, when the stock trades between a support and a resistance level. If a stock consolidates by trading in a range, let's say for the sake of argument between 30 and 45 dollars, looking at volume provides important investment guidelines. If volume increases as the stock trades in that range, this action suggests there is accumulation of the stock, and this should be an indication that the stock may soon be poised for a rise.

This is particularly so if volume increases every time the stock hits the low end of the range (the 30 dollars we have chosen for an example), and then decreases as the stock reaches close to the (45 dollar) upper range level (Figure 11-2). A very profitable pattern happens when, after trading for, say, three to four months in the 30–45 dollar range, volume slowly picks up and the stock breaks above the upper level of 45 dollars with soaring volume. This is a major bullish signal for the stock. It is not unusual, however, that after this break the stock declines again and retests the 45 dollar level.

PRICE-VOLUME PATTERN

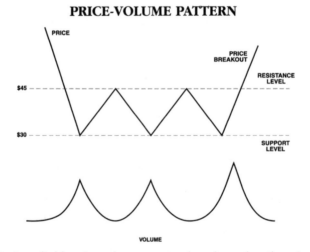

Figure 11-2. A profitable price-volume pattern takes place when the price of a stock declines sharply and volume increases well above average. Note the breakout of the trading range accompanied by very strong volume.

If volume increases and remains very strong, that is a significant signal that the stock will eventually break out of its range because there have been so many shares accumulated and just a small demand will push the stock much higher. On the other hand, if volume remains subdued and then the stock trades below the lower end of the range, that is, $30, this is a bearish signal because there has been a breakout on the downside of an important support level accompanied by very slow volume

Sentiment Indicators

Several organizations measure the level of bullishness of professional and nonprofessional investors. They poll market participants and writers of investment advisories and establish how many of these advisories are bullish, bearish, or neutral. The percentage of bullish investors provides some important clues about the position of the market. When the percentage of bullish investors is very high, it means the market is very strong and the outcome is that investors believe the market cannot go anywhere but up. Clearly, at that point, the majority of investors is fully invested, and therefore, the risk is that there is no new money coming into the market. At these times, the odds favor the market to consolidate or decline.

When the percentage of bullish investors is very low, the majority of investors have sold their stocks and there are no more stocks to be sold. It is clear, then, that this extreme represents a buying opportunity because there are no more sellers. In this case buyers need to bid up the price of stocks to induce investors to sell their share.

The most important sentiment indicators can be found every week in *Barron's*, like most of the other data that have been discussed in this chapter. Sentiment indicators represent what are called *contrary opinion indicators*. In other words, when everybody thinks the same thing, the odds are that the opposite is going to take place. When investors are extremely bullish, then one should expect exactly the opposite—that is, the market will go down. When, on the other hand, investors are extremely bearish, one should expect the market to bottom and rise.

The American Association of Individual Investors releases weekly the percentage of bullish sentiment of it's members. The record shows that when this percentage rises above 50 to 55 percent, the odds are that the market is very close to a period of consolidation or decline. On the other hand, when this percentage decreases to 25 to 30 percent, the odds favor that the market is close to a bottom, especially when this measure begins to rise.

Another important sentiment indicator is released by Investor Intelligence, and it shows the percentage of all the investment advisories that are bullish, bearish, or neutral. The bullish percentage signals that the market is close to a top when the bullish percentage is above 55 percent. Bullishness above this level is usually associated with a very erratic market. On the other hand, a bullish percentage close to 30 to 40 percent is a signal that the market is oversold and a bottom is close.

Another way of measuring sentiment is by taking the Investors Intelligence bullish and bearish percentages and computing the ratio of bulls and bears. The resulting sentiment indicator shows that investors should exercise caution when there are twice as many bulls as bears. On the other hand, when the bullish percentage is roughly the same as that for bears, giving a ratio of close to 1, then the market is usually close to a significant bottom (Figure 11-3).

Another service that provides bullish percentages is the Consensus of Kansas City; it provides the bullish percentage of professional investors. The market becomes overbought when the bullish percentage in this indicator goes above 70 to 75 percent. On the other hand, a major bottom is close when the bullish percentage falls below 40 percent. Sentiment indicators are one of the many tools that investors should follow. They are important because they provide a view of what other investors are thinking, and usually it pays in the investment field not to go with the crowd or have a herd mentality. Therefore, knowing what

INVESTORS' SENTIMENT

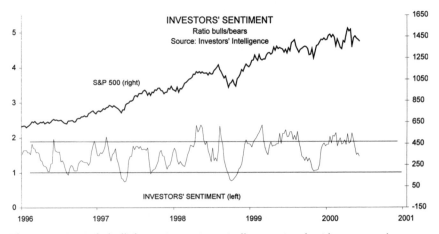

Figure 11-3. High bullish sentiment is typically associated with poor market performance, while low bullish sentiment precedes strong market performance.

most people are thinking and then going against them is usually a profitable strategy.

Moving Averages Envelopes and Bollinger Bands

A way of visualizing the trend is not only by drawing channels using straight lines, but also by using moving averages. For instance, the 40-week moving average of the S&P 500 is computed and overlaid on the values of the S&P 500 itself. Let's call this moving average "M." Then another line is computed by adding 10 percent of the value of the previous moving average. Let's call this moving average "U." The outcome is a line that is parallel to and above the previous moving average. Another line is computed by subtracting 10 percent from the centerline moving average. Let's call this moving average "L." By doing so, an envelope is created, with a moving average going through roughly the middle of the market average (moving average "M"), and the two other moving averages which roughly envelope the value of the S&P 500. The moving average "U" is the upper line of the envelope and the moving average "L" is the lower line of the envelope.

The use of this envelope is the same as that used with channels identified by trend lines. When the market goes very close to the upper moving average, the market becomes overbought. Of course, this is no guarantee that the market will decline, because a strong market can follow the upper range of the envelope very closely for a long period of time. The same can be said when the market falls close to the lower moving average. The market becomes oversold, and a turning point may be likely. Although, even in this case, when momentum on the downside is pronounced, the market could decline substantially and remain close to the lower moving average.

A variation of this concept is what is called the *Bollinger bands*, which were created by John Bollinger. Bollinger bands are plotted at standard deviation levels above and below a moving average. Since standard deviation is a measure of volatility, the bands are self-adjusting. They widen when the market is very volatile, and they contract during a calmer period. The basic interpretation of the Bollinger bands is that prices tend to stay within the upper and lower band. The distinctive characteristic of Bollinger bands is that the spacing between the bands varies based on the volatility of the prices. Bollinger bands are not easy to compute, but most services and websites showing stock market charts provide the charting capabilities to produce the bands.

Seasonality

Considerable effort has been spent to determine if stock prices have seasonal tendencies. Do they rise during specific days? Do they rise more during specific months or periods? One of the most important seasonal indicators is the so-called January barometer—as January goes, so goes the rest of the year. The main idea is that January is the first month of the year, and if investors feel bullish in January, they're likely to feel bullish throughout the year because they see positive developments that will benefit stock market trends.

A lot of research on the January barometer has been done, but the research reported is flawed. Most statistics reported include January in the performance of the year. It makes, however, no sense to include market returns for that month if that month is used to forecast the rest of the year. For instance, say the market rose 4 percent in January and rose 5 percent over the rest of the year, then it's not correct to say that the market rose 4 percent in January plus 1 percent for the rest of the year—that is, 5 percent. Actually, the 4 percent in January should be excluded from the total return, and therefore, the market rose only 1 percent for the rest of the year. So, really, January was not a forecaster of the trend of the rest of the year. In spite of this misunderstanding, the forecasting capabilities of January have entered the folklore of Wall Street.

Other research has been done on seasonality. Research has shown that the last four days of a month and the first five days of the following month are the most profitable periods, and investing in only those eight to nine days, depending on holidays and weekends, provides well-above-average performance. Although it's difficult to use this rule as an investment tool, it might suggest that if one wants to sell, a good selling time is always the first week of the month. If one wants to buy, buying toward the end of the month probably provides a more profitable entry point.

Another pronounced seasonality trend in the stock market is the one that shows strong stock market performance between the end of October and the end of May. On the other hand, the market performs poorly between June and the end of October. This provides a fairly reliable investment guideline, suggesting that investors should be fully invested between the months of November and May and should raise cash and sell their weak positions in the months of June through September.

Dow Theory

The Dow theory was developed by Charles H. Dow around the turn of the last century and was later refined by William Hamilton and Robert Rhea. A modified version of the theory is based on the analysis of three indicators: the Dow Jones Industrial Average, the Dow Jones Transportation Average, and the Dow Jones Utilities Average. In order to gain an appreciation of the value of the theory, we need to understand the meaning of these three averages.

The Dow Jones Industrial Average is computed using the stocks of the largest and most dominant companies in the United States. These companies are the major producers of goods and services in the country. The Dow Jones Transportation Average represents the stocks of the largest transportation companies—companies that have the purpose of moving people and goods throughout the country. The Dow Jones Utility Average has the property of being very closely related to interest rates, because the utility companies have large long-term debts, and interest expenses represent one of the predominant cost items in their financial statements. As such, utility stocks perform well when interest rates decline because the profitability of utility companies increases. On the other hand, when interest rates rise, utility stocks tend to perform poorly, and therefore, the profitability of these companies is hurt.

The Dow Jones Industrial Average and the transportation index are closely related. When the Dow Jones Industrial Average rises, it reflects a strong economy and strong sales and profits for the major industrial companies. A strong market is also accompanied by a strong transportation index, reflecting the fact that a large number of people and goods are being moved through the country due to strong business conditions. In a way, the transportation index confirms the action of the Dow Jones Industrial Average.

The third indicator, the Dow Jones Utilities Average, is used to determine if the economic environment is sound. A sound economic environment is one in which interest rates are stable or declining, and so you should expect the utility average to be quite strong. As a result, the ideal positive market climate is when the Dow reaches new highs, accompanied by new highs in the Dow Jones Transportation Average and also by new highs in the utility average. This configuration reflects the fact that the economy is strong, business is strong, and goods and services have moved through the pipelines in a climate of stable inflation and interest rates, as reflected by the positive trend in the utility average.

A sign that the market may be close to a period of consolidation and a possible change in trend comes when the Dow Jones Industrial Average moves to new highs, but the Dow Jones Transportation and/or the Utility Average is not confirming the new highs in the Dow Jones Industrial Average. This is a signal that there is something wrong in the system. Somehow, transportation companies are not moving the same amount of goods and services, or another possibility is that the cost of transportation may be rising more rapidly.

Certainly, rising cost is the case when there is a sharp increase in oil prices. The fact that utilities do not confirm the action of the Dow Jones Industrial Average is associated with higher inflation and rising interest rates. The main usefulness of the Dow theory from an investor's viewpoint is that the three averages have to be in gear. A new high in the Dow Jones Industrial Average has to be confirmed by a new high in the Dow Jones Transportation and Utility Averages. Investors should exercise caution when a strong move on the upside of the Dow Jones Industrial Average is not accompanied by a similar action of the transportation and utility averages. The market is getting narrower, there is less participation on the upside, and there are also problems on the interest rates and inflation fronts. Therefore, investors, in the case of nonconfirmation of the three averages, should use caution.

Investment Implications

The use of technical analysis of stock market trends has considerable value because it provides guidelines for determining what is the level of risk in the market, how much the market is overbought or oversold, and what is the majority view about its outlook. This information is crucial because it helps to refine the judgment that you have about the market, using business and financial cycles as discussed in this book. One word of caution concerns the level of overbought, oversold, or sentiment indicators. The market can keep rising and remain overbought for months. This is not necessarily an indication that you should sell.

The opposite is also true—the market can be oversold for protracted periods of time and keep declining; therefore, it is not providing conclusive information that this is the time to buy. However, if fundamental analysis of business and financial cycles says that the market risk is high or low, technical analysis tends to confirm that a buy point or a sell point is reached. The main idea is that the two fields complement each other and can be used quite profitably by the informed investor.

Chapter
12

MANAGING YOUR STOCK PORTFOLIO RISK

Managing your money successfully is a very difficult and time-consuming endeavor. If you're looking for a formula to get rich, you will be disappointed, because no matter how good the formula looks, eventually it will fail. Managing money successfully is a very disciplined process requiring a considerable portion of your time. The more time you devote to the process, the more successful you will be.

One of the main objectives of this book has been to provide you with a framework and process for making decisions, for developing strategies in order to manage risk. The process and methodology you will eventually adopt will fit your personality. No one can tell you what is best for you. You, and only you, will have to decide.

This chapter will deal with how to select a stock portfolio, what frame of mind you should have in the process of doing so, how to manage risk, when to buy and when to sell, and other issues every investor eventually has to face.

The success of any investment program depends on the information collected and the process used to review the information. A crucial aspect is the frequency with which the information is reviewed. Professionals who spend 24 hours a day managing money are likely to absorb data from the markets and the economy every minute; and every minute they are asking themselves what it means, what should be done about it, and what the impact is on the current portfolio. These are the people you are playing against—people with sophisticated models, approaches, and stock selection techniques. Their timing in reacting to markets is almost instantaneous.

Therefore, it's up to each person to determine when and how often to review his or her strategies. The closer a person looks at his or her portfolio and its performance, the more satisfactory the results. Making money requires a lot of work—there is no easy way out of this proposition.

Frame of Mind, Investment Style, and Risk Management

Most successful investors will argue that your frame of mind in approaching the management of your money is one of the most crucial aspects of the process of investing. Every effort should be made to look at the process of managing your portfolio as a professional because you are competing against professionals.

The first step is to look at the process of managing your portfolio in a detached way—as a professional would, with no emotions. When emotions take over, poor decisions are made. Emotions lead to sudden decisions because you are experiencing stress. But it's just when you're overly emotional that you need to exercise self control, because these are times when you are more likely to lose money. Losing money greatly penalizes the overall long-term performance of your portfolio. Always remember the equation: +15 percent +15 percent +15 percent -15 percent = 6 percent annual return. In other words, if your portfolio increased 15 percent per year for three consecutive years and you lost 15 percent the fourth year, then the total return for the four-year period would be slightly higher than 6 percent per year. One loss destroys the return of many successful years.

The only way to control emotions and to avoid rushed decisions is to act slowly and deliberately. This is the most important concept in managing your portfolio—act slowly and gradually. If one decides to sell or decides to buy, no matter how professional one is about the issue, emotion is always involved. For this reason, to minimize the error, it is important to buy or to sell small quantities and to develop a program to buy or a program to sell. *Gradually* and *slowly*—these are the key words.

Winning out over your emotions is the most difficult part of the process. You must be detached from them. One has to not think about what is happening, but look at your portfolio as running horses. If they run well, you are pleased. If they run poorly, what do you do? You discard the losing horses. You have to think about the elements of your portfolio as tools for building wealth, not as personal possessions. Sometimes people talk about the stocks they own or their advisers as though they had an emotional attachment to them. The decisions you make about money must be cold-blooded, detached, and emotionless. What matters is performance.

Some very famous traders think about concepts such as meditation and Zen, because the Oriental philosophies help them to reach a state of relaxation that is conducive to helping them assess the situation. One of the most dangerous aspects of an emotional state is that it may lead you *not* to act. But one of the important teachings of Zen is that when you are in a dilemma, you must act—you must make a decision. Take a small step. Do not wait until your losses become too great. Do something about them. The first step will lead you to the next step. But the significant point is that you must make a decision.

Always keep in mind the question, what is the objective? If you decide to invest in stocks and to build your stock portfolio, you have to have an objective. One objective is to outperform the stock market; otherwise one would buy an index fund or the Spider for the S&P 500 (symbol SPY) traded on the AMEX. This stock moves exactly like the S&P 500. In other words, when you buy this stock, you are going to perform exactly like the market. Therefore, if you decide to invest in stocks, you have to have the objective of outperforming the stock market.

The second objective, of course, has to be to minimize volatility. Buying the Spider (SPY) allows you to perform like the market. However, if the market declines 20 or 30 percent, you would suffer major capital losses. If you decide to actively manage your money, it is because you want to avoid a loss and seeing your capital shrink. These two objectives—outperforming the market and minimizing volatility—are the main reasons you are willing to undertake the management of your stock portfolio.

How large should your stock portfolio be? Successful investment portfolios are concentrated on a few stocks. Buying a stock everytime someone gives you a tip is not the proper—or the smart—way to do it. The best size of a portfolio is close to 10 stocks, 15 maximum. This allows you to follow them very closely. They are easy to control and monitor, and it's relatively easy to measure their performance.

If your portfolio becomes too diversified and you can't readily keep track of how much money you have and how your stocks are performing, your portfolio has become too big and unmanageable relative to the time you can devote to it. The issue is not how many stocks you have, but do you have the time to follow them?

One of the objectives of managing your portfolio is to manage risk—that is, manage volatility. The best way to approach this issue is not to think in terms of buying or selling. It is much better to think in terms of how much to buy of a stock or how much to sell.

Many times people have a good stock that has appreciated tremendously, and (again the emotions) they are uncertain whether they should sell it to lock in their profit. Remember the key terms *slowly* and *gradually*. Why not sell just a portion of it? For instance, if an investor owns 100 shares, why not sell 10 shares and see what happens? If the stock continues to rise, selling the 10 shares was a good idea because most of the money, 90 percent to be exact, is still invested in the stock. If, on the other hand, the stock begins to decline, this confirms the view of the investor that the stock was overvalued, thus giving him or her the chance to sell more of it. This approach allows you to keep your emotions under control and lets the market tell you what to do.

The same approach applies when a stock starts going up. Should you buy? You don't know for sure if the market or the stock is ready to go up. Why not then buy only a few shares rather than investing a lot of money in a single position. If the stock goes up as you expected, it was a good decision. You have the money to buy more shares. If, on the other hand, the decision was wrong and the stock goes down, you were exposed for only a few shares, and so your capital losses are not significant.

Making decisions slowly and buying or selling a position gradually provides you with a way of managing the risk and the volatility of the returns and at the same time controlling the emotional aspect involved in that decision. It is crucial to think not in terms of buying or selling, in or out, but rather in terms of increasing or decreasing a position and in terms of increasing or decreasing risk.

We've seen that investing is like playing poker. Poker players invest gradually, increasing their bets as the odds of making money increase, and fold when the hand they hold does not have a chance of winning. This is much like the process an investor goes through when buying or selling a position. As the odds of making money increase, so does the amount of money invested. On the other hand, when the odds of making money decrease, the investor should decrease the amount of money invested. It does not make any sense to invest a lot of money in a position when there is low probability of making money.

Sometimes reporters and analysts talk about investment styles and how they have an impact on returns. The fact is some investment styles work sometimes, and at other times, when conditions change, they do not work anymore. It's best not to endorse any particular investment style. Small caps, large caps, growth and income, buy and sell, relative strength, balanced portfolio, these are all investment styles that sooner or later become popular because they worked for specific and temporary conditions. But if those conditions change, the investment will not show the same performance as it did. Only business and financial cycles stay in style. They provide you with information about risk and what assets are more likely to offer the best returns. Investors must, therefore, be aware of changing trends and adapt to them.

There is no formula that will make you wealthy. What you do have to do is maintain flexibility in your approach to investing. If the approach you have been following isn't working, you have to have the courage to recognize that and make gradual changes toward what seems to be working. If the market, or a stock, moves against your expectations, you need to decide quickly what to do. You cannot afford to wait too long to make a decision. You have to act and then gradually correct what seems to have been an incorrect investment decision. If an approach you are using is not working, don't fall asleep and think that things eventually will work out, because they may not. Any period of poor performance should be interpreted as an opportunity lost, because your money could have worked in a much better way if you had invested it in a different asset or had followed a different approach.

Look at the performance of your portfolio. If some stocks, even those of great companies, are not performing, if the stocks do not rise or are underperforming the market, you should gradually sell them and slowly reduce your position in them. Then you should move that capital toward approaches that are working. Investing is a constant transition from assets that do not perform toward those that perform better. Although it's important to react quickly to a disappointing result, the transition has to be done slowly and gradually.

Stock Selection: What Portfolio Would You Like to Have?

If your objective is to outperform the market with a portfolio providing low volatility of returns, the answer to what portfolio you would like to have is simple: stocks that are rising; stocks that are in great demand, and more often than not are in the list of new highs; stocks that, when you look at their graphs and charts, you know you would like to own, whose volume is strong and whose price action is steady in its rising trend.

If you accept this approach to stock selection, then it is baffling to see people hold stocks that are reaching new lows that they are hoping will turn around and make some money. Clearly, there is no room in your portfolio for weak stocks or for stocks that are underperforming the market. Think like a professional. If a doctor recognizes that you have a physical problem, he does not hide the fact from you. He tells you what to do, because that is in your interest. If you have a poorly performing position, you must eliminate it or reduce it. There is no question about it. It is in your interest to do so.

There are two types of stocks to choose—stocks that are rising and stocks that are declining. This is not intended to sound funny, but sometimes people forget they have this choice. Choosing stocks that are declining, hoping that they will turn around and rise, is a great challenge for any investor, but it is really a low-probability way to make money.

Instead, of course, the best investors strive to invest in rising stocks. There are three types of rising stocks. There are stocks that rise slower than the market, stocks that rise with the market, and stocks that tend to outperform the market. Clearly, your main focus has to be on stocks that outperform the market and have the tendency to rise faster than the market. These are the best bets for your portfolio if your objective is to outperform the overall market.

You also have a choice of large-capitalization stocks and small-capitalization stocks. Large-capitalization stocks are issued by companies that are fairly large in size. Small-capitalization stocks are stocks of companies of smaller size. Smaller-cap stocks tend to appreciate the most, but they also have higher volatility, and for this reason they increase the risk of your portfolio. Larger-cap stocks have lower volatility, but they rise more slowly and offer less risk. Which one should you choose?

There is no formula. One has to follow a process that is flexible and allows for selecting the stocks that are best for the times. You find them by analyzing the strongest sectors of the markets over the past three or six months. Many websites on the Internet, for instance BigCharts.com, provide this analysis and also provide exhaustive reports on which sectors of the stock market are the strongest. You want to invest in stocks that most investors want. You want the stocks that belong to those groups that are considered most attractive by market participants. Therefore, you should start by selecting stocks from the strongest sectors. They are likely to continue to remain strong.

Within the strongest sectors, choose the stocks that have the strongest performance. Clearly, you want stocks from the new highs. This is a good starting point for selecting stocks. You also want stocks that are on the most active list. You want stocks where volume is increasing, because rising volume means that there is buying behind the price action of the stocks.

Once you have the names of the stocks, list them all. Choose those that have strong earnings and sales growth, that have a product that is unique, with exclusive characteristics in its industry, and with strong and innovative management. Then go through an analysis of their charts.

They have to have a definite rising trend, and of all those stocks that have a rising trend, choose the stocks that have the lowest volatility—that is, their rising trend is the smoothest. Those stocks are more likely to continue in their trend than the very volatile stocks. If you choose volatile stocks, it is very difficult to determine an entry point, because you could be at a temporary top and it could take some time to break even or make money.

When you accumulate stocks with lower volatility, you see the results in performance. The stocks you want to choose are stocks that have been rising faster than the market in the last three to twelve months. An important factor in deciding which stocks to accumulate is volume. If a stock is going up on strong volume and volume has been declining for a while, that stock is probably close to a peak and so you may want to wait.

If a stock goes through a period of trading in a range and volume rises sharply at the low point of the trading range, it means there is accumulation. If the stock breaks and rises above that trading range with strong volume, it is time to buy.

At the end of this process the kind of stocks that one ends up with in her portfolio are stocks of strong companies—companies with the highest innovation factors and, with the strongest management teams. They have product leadership, and this is reflected in double-digit earnings growth and double-digit sales growth. Of course, you have to pay for all these qualities, and the price you have to pay is a price-earnings ratio well above the PE ratio of the market. In this case the PE ratio represents the dollar paid per each dollar of earnings, obtained by dividing the price of the stock by the earnings per share of the company. You are paying because you are buying the best and most attractive companies in the country.

When to Start Selling

The performance of a portfolio and the management of risk depend not only on the buying strategy, but especially on the selling strategy. The first reason for selling stocks depends on the market risk, since 80 percent of the movement of a stock is dependent on the action of the overall market. When the odds of the market rising have declined significantly, economic conditions and the indicators we have reviewed above suggest risk is increasing, and so investors have to start selling. The only way to manage risk and minimize losses is to raise cash. There is no other substitute.

Another reason to start selling is poor stock performance. When a stock is performing worse than the market, the position should be reduced gradually and slowly, and the proceeds should be invested in a better alternative.

A third reason for selling stock is a 10 to 15 percent decline in the price of a stock. A decline of this magnitude is a warning that action on the upside for that stock is over for some time. Declines of this type mean market participants have decided to shift their attention to other sectors or other stocks within that sector, because that particular company is having problems not evident yet to the broad investing public. A decline of 10 or 15 percent implies that money tied up in that stock is likely to provide very little return for several months. Sharp and sudden declines are a sign to reduce the position in that stock.

It is important to look at volume before making a final selling decision. If the stock declines but volume increases well above average, it is a strong sign investors have decided that the stock has reached a very attractive level. In that case one should wait and see what happens to the stock. Usually the stock, after a few days or weeks of consolidation, will start going up again. However, if volume remains low and the stock declines with low volume, investors should start eliminating that position.

Because of the analysis and decision process involved in managing risk, it is easy to recognize the impracticality of owning too many positions. In fact, what is the reason to own two stocks if one is performing better than the other? This is an extreme situation, but it helps illustrate the point that it is important to concentrate your capital in the best-performing stocks only. And managing your portfolio should be directed toward that task.

Portfolio Management Strategies and Stock Market Cycles

Establishing and following an investment strategy provides the investor with the capability of keeping portfolio volatility within limits that are acceptable. These limits depend on the personality and psychological profile of the investor. The most important step in developing a successful strategy is to recognize in which phase the stock market is. Is the stock market at the beginning of a major bull market? Is the bull market in full swing? Or is it close to a top? We have discussed in previous chapters how to recognize these phases.

The most significant developments in phase one of a stock market cycle are:

- The market has been flat or declining for many months.

- The economy has been slowing down after years of strong growth.

- The growth of the money supply begins to rise after more than one year of decline.

- Short-term interest rates are declining after rising for more than 12 months.

- Inflation and bond yields are declining following more than one year of a rising trend.

- Commodities are weak after showing considerable strength for more than one year.

- Trading volume expands sharply as market participants recognize new opportunities and liquidity expands.

- The dollar strengthens in anticipation of sounder economic conditions accompanied by lower inflation.

- Valuation measures show that the market is more reasonably priced than it was several months earlier.

This is the time to establish the investment portfolio that typically includes not more than 10 to 15 stocks. Each stock is chosen among the strongest sectors in the market. Each stock in the portfolio is also the strongest stock in each sector. The 10 to 15 issues should be selected from different groups, and the amount invested should be low. When developing the portfolio, 2 to 3 percent of the total funds seems reasonable as an initial investment in each stock, with the possibility that the position could grow to 100 percent if the stock—and the market—moves up. The reason is that if the timing is wrong, the loss is minimal because of the small amount invested. On the other hand, if the market rises as expected, more funds can be allocated to the portfolio. Furthermore, the reason for selecting stocks from different sectors is to diversify the portfolio and not make it vulnerable to the whims of any particular group of stocks.

In phase two of the market cycle, stocks rise, with very few corrections. The bull market is in full swing, and the investor should be fully invested. In this phase, it is typical to experience the following developments:

- The economy stabilizes and then starts growing more rapidly.

- The growth of the money supply continues to increase as businesses and consumers need credit to finance purchases and investments.

- Short-term interest rates continue to decline and then stabilize as the economy begins to grow more rapidly.

- Inflation and bond yields continue to decline and then stabilize as investment needs increase.

- Commodity prices continue to weaken and then stabilize as demand for raw materials increases due to a stronger economy.

- Trading volume remains close to previous high levels.

- The dollar remains strong, reflecting an improving economy with no inflationary pressures.

- Valuation measures remain within historical limits and do not reflect excessive valuation.

During this phase of the stock market cycle, investor have to reposition their portfolio and maintain a fully invested posture. The weakest stocks are sold gradually, and at the same time, the money generated is rein-vested immediately in new strong sectors and in the strong stocks in these sectors. It helps to have visibility on the performance of each stock relative to the performance of the overall portfolio and of the market. If following the performance of the portfolio becomes too complex, it is time to eliminate positions from the portfolio to facilitate the function of managing its performance.

Eventually, the market reaches phase three of its cycle. This is the most dangerous and most difficult to act on. The typical signs the market has entered the final phase of its cycle are:

- The economy is now growing very rapidly.

- The growth of the money supply begins to decline as demand for credit subsides.

- Short-term interest rates have bottomed and are now rising for more than two months as the Fed begins to inform the public that it is con-cerned about the overheated economic conditions.

- Inflation and bond yields are now rising as inflationary pressures build up. The main causes are rising commodity prices, rising crude oil prices, and higher wages due to a tight labor market.

- The major commodity indexes are rising rapidly.

- Trading volume begins to decline.

- The dollar weakens, reflecting the inflationary environment.

- Market valuations are now in the upper range of what has historically been reasonable.

During phase three of the market cycle, the main focus of the strategy is to protect the value of the portfolio. New investments should be avoided, and the weakest stocks should be gradually sold. They can be purchased later at a cheaper price when phase one begins again. Stocks should be sold gradually, and emotional and sudden decisions should be avoided. Just as new positions were added gradually in phase one of the stock market cycle, they now should be eliminated slowly. The amount sold should be kept in cash, and the portfolio should contain only the strongest sectors and the strongest stocks within those sectors. The main idea of the strategy in phase three is to slowly raise cash as the stocks in the portfolio begin to decline and weaken. It is crucial to recognize that what is suggested here is not a strategy based on a buy or sell decision; rather it is a process based on gradually increasing and decreasing positions in order to adapt to the continuous transition of the market through its phases.

The tax issue always arises in managing a portfolio. Investors have to make a personal decision based on their risk profile and tax position. They need to resolve whether it is better to raise cash and become more conservative or stay in the market and see the value of the portfolio shrink.

Issues

Conventional wisdom suggests several ways to manage your portfolio. Each approach is based on a simple formula, which on the surface seems to be attractively straightforward. But these approaches raise important issues that need to be analyzed, and this is the objective of this section.

Issue 1: Diversification

Many commentators suggest that the only way to minimize risk is to diversify. Diversification implies buying several assets in order minimize volatility. Although it does provide a way of managing volatility, the problem with diversification, is that the portfolio is bound to perform like the broad averages. For this reason, the investor would be well served by simply investing in a mutual fund, thus avoiding trading commissions. Furthermore, diversification does not reduce the issue of risk, because if the market declines, the odds are that the portfolio will decline also. Diversification does not eliminate volatility and risk. The investor still has to manage them.

Issue 2: Dollar Cost Averaging

Averaging down is the process of buying stocks as the market declines, with the belief that eventually the market will again rise. There are several problems with averaging down. The objective of stock selection is to own stocks that are appreciating in price. If money has to be invested, it should be directed toward rising stocks, not declining ones. Why add money to a position that is already losing money? This is not the way to become rich. Why own that company's stock? Last, but not least, where is the money to be invested coming from?

If investors want to outperform the market, they must own stocks that rise, not stocks that decline. Investors obviously want to own stocks that are going up and reaching new highs, not stocks that are going down and reaching new lows. If you are putting money in stocks that are going down, that is clearly an opportunity lost, because that money could have been used to invest in other assets or in other stocks that are rising.

Averaging down is like playing poker with losing cards and increasing your bets because eventually you have to win. No poker player would follow this strategy and hope to make money in the long run.

Issue 3: Buy and Hold

Buy and hold is a valid approach if one knows that he is going to live long enough to reflect the long-term nature of the stock market during his or her lifetime. *Long term* in stock market terms is a vague concept, as we saw in a previous chapter. Buy and hold for the long term requires a belief that the market will continue to rise, but we know from history that one can absorb a 30 or 40 percent decline in stock prices if a bear market materializes. Buy and hold is easier said than done. It is important to remember that, historically, the market is up an average of 8 percent per year. However, 8 percent is an average of periods when the market was up 20 percent or more and periods when the market was flat or down.

The brief discussion of these three issues suggests once again that there are no easy formulas to manage money, especially when managing risk. And just as investors must manage risk in their portfolios, so must business leaders manage risk in their organizations in order to improve shareholder value. It is to this topic that we turn next.

Chapter

13

IMPROVING SHAREHOLDER VALUE

The previous chapters had two prime objectives. The first objective was to explain the dynamics of the business and financial cycles and then to examine the behavior of the forces that act on business growth and the financial markets. As business and financial cycles move from one phase to the next, major cause-and-effect relationships take place. These relationships were formalized in the late 1930s and refined throughout the years in a system of economic indicators currently being maintained by the Conference Board. Changes in the growth of the composite indexes of leading, coincident, and lagging indicators synthesize the behavior and the dynamics of the most important economic forces.

The discussion on the functions and objectives of the central bank, and in particular of the Fed, provided the opportunity to introduce the behavior of financial cycles. This allowed the study of the interaction of financial variables and markets. By combining the two cycles, the following are the main developments that take place in each phase.

Phase One of the Financial Cycle

• Growth in the money supply increases.

• The stock market rises.

• The dollar improves.

• Productivity growth rises.

• Growth in the economy (income, production, sales, and employment) bottoms and then increases.

• Commodity prices decline and then bottom.

• Short-term interest rates decline and then bottom.

- Inflation declines and then bottoms.
- Growth in wages declines and then bottoms.
- Long-term interest rates decline and then bottom.

Phase Two of the Financial Cycle

- Growth in the money supply rises and then peaks.
- The stock market rises and then peaks.
- The dollar rises and then peaks.
- Productivity growth rises and then peaks.
- Growth of the economy rises.
- Commodity prices rise.
- Short-term interest rates rise.
- Inflation rises.
- Growth in wages rises.
- Long-term interest rates rise.

Phase Three of the Financial Cycle

- Growth in the money supply declines.
- The stock market declines.
- The dollar declines.
- Growth in productivity declines.
- Growth in the economy declines.
- Commodity prices rise and then peak.
- Short-term interest rates rise and then peak.
- Inflation rises and then peaks.
- Growth in wages rises and then peaks.
- Long-term interest rates rise and then peak.

Phase Four of the Financial Cycle

- Growth in the money supply declines and then bottoms.
- The stock market declines and then bottoms.

- The dollar declines and then bottoms.

- Growth in productivity declines and then bottoms.

- Growth in the economy declines.

- Commodity prices decline.

- Short-term interest rates decline.

- Inflation declines.

- Growth in wages declines.

- Long-term interest rates decline.

As we discussed all these forces and why and how they behave the way they do, the approach was to learn how the investor could take advantage of their movement.

The second objective of our analysis was, therefore, to learn how to recognize risk and opportunities for an investor and the conditions that make different classes of assets more attractive. The objective was to suggest how investors could manage these assets and maximize the value of their portfolio by keeping in tune with economic and financial cycles.

The purpose of this chapter is to discuss how the management of a corporation, by examining the same forces that act in the decision-making process of an investor, can develop corporate strategies that improve shareholder value. By doing so, business leaders can maximize the performance of a company and improve the returns to the investors. To that end, we will discuss the main corporate functions and will briefly review the planning process, together with the role played by the chief economist of a corporation. Finally, we will examine how the corporation can capitalize on the immutable forces driven by the business and financial cycles. They take place anyway. Why not take advantage of them?

The forces that develop, because of the changes that take place as the business and financial cycles move from one phase to the next, can be used by corporations to maximize shareholder value. This is achieved by taking advantage of what is happening in each phase.

The second important point is that profit maximization can be achieved when all functional units of an enterprise act on the basis of the same business cycle assumptions. The function of the chief economist is to present and discuss these assumptions with the functional units, after receiving the stamp of approval from top management. The purpose of this chapter, therefore, is to present an approach on how to organize information and how to interpret it. Finally, we will look at the decision-making process of top management to maximize shareholder value.

The Setting for Decision Making

Let's begin by reviewing the main strategic corporate functions and identify the main parameters of responsibility. By doing so, it will be easier to understand the interaction among top management functions, the chief economist, and the interpretation of business cycle developments to implement and time corporate strategies.

The chairman of the board has the main function of identifying the vision of the corporation and the direction of the business. His or her role is to understand the business climate for the products of the company and to direct the company toward the fast-growing areas. The leadership of the chairman of the board is measured by the capability to reconcile political constraints, market constraints, and the utilization and development of management talent.

The president of an enterprise has the main role of making sure that the operations of the company run smoothly and meet the objectives set by the chairman. The president will have to deal in more detail with what all the functional areas do and how they perform.

The chief financial officer and the treasurer have the main function of organizing the company data flows and consolidating them into financial and control statements. From an operational viewpoint, the function of the CFO and the treasurer is to keep in contact with the banking institutions to arrange borrowing to finance the investments approved by the board of directors. Their responsibility is also to manage debt by establishing the ratio of fixed debt versus floating debt. An additional function of the CFO and the treasurer is to hedge exposures deriving from foreign exchange risk and interest rate risk.

Another important function in an enterprise is the purchasing function. The vice president of purchasing has similar responsibilities to those of the CFO and the treasurer, but the vice president's concern is to contact the major vendors and make sure that supplies are delivered in time for the enterprise to produce the products. The other responsibility of the purchasing vice president is to manage the portfolio of commodities and to put in place the necessary hedges to minimize the cost and volatility due to increases or declines in commodity prices.

The vice president of marketing has the responsibility of delivering the product to the marketplace at the right price and in the right mix. The vice president of marketing, therefore, represents the connection between the marketplace and the production function, by providing the production department with the necessary information on what kind of products to produce, what quality, and at what price they could be sold.

The vice president of production has the responsibility of planning the production of the products required by marketing and of controlling the inventories, so that there is a smooth delivery of products from the plants to the marketplace, according to the requirements stipulated by the marketing department.

Finally, another important responsibility of an enterprise is that of the vice president of engineering, who is responsible for acquiring the machinery and developing the design of capacity expansions or productivity enhancements.

The people responsible for these functions meet periodically, usually once a week, and the chairman of the board reviews the status of the major projects in each functional area. In some companies this group is called the policy committee, which has the responsibility, under the direction of the chairman of the board, to develop the plans of action to meet the visions defined by the chairman.

Timing Management Strategies to Improve Shareholder Value

There are several ways of managing a business and of growing shareholder value. Strategic alliances, mergers and acquisitions, product development, and leadership are all ways to reach a predominant market position that translates into above-average growth in sales and earnings. Whatever the formula for growth, management can further enhance shareholder value by timing strategic corporate decisions using the concepts discussed in this book (Figure 13-1).

Business and financial cycles put powerful forces into motion that directly or indirectly impact all businesses, regardless of whether the manager of the business is aware of them. Why not, then, take advantage of business and financial cycle developments to maximize shareholder value?

The following discussion is an outline of how to time the main strategic decisions an enterprise has to face, including:

- Acquisitions and divestitures

- Capacity expansion

- Productivity enhancement processes

- Hiring of new personnel

- Purchasing

BUSINESS CYCLES AND DECISION MAKING

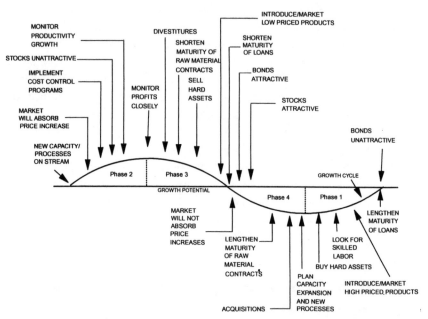

Figure 13-1. Timing management and investment decisions based on business and financial cycle developments greatly enhances shareholder value and investment performance on a risk-adjusted basis.

- Treasury
- Product pricing
- Production and inventory control

Acquisitions and Divestitures

There is always a major strategic reason to acquire a new company or sell a division of an enterprise. The need for a corporation to acquire a company may arise from the need to diversify into new product areas with higher growth potential. Increasing market share and presence in the marketplace of the acquired business will provide strategic advantages against the competition. Some companies may feel compelled to acquire a new company to increase productive capacity that otherwise would be too expensive and too lengthy to put in place.

Usually the strategic need for a corporation to divest of an existing business is to reduce the number of business units so it can concentrate on its core business. At other times, the need to divest arises because a business is not doing well and management is hard-pressed to show earning improvements to Wall Street to support the price of its stock. For this reason, divisions are sold, and as a result, new fresh capital flows into the corporation.

Whatever the reason for divesting or acquiring, the issue of determining the ideal time to implement these decisions and take advantage of the forces of the business cycle becomes particularly relevant. The ideal time to acquire a company is when the economy is slowing down rapidly, commodity prices and interest rates are declining, inflation is heading down, and profit margins are under downward pressure because of overall poor business conditions. These are the times when a poorly managed business feels compelled to sell assets to survive. These are the times when a poorly managed business finds itself strapped for cash and with no strategic options but to sell assets. These are the times a well-managed company is poised to shop for acquisitions, to find value, and to increase shareholder returns. For this reason, during the economic slowdown, the well-managed company has raised and saved enough cash to invest, waiting for the right economic time to go shopping. Buying at a trough, just before the economy picks up again, provides the added advantage of improving the return on the investment made as sales pick up and as the stronger economy further enhances the value of the purchased assets.

The ideal time to divest of a company asset or division is exactly the opposite of when to acquire a company. A company will receive the most from the sale of an asset if it is sold when the economy is very strong, commodities are rising, short-term and long-term interest rates are heading higher, wages are accelerating, and inflationary pressures are increasing. The value of the asset being sold is maximized under these conditions since sales and profits are more robust than usual and they represent an incentive for the buyer to acquire the asset. Furthermore, the buyer may need the asset to increase capacity of existing product lines, thus creating a feeling of urgency in making the deal.

Capacity Expansion

Timing a capacity expansion is one of the most difficult decisions because it needs a forwarding-looking management. It is quite typical to recognize the need for new capacity when business is booming and costs are soaring. This is the easiest time for operating managers to justify and sell the need for new capacity to top management. It is clear at these times that products cannot be produced because of lack of equipment and manpower availability.

Unfortunately, this is the worst of times to make such a decision and allocate capital to implement it. The reason is that it takes time to implement a large project, and it is not unusual that by the time a new plant is on-stream, the economy slows down to a point where the new capacity is not needed.

The ideal time to make a capacity expansion decision and implement it is when business is very slow, commodities are declining, interest rates and bond yields are rapidly heading down, the unemployment rate is rising, and the dollar is weak. There are the times when a rapidly rising growth in the money supply points to a much stronger economic growth in about two years. This is the time when new capacity will be needed to meet the strong demand and rising costs.

Making a capacity expansion decision when the economy is growing slowly is advantageous from several viewpoints. The enterprise will find it easy to find vendors willing to provide their best effort to implement the projects. Interest rates are low, and so the financing costs of the project are minimized at these times. Furthermore, because of the rising unemployment rate and the declining growth in wages, it becomes much easier and much less expensive to find the needed personnel to expedite and implement the capacity expansion.

Productivity Enhancement Processes

The implementation of productivity enhancement processes is an ongoing activity for all enterprises. However, they are particularly needed when costs are rising rapidly. The period of the business cycle when having the right cost-cutting process in place is a must is when the economy is booming, following about two years of rising growth in the money supply. During such times, it is imperative for companies to have growth in productivity that outpaces the growth in costs—only in this case, costs have no impact on profitability.

Let's say, for instance, costs are rising at 4 percent during a boom period, when the economy is growing at well above its long-term average growth rate of 2 to 3 percent, Productivity growth for the enterprise (that is, increase in output per man hour) of at least 4 percent is mandatory if unit costs are intended to have no effect on profitability. The ideal time to make a decision to implement a productivity enhancement process is when the economy is very slow. The reasons are exactly the same as those discussed in the case of capacity expansion decisions.

Hiring of New Personnel

The hiring of new personnel is one of the most important long-term strategic decisions of a company can make and involves great efforts on the part of any human resource area of the company. The ideal time for hiring new personnel, especially those individuals with specialized and hard-to-find skills, is when the supply of labor is the greatest. The ideal time to implement such decisions is when the economy is growing slowly, well below the long-term average growth rate; growth in wages is declining; and the unemployment rate is rising. These are times when commodities are declining and interest rates are heading down.

The worst time to make hiring decisions is when the economy is booming, growth in wages is rising, and the unemployment rate is declining to new lows. These are also times when commodity prices are rising sharply accompanied by higher interest rates. It is very difficult to find the right people with the right skills at this time without paying a premium to convince them to change companies.

Purchasing

Keeping a steady flow of raw materials from vendors to the company is a major endeavor of the purchasing department. The challenge is to acquire raw materials at the lowest possible cost within the limits of quality requirements. In order to achieve the lowest costs of purchased materials, the purchasing department has to manage the commodities acquired as a portfolio whose value is minimized relative to the current price listed in the marketplace.

This can be achieved by recognizing that the lowest prices for the overwhelming number of commodities are obtained when the economy is slowing down and its growth is well below its long-term average growth rate. These are the times when the unemployment rate is rising, interest rates are declining, and the media headlines begin to emphasize a soft landing or possibly a recession.

Periods of slow growth provide the opportunity to the purchasing department to start gradually lengthening the maturity of the contract with suppliers, in order to fix current prices for several months. As prices start increasing, confirming that the economy is turning around and commodities are close to a bottom, maturities should be lengthened aggressively.

As the economy reaches a boom stage and the signs are evident that it will slow down in the coming months, maturity of the purchasing contracts should be shortened to take advantage of declining commodity prices. The portfolio management issues of a purchasing department are very similar to those faced by the treasury department of the company in managing debt.

Treasury

The treasury department of an enterprise has the function of establish-ing contact with the banks and assuring a financing relationship, so that the company can meet its investment and spending objectives at the low-est interest cost. While it is true that borrowing floating-rate debt may add volatility to interest rate costs, historical evidence shows that bor-rowing in short-term money markets is the cheapest form of financing. However, because of the volatility of short-term interest rates, all com-panies decide to have part of their debt as fixed—that is, borrowing with long-term maturity.

One of the functions of the treasurer, therefore, is to manage the debt portfolio. The treasurer will have to decide how much floating (short-term) debt and fixed (long-term) debt to have. The issues that the treasurer has to face are exactly the same as those of the purchasing department.

The treasurer should increase floating debt when the economy is slow-ing down and there is strong evidence that its growth will fall below its long-term average growth rate. These are the times when interest rates decline, the unemployment rate rises, inflation declines, and commodity prices are weak.

The treasurer should decrease the amount of floating debt and increase the maturity of the debt portfolio when there is strong evidence that the growth of the economy is likely to rise above its long-term aver-age growth rate and commodity prices have bottomed. This usually hap-pens as the growth of the money supply keeps rising very rapidly and the unemployment rate heads down.

Product Pricing

Changing the price of a product is an important decision for any enter-prise because the wrong choice of prices might involve a negative reac-tion on the part of the consumer and a resulting loss in market share. Poorly managed companies are forced to raise prices to improve mar-gins when the economy is growing slowly, commodity prices are declining, inflation is heading down, the unemployment rate is rising, and consumers are particularly sensitive to finding value at a very low price. These are the worst times to increase prices because consumers will easily switch to buying goods or services from a competitor that recognizes what is happening and keeps prices low. The outcome is likely to be lower market share and possibly even lower profits for the company that raised prices.

The best time to increase prices is when consumers can rationalize a reason for higher prices. This occurs when inflation is rising and the prices of most products in the marketplace are rising. These are the times when the economy is growing above its long-term average growth rate, commodities are rising, interest rates are heading higher, and the unemployment rate is declining. Higher prices during these times, in order to pass cost increases to consumers, is likely to be accepted and will not result in lower market share.

An alternative way of raising prices is changing the product mix or introducing new products. This is also called the "shrinking candy bar strategy." When profits are under pressure because of poor overall economic conditions, rather than raising prices to improve margins, the alternative could be to introduce products that can be produced at a lower overall cost and that have less material. An alternative to raising prices in a boom period is to produce products that emphasize new luxury features that give the idea of more exclusive characteristics, thus providing a higher margin.

Production and Inventory Control

Production and inventory control have to be kept informed about sales projections and business cycle developments so that production management controls the level of inventories to have the right products at the right place at the right time. Marketing and sales departments and the chief economist have to work very closely with production and inventory control to closely follow how business cycle developments will impact sales, inventory, and overall production costs. This information is also needed by the engineering department to devise new productivity enhancement processes during times of upward pressure in manufacturing costs.

The Role of the Chief Economist

The main role of the chief economist in the decision-making process of the enterprise is to collect information about business and financial cycle developments. The chief economist's function is also to remain informed about the information that is available from all sources about forecasts of economic growth. Each month, the chief economist will present to the policy committee—that is, the chairman of the board, the president, the CFO, the treasurer, the purchasing vice president, the marketing vice president, the production planning and the control vice president, and the engineering vice president—the information about the economy and its trends.

The crucial aspect of the chief economist's work is not to present an accurate forecast. This is impossible. The purpose is to provide assumptions on what is happening in the economy and also provide input to the policy committee on the position of the business cycle. The next step is for the policy committee to agree on the assumptions and refine the input provided by the chief economist.

The chairman of the board and the president of the company then have the role of asking each of the policy committee members what their plans are, based on the assumption that the business cycle is in the position that has been decided. Each of the decisions of the various operating departments will, therefore, be consistent with trends in costs, commodities, the labor market, interest rates, sales, and inflation. Only by having this coordinated decision-making process in tune with the business cycle will the corporation have better opportunities to improve shareholder value.

Conclusions

Business and financial cycles unleash powerful forces as they go through various phases. These forces are the result of previous events and tend to bring the economic and financial system back into equilibrium. For instance, too strong a growth in the money supply is followed by a very strong economy, which is then followed by rising inflation and interest rates.

Through the process of negative feedback, the rise in inflation and interest rates causes the demand for money to slow down, resulting in slower growth in the money supply and, eventually, in the economy. The economic and financial systems, therefore, contain self-regulating mechanisms that cause, over the long term, the economy to grow somewhere between 2.5 percent and 3.5 percent, depending on levels of regulation and inflationary pressures in the country.

As the forces released by the business and financial cycles evolve, we have seen that they create opportunities and risks for investors. The same trends, crucial to establishing a successful investment strategy, also have an important impact on the decision-making process of the management of the enterprise. All the major functional areas are not immune to the effect of the business and financial forces. Management can take advantage of them to improve shareholder value.

However, decisions should not be made in isolation. It is important that strategic plans be based on accepted business and financial cycle assumptions by all top managers. The function of establishing these assumptions is assigned to the chief economist of the company. The acceptance of the economic and financial assumptions should be made by the chairman of the board and the policy committee.

Once an agreement is reached on the assumptions, the current position of the business and financial cycles, and the implications for the company, the president's responsibility is to ensure that all the near-term plans or strategies are implemented.

The improvement of shareholder value comes from the fact that all operating units are now making decisions based on the same assumptions and expectations, not in isolation and sometimes in conflict (Figure 13-1). Of course, the outlook as presented by the chief economist and approved by the chairman and the policy committee is likely to be off the mark. That's the risk of any forecast. However, what is important is that at next month's meeting with the chairman of the board, the policy committee, and chief economist, the new assumptions will be reviewed, and any divergences between previous assumptions and new assumptions will be discussed in detail so that management understands and gains an appreciation of what is happening to the business and financial cycles and how best to make corrective actions to previous decisions. This is the same process investors go through in devising corrective actions to improve the performance of their portfolio.

Chapter

14

CONCLUSIONS

The equation + 15 percent + 15 percent + 15 percent − 15 percent = +6 percent, discussed in Chapter 1, shows that the main objective of investors should be *not to lose money*. Clearly, we can see that losing money only once penalizes the return of many years of solid gains. With this idea in mind, this book has attempted to answer two main questions. What is the level of risk? And is risk increasing or decreasing? The first question was answered by providing a list of indicators that investors should follow to determine the level of risk when investing in stocks.

In order to answer the second question, this book has provided an approach to establish the likely future direction of each parameter. By doing so, the investor is also able to find alternative investments to stocks when they reach a high-risk area.

For instance, we know that short-term interest rates are one of the parameters investors should use to establish the risk of investing in the stock market. Rising interest rates signal that risk is rising. If interest rates have been rising for two to three months, risk is very high and the market environment is more for traders than for long-term investors.

The important question to answer concerns the future direction of interest rates. If short-term interest rates are going to decline in the near future, the risk is likely to be at its highest point and is going to decrease in the coming months. On the other hand, if short-term interest rates are likely to continue to rise, then risk would increase even further. Under this scenario, a more prudent investment approach becomes the best alternative.

You now have the tools to resolve these issues. If the growth of the money supply has been declining for more than a year and is now close to 0 to 3 percent, if the economy is growing below potential (average growth rate over the previous 5 to 10 years), if commodities are weakening, and if the purchasing managers index is below 50, then the odds favor a near-term peak in short-term interest rates.

Recall that at the beginning of this book it was mentioned that the subject of assessing the risk of investing in stocks would be the last topic explored. The reason was that the book was like a mosaic, and all the various parts of the mosaic had to be discussed first; only then, at the end, could you see how the pieces would fit together.

Thoughts about Investing

You can make money in different ways. You can make money just for income. Another way is to invest your funds just for the purpose of achieving capital gains. Some investors recognize that dividends are an important part of their income, together with interest from bonds. They try to manage the total return of their portfolio, which is interest plus dividends plus capital gains. The approach, which has been discussed in this book, is managing the total return on a risk-adjusted basis—that is, managing the total return of your portfolio by managing its volatility and therefore managing its risk.

By managing risk you will avoid painful losses and you will make your returns more predictable. As mentioned earlier, it takes just one year of losing 15 percent, even if you made 15 percent the previous three years, to reduce your total return close to only 6 percent on an annual basis. The markets heavily penalize those who lose money because it is an opportunity lost. It is much better to manage risk on the downside than manage opportunities on the upside.

The approach followed is an approach that is designed for the management of all your money, not play money. You have to look at the entire portfolio, managing the whole volatility of returns of your total portfolio. It is important to set reasonable objectives. It is true that with the market and some types of investments, there are times that they provide 10, 20, 30, and even 100 percent returns over a few months. Clearly, that is not the norm. The norm is much closer to 9 or 10 percent per year. By scaling down your objectives, you are also scaling down the risks for your portfolio.

There are times when bonds become an attractive investment because of the capital gains and interest they provide. One should not think of stocks only, because bonds are attractive after a period of high inflation. When long-term interest rates decline, there are substantial capital gains to be made. It is true that the odds favor that the stock market will strengthen, but the probability of being right is higher with bonds than with stocks.

One of the most important aspects in the management of your portfolio is to measure its performance at least weekly. Every week the total value of your portfolio should be assessed and compared with the previous week's. A graph of the return of your portfolio compared with an average like the S&P 500 or the Dow Jones would help assess the relative performance of your portfolio versus the broad market.

Part of the weekly review should be to analyze the graphs of the stocks and mutual funds that are part of your portfolio. In this way, you can quickly assess which stocks contribute positively to the increase of your portfolio and which ones are performing poorly or declining. The purpose of a weekly review is to assess the investments in your portfolio and decide if some of that exposure should be reduced. The charting aspect is easy to obtain. There are several tools available on the Internet.

Finally, as for any game of strategy, investment is a knowledge game. It is very important to increase your knowledge of investment tools, techniques, and strategies, and review periodically the indicators needed to manage the investments of the portfolio. The outcome of this review is to establish your investment framework, your set of measures, your set of guidelines that have proved to be successful for you because you have tested them and fit them to your personality.

Before you start, you must determine the odds of being right. You have to prove to yourself that those guidelines are going to meet your investment objectives and that historically they have not caused serious losses. When you are not sure, always start with a small investment and see how it works and be patient. Increase your investment as you become more confident about the performance of your portfolio, a performance that meets your expectations. But above all, stick to guidelines and be disciplined. Only in this way can you reduce risk. Always increase your investments when risk is decreasing, and decrease your investments when risk increases. Every move and change you make should be gradual—never in and out—always very slowly. Think like a poker player.

Developing Reliable Investment Scenarios

The importance of looking at the financial markets as an integral part of the business and financial cycles lies in the fact that they can be considered within the context of leading, coincident, and lagging indicators. By doing so, investors have a very powerful tool to make an assessment of what is happening and what is likely to happen, and establish an investment strategy consistent with the current configuration of leading, coincident, and lagging indicators.

One of the main themes of this book has been that all the indicators investors need to follow are related by the following model (see also Chapter 5, Figure 5-1).

• A peak in the leading indicators is followed by

• A peak in the coincident indicators, which is followed by

• A peak in the lagging indicators, which is followed by

• A trough in the leading indicators, which is followed by

• A trough in the coincident indicators, which is followed by

• A trough in the lagging indicators, which is followed by

• A peak in the leading indicators

The business and financial cycles continue to repeat themselves with precise regularity. The above relationships have another very crucial property for investors. In each position of the business and financial cycles, there is only one outlook investors should expect. In other words, for each configuration of leading, coincident, and lagging indicators, there is only one answer, only one logical outlook investors should utilize to develop their investment strategy.

In order to illustrate how this can be achieved, let's consider a number of typical configurations of leading, coincident, and lagging indicators (Figure 14-1). The terms *leading, coincident,* and *lagging indicators* are used to make the explanation easier to discuss. However, instead of leading indicators, you can easily use the growth of the money supply or stock prices; instead of coincident indicators, you can substitute the growth of the economy; and instead of lagging indicators, you can speak of growth in commodity prices, inflation, short-term interest rates, and long-term interest rates.

Configuration A

Looking at the graphs of the indicators, the investor recognizes that:

• The leading indicator is rising.

• The coincident indicator is rising.

• The lagging indicator is rising.

The investor, based on this configuration of indicators, should have the following expectations.

• The leading indicator will continue to rise because it's showing no signs that it may be peaking.

BUSINESS AND FINANCIAL CYCLE CONFIGURATIONS

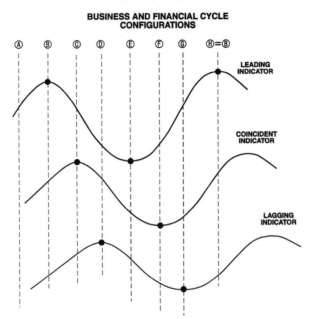

Figure 14-1. The logic developed in this book will help investors recognize configurations and patterns between leading, coincident, and lagging indicators. For any configuration and pattern, there is only one likely conclusion about the future of the forces acting on the business and financial cycles under consideration.

- The coincident indicator will continue to rise because of the upward trend of the leading indicator.
- The lagging indicator will continue to rise because of the upward trend of the coincident indicator.
- The next important cyclical development will be a peak in the leading indicator because of the rise in the lagging indicator (Configuration B).

Configuration B

Looking at the graphs of the indicators, the investor recognizes the following configuration:

- The leading indicator has not been making any progress for some time.
- The coincident indicator is rising.
- The lagging indicator is rising.

The investor should have the following expectations:

• The leading indicator is very close to, or at, a cyclical peak. Its action is caused by the rising lagging indicator.

• The coincident indicator will continue to rise because there has not yet been a prolonged decline in the leading indicator.

• The lagging indicator will continue to rise because the coincident indicator is still rising.

• Following the peak in the leading indicator, the next important cyclical peak is that of the coincident indicator (Configuration C).

Configuration C

Looking at the graphs of the indicators, the investor recognizes that:

• The leading indicator is declining.

• The coincident indicator has not been making any progress for some time.

• The lagging indicator is rising.

The investor should have the following expectations:

• The leading indicator will continue to decline because the lagging indicator is still rising.

• The coincident indicator is very close to, or at, a cyclical peak. Its action is caused by the declining leading indicator.

• The lagging indicator will continue to rise because the coincident indicator is not showing a prolonged decline.

• Following the peak of the coincident indicator, the next important cyclical peak is that of the lagging indicator (Configuration D).

Configuration D

Looking at the graphs of the indicators, the investor recognizes the following configuration:

• The leading indicator continues to decline.

• The coincident indicator is declining.

• The lagging indicator has not been making any progress for some time.

The investor should have the following expectations:

- The leading indicator will continue to decline because the lagging indicator is not showing a visible downtrend.

- The coincident indicator will continue to decline because of the declining leading indicator.

- The lagging indicator is very close to, or at, a cyclical peak. Its action is caused by the declining coincident indicator.

- Following the peak in the lagging indicator, the next important cyclical turning point is a trough in the leading indicator (Configuration E).

Configuration E

Looking at the graphs of the indicators, the investor recognizes that:

- The leading indicator has stopped declining.

- The coincident indicator continues to decline.

- The lagging indicator is declining.

The investor should have the following expectations:

- The leading indicator is very close to, or at, a cyclical trough. Its action is caused by the declining lagging indicator.

- The coincident indicator will continue to decline because the leading indicator is not showing a visible uptrend.

- The lagging indicator will continue to decline because of the declining coincident indicator.

- Following the trough in the leading indicator, the next important cyclical turning point is the trough in the coincident indicator (Configuration F).

Configuration F

Looking at the graphs, the investor recognizes the following configuration:

- The leading indicator is rising.

- The coincident indicator has stopped declining.

- The lagging indicator is declining.

The investor should have the following expectations:

- The leading indicator will continue to rise because of the declining lagging indicator.

- The coincident indicator is very close to, or at, a cyclical trough. Its action is caused by the rising leading indicator.

- The lagging indicator will continue to decline because the coincident indicator is not showing a visible uptrend.

- Following the trough in the coincident indicator, the next important cyclical turning point is the trough in the lagging indicator (Configuration G).

Configuration G

Looking at the graphs, the investor recognizes the following configuration:

- The leading indicator is rising.

- The coincident indicator is rising.

- The lagging indicator has stopped declining.

The investor should have the following expectations:

- The leading indicator will continue to rise because the lagging indicator is not showing a visible uptrend.

- The coincident indicator will continue to rise because of the rising leading indicator.

- The lagging indicator is very close to, or at, a cyclical trough. Its action is caused by the rising coincident indicator.

- Following the trough of the lagging indicator, the next important cyclical turning point is a peak in the leading indicator.

At this point, the cycle starts again and the investor should expect configuration B.

The periods involved between cyclical points vary considerably between financial cycles because not all cycles have the same characteristics. The following are simply guidelines and should not be applied mechanically without first thoroughly investigating what is happening in the current financial cycle and then comparing that finding with previous ones.

From historical financial and business cycles, the following relationships are provided as an order of magnitude.

- The peak of the leading indicator leads the peak in the coincident indicator by one to two years.

- The peak in the coincident indicator leads the peak in the lagging indicator by about six months.

- The peak in the lagging indicator leads the trough in the leading indicator by less than six months.

- The trough in the leading indicator leads the trough in the coincident indicator by one to two years.

- The trough in the coincident indicator leads the trough in the lagging indicator by about one to two years.

- The trough in the lagging indicator leads the peak in the leading indicator by one to six months.

These lead-lag times are found when the growth of the money supply and stock prices are used as leading indicators; the industrial production index is used as a coincident indicator; and inflation, interest rates, and growth in commodities are used as lagging indicators. Again, remember that the above figures are rough guidelines, and should be refined depending on the financial and business cycle under examination.

Investing in Stocks

Risk changes, and its direction has to be assessed every minute, every day, every week, and every month. As risk changes, whatever the time span you choose, the amount invested should change. As a good poker player would, you should match your investment with the probability or odds of making money.

When everything is favorable, investors should be 100 percent in stocks. Great buying opportunities happen when:

- The economy is weak and is slowing down. This happens when the growth of the money supply has been declining for at least a year and is close to 0 to 3 percent, and the average growth rate of business activity is below 2.5 to 3.0 percent a year. Several leading indicators are declining or are growing very slowly. Consumer confidence is very low, and the index of the National Association of Purchasing Managers is below 50.

- The financial cycle is in a phase characterized by rising growth in the money supply, reflecting the decision of the Fed to let liquidity in the system increase to stimulate the economy.

- Short-term interest rates decline or are stable. This trend reinforces the idea that growth in the money supply will continue to rise and the Fed is determined to increase liquidity in the system.

- Commodities are declining or are stable. Their trend suggests the economy is still weak and inflationary pressures are under control.

- Inflation is still declining or is stable. This trend reinforces the idea that the economy is still in a favorable phase of the business cycle. Even in times of "low inflation," a closer look at the economy's growth pattern provides important information on the position of the business cycle.

• Bond yields are declining or are stable. Lower or stable bond yields confirm that inflation is also declining and the business cycle is in a phase favorable to stocks. The level of real short-term interest rates should be used to assess the degree of inflationary pressures on bond yields.

• Valuation should be reasonable when comparing the yields on 10-year government bonds and the PE ratio of the market. The market is particularly attractive when valuation is close to the lower end of the range for the particular level of 10-year Treasury bond yields.

• The yield curve is flattening or is still relatively flat, suggesting the odds favor slower growth in the economy.

• The U.S. dollar is strengthening, reflecting the confidence of the international market in the U.S. economy.

• Trading volume is climbing and expanding to new highs. This is a very important technical indicator because the stock market cannot rise without increasing buying activity.

These are important parameters to follow to assess the risk of the market. As these parameters change their trends, so does the risk. When their trends start becoming negative, risk begins to increase and the probability of lower returns increases.

The investor needs to take a snapshot of these trends and determine the direction of risk. The next step is to attempt to predict the direction of these parameters to assess the likely direction of risk, as discussed above. You now have the basic tools to achieve this goal.

If the outcome of your analysis is that risk is decreasing, or is low, then you should become more aggressive and increase your investment in stocks. However, if your analysis concludes that risk has been steadily increasing for more than two to three months, then a more conservative investment posture is fully justified and your portfolio should become more defensive.

It is important to remember that the stock market goes through three distinct phases: the beginning of a bull market, the continuation of the bull market, and then the final stage of the bull market. We have discussed in Chapter 10 and 11 how to recognize the economic and financial conditions that identify each of these phases. The crucial aspect in following the framework that has been proposed is to be objective enough in recognizing what is happening and what the data are saying.

Sometimes, because of lack of time or due to your emotional state, it is difficult to accept what the data are saying and act upon their message. For this reason, it is important to achieve a state of mental tranquility, calm, and isolation when the time to make important strategic decisions has arrived.

Investing in Assets Other Than Stocks

Are there any alternatives to investing in stocks? The answer is no when conditions for investing in stocks are the right ones and the risk is low for equities. The reason is that, as it has proved many times in the literature on this subject, stocks outperform all other assets when economic and financial conditions are favorable to equities.

However, assets other than stocks should be considered by an investor as a form of diversification. Long-term bonds become particularly attractive when the business environment changes due to much slower economic growth, declining commodities, high real short-term interest rates, and declining inflation.

Investment in hard assets such as real estate, commodities, precious metals, coins, and art should be made when the economy is becoming very strong, there is rapid growth in monetary aggregates, and real short-term interest rates are close to or below their long-term average. The 1970s have shown that low real short-term interest rates were the main reason for soaring inflation and rising prices of hard assets.

Managing Risk

You have been armed with guidelines that have proved to be sound over a long period of time. They provide you with the information you need to establish the risk level for investing in the stock market. And you are well aware of the relationships between various indicators and the relationship of those indicators to the stock market. So you have now acquired knowledge of how to process the information that you need.

The third important step is to evaluate risk. You must evaluate risk by listing the points made about the economy, the direction of the financial cycle, short-term interest rates, the dollar, inflation, commodity prices, long-term interest rates, the yield curve, and valuation by looking at the 10-year Treasury bond yield versus the PE ratio of the S&P 500. A snapshot of these measures tells you what the risk is.

The fourth step is to use the structure and material presented to make a simple assessment of what the trends are to see in which way risk is moving. You do not need to be sophisticated, but by following the indicators it should be fairly easy to assess if the odds favor the market.

These four steps: obtaining the information, processing the information through the knowledge acquired through this book, evaluating the risk, and sensing the direction of the risk should be enough to establish a strategy. The outcome of the strategy should help you determine whether you should increase your investment or decrease your investment and in which asset. Or, instead, if you should reduce 10 percent of your investments and put your proceeds in cash, and then go back to your stock selection and start selling your weaker stocks. Remember that this process should be done periodically. Some do it daily, some weekly, and some monthly. It is a good idea to measure the performance of your portfolio on one day and devote another day to assessing the risk of the marketplace and the strategy you should follow.

These are the four important steps in managing the dynamics of your portfolio. Process the information through the knowledge you have acquired in this book, assess the risk of the markets, make an assessment of the direction of risk, and develop a strategy based on that assessment. Measuring the performance of your portfolio is the final report card on how well you are doing. This should be repeated every week. The objective of this activity is to reduce the volatility of your portfolio and strengthen the structure of your portfolio by staying in assets that are performing the best. Always use a very disciplined stock selection process and always invest in the best mutual funds.

Investing takes a lot of time, and professional investors spend a lot of time and energy to be successful. If you want to be more successful than the professionals are, you must work very hard. Investing is a two-person zero-sum game. Whatever you lose, someone else wins. The people sitting on the other side of the table are shrewd, are extremely well prepared, and have excellent tools. It is a knowledge-based game, and therefore, you have to acquire knowledge. Above all, it is a disciplined game. You now have the information you need to follow, and you know how to interpret it and how to establish the risk involved. Investment strategies have to be developed as a result of this process, which will make you more aware of the risk of being in the market. The only way you can be successful is to apply this material in a very disciplined way.

Chapter

15

WHAT TO DO NOW?

We have reached the end of this book, but the question remains—what to do now? How does a beginning or intermediate investor take this material, all these theories, relationships, and information about business and financial cycles, and make sense out of it? The answer is outlined in this chapter.

This chapter, set up in terms of questions and answers, is divided in six sections. From collecting data to measure performance, we'll address same key questions to help manage your interests. The first section deals with the data you'll need to collect. We'll start in a simple way and then discuss other data that can be added. We also will examine the way the data are computed and the sources of these data. The second section will show how to analyze the data.

In the third section we'll analyze how to make a forecast. This phase is really more of a scenario-building phase to recognize the alternative options available to investors and the risk involved with each one of those options.

Collecting Data

Q   Give me an idea of the type of data I need to collect.
A   Several types of data are important. First, there are data about the economy. They provide information about the business cycle, the speed with which the economy is growing, and the degree of acceleration or deceleration of the business cycle.

The second set of data is monetary data. These data will provide information on the financial cycles, as well as information on what the Fed is doing and how it is going to impact the financial markets and the future of your investments.

The third type of data that you need is interest rate data. This is important information because you need to assess the effect of the business and financial cycles on interest rates. Since interest rates have an important impact on financial markets, these data have to be collected and interpreted.

Because of the impact of inflation on the business and financial cycles experienced, inflation information is also crucial. In collecting data about inflation, it is important to collect information about the major commodities, because they provide very useful information on inflationary pressures. Since those are market data, they are not going to be revised by the government, unlike most other data that you will be following. They provide, therefore, a real-time feedback on what is happening now in the business cycle.

Finally, there are data about the stock market itself that will provide you with information on the internal strength of the market and the degree of speculation of the market itself.

Q How will the data be represented so I can look at them?
A First of all, you have to transcribe the data into a book and then enter the data in a spreadsheet software. The spreadsheet will provide you with the tools you need not only to graph the data that you have entered, but also to graph the data that you will eventually manipulate. In fact, I suggest you graph two or three series of data on the same chart, so you can superimpose the graphs and, therefore, find the relationships that have been discussed in this book. By overlapping graphs on the same chart, you will see patterns repeating with amazing regularity. Once you have become familiar with the technique, you will eventually find your own relationships.

Q Give me an idea of what kind of data you feel are relevant for me to start the analysis of the business cycle.
A To have a good idea of the business cycle and how it is growing, the important data are:

• *The industrial production index.* This monthly information about the man-ufacturing sector provides an excellent approximation of overall business activity and its growth. It also offers clues on trends in commodities.

• *The National Association of Purchasing Managers index.* This index pro-vides information on the direction of the economy and how fast it is grow-ing, depending on far this index is above or below 50.

• *The gross domestic product.* This information is released late, and has little tactical significance. However, it is useful to give you a sense of what the economy is doing and its patterns of growth.

• *Retail sales.* These data reveal the strength of the consumer sector.

• *Housing starts.* These data give a sense of the impact of interest rates on the construction sector and overall economy.

• *Car sales.* The trend in car sales confirms overall strength or weakness of the business cycle.

• *Business inventories.* The growth of business inventories depends on sales.

If sales are very strong, odds are that inventories are going to be built more rapidly, which means the economy is going to be strong.

- *Orders for durable goods.* An important leading indicator of trends in the manufacturing sector and in the economy.

- *The three indexes published every month by the Conference Board.* They show the trends in the index of leading, coincident, and lagging indicators.

- *Jobless claims.* They provide information about the strength of the economy and the tightness of the labor market.

- *Employment.* Released at the beginning of each month, it provides information about the tightness of the employment market and how strong the economy is.

- *Foreign data.* There are three major sources of information. One is the Organization of Economic Cooperation and Development (OECD) in Paris. The Federal Reserve Bank of St. Louis also makes available foreign economic data. The IMF also provides comprehensive statistics on all countries.

- *Brokerage houses and major banks.*

Q Give me one or two pieces of information that I need to follow.
A A very simple index to follow, and one that definitely provides a lot of information on the strength of the economy, is the National Association of Purchasing Managers overall index. Another good one is the National Association of Purchasing Managers deliveries index, which shows the percentage of purchasing managers experiencing slower deliveries. The change in industrial production index should also be followed.

Because slightly more than 60 percent of the economy is driven by consumer demand, retail sales also provide important information. For the same reason, employment reports offer important clues about the tightness of the labor market and possible inflationary pressures.

Q Where do I find these data?
A The industrial production index, which is a measure of output of the manufacturing sector, retail sales, and employment, can be found at the website of the Federal Reserve Bank of St. Louis in the database called FRED. The National Association of Purchasing Managers overall index and deliveries index are released by the National Association of Purchasing Managers monthly and can be retrieved at the NAPM's website.

Q What other data do I need to follow?
A Monetary data provide a sense of what the U.S. central bank is doing and how it's likely to impact the economy. The most important information

released by the Federal Reserve is data concerning the growth in the money supply and the total debt of the nation. The most important money supply numbers are M1, M2, and M3. The Federal Reserve Bank of St. Louis provides in its database data about MZM and the adjusted monetary base, as adjusted by the Federal Reserve Bank of St. Louis.

All these data (M1, M2, and M3) can be found weekly either on the Federal Reserve website or on the website of the Federal Reserve Bank of St. Louis. I also strongly recommend that you follow the releases of each meeting of the Federal Open Market Committee that come out about every eight weeks. You can find the schedule on the Federal Reserve website.

Q   Is there any other information on monetary data that provides further help in managing my money?
A   The total debt of the nation is reported every week by the Federal Reserve and provides the growth rate of the debt of the nonfinancial sector of the nation. The growth rate of that debt also adds to further insights on the health of the country. It should grow at about 5 percent year on year. Anything higher than this suggests strong imbalances, a negative development for the economy and financial markets.

Q   Of all these monetary data, which ones are the most important?
A   All data on money supply are important because they help you identify the financial cycle. MZM is the most reliable and useful one. This measure of the money supply is closely related to financial and business cycle developments.

A second one would be the adjusted monetary base of St. Louis and then all the other money supply numbers.

Q   What is the next set of data that you feel is important?
A   Interest rates offer important information. The most important interest rate to follow is the interest rate on 13-week Treasury bills. This rate is very sensitive to small changes in market conditions because it's affected most immediately by the action of the Federal Reserve. Although on the list is the 90-day prime commercial paper, which measures the short-term interest rates offered by the markets. The spread between prime commercial paper and Treasury bills is also important to assess risk in the financial markets. A rising spread suggests rising risk. It is not unusual to see a strong stock market during periods of declining spreads.

In the longer-term maturities, the 5-year, 10-year, and 30-year Treasury bond yields are important.

Finally, the yield on BAA bonds should also be followed. This is very crucial because the spread between yields on BAA bonds and Treasury bonds is closely related to growth in the money supply, growth in stock prices, and financial cycle developments.

Q   Where do I find all these data?
A   These data are found in almost any financial paper. Other good sources are the database FRED at the website of the Federal Reserve Bank of St. Louis and the website of the Federal Reserve in Washington.

Q   Of all these interest rates, what are the most important to follow?
A   The rate on 13-week Treasury bills. It provides a sense of what's happening in the short-term market because it is sensitive to changes in monetary policy and tends to move ahead of all the other interest rates.

The 10-year Treasury bond yield is also important because it provides information on the returns from investments in bonds. It also confirms trends in inflationary expectations.

Q   What about inflation—where does it fit?
A   Trends in inflation are very important because of their impact on the financial markets and the economy. Inflation is measured by using the consumer price index, the producer price index, the National Association of Purchasing Managers price index, the employment cost index, and data on commodities such as copper, aluminum, lumber, gold, and crude oil. The CRB spot index of raw materials is also crucial because it provides information not only on inflation, but also on the strength of the economy, because it is closely related to the growth of the industrial production index.

Data not directly measuring inflation, but related to inflation, are the value of the dollar against major currencies, the exchange rate of the Euro or of the yen, productivity growth, and unit labor costs.

Q   What is the essential information I need in order to follow the overall stock market?
A   This is going to be the focus of your work, and therefore, it will require more effort. For the stock market, you need to follow:

• The S&P 500 index

• The NASDAQ index

• The Wilshire 5000

• The price-earnings ratio of the S&P 500

• Earnings per share on the S&P 500

• Yields on the S&P 500

Other internal numbers of the stock market are number of issues advancing, declining, reaching new highs, and reaching new lows, and total issues traded on a weekly and, for most investors, daily basis.

There are also sentiment indicators, trading volume of rising issues, trading volume of declining issues, and total volume. *The Wall Street Journal* makes available daily the most active stocks. It's a good idea to follow, as discussed in the previous chapter on the technical analysis of stock market trends, the advance-decline ratio based on the 15 daily most active stocks. This is an excellent indicator that should be closely followed.

Finally, other data include foreign markets and foreign bond yields.

Q Do you feel that some of them are more important than others?
A The number of issues advancing and declining, trading volume, stocks rising and declining, total volume, and total issues traded are the most important ones, together with market indexes, such as the S&P 500 and the NASDAQ.

Q Which one of the sentiment indicators do you recommend?
A Barron's shows every week the number of bullish investors who are members of the American Association of Individual Investors (AAII). Another sentiment indicator is the Investors Intelligence bullish and bearish percentage.

How to Analyze the Data

Q Now that I have collected all the data, what do I do?
A You need to prepare them, so that you can analyze them and understand their meaning. The following step is to make a forecast to build a scenario of possibilities (which will be discussed in the next section). This is preparatory work for the next step to make the forecast.

Q Can you give me an idea of how to prepare a few data?
A The preparation of the data needs to be in graph form.

Q You mentioned various types of information; some are indexes; others are employment, retail sales, etc. How can you prepare all these data in one chart?
A In order to compare apples and oranges, the only way to do it is to use rate of change. This allows the possibility not only of comparing apples and oranges, but also of understanding the dynamics of the environment. Small changes in the rate of change of these indicators produce widespread effects that eventually impact the financial markets.

Q What exactly the rate of change?
A The rate of change is the percentage change over 12 months and is obtained by computing the percentage change from the current month relative to the same month a year earlier. Repeat this process for each of the following months.

For instance, if we are in January of this year, we compute the percentage change from January of this year to January of last year and so on.

Q Which of the data discussed above need to be analyzed and how they should be represented on a graph?

A The first step is to prepare the data for the analysis of economic trends. The first chart is composed of the graphs of the National Association of Purchasing Managers index and the National Association of Purchasing Managers deliveries. These data, oscillate around the value of 50, and they have roughly the same scales. They tend to match each other pretty well, but the use of both series helps to better understand what is happening.

The next graph that is important is the percentage change over 12 months of retail sales. This can be computed before or after inflation, and usually sales oscillate between zero and 12 percent.

The next chart needed is the growth in the employment rate and here we can use the total employment and employment in manufacturing. These series are also represented on a graph using the percentage change over 12 months where manufacturing employment is more volatile than total employment and provides more insights into employment trends and the economy.

The next chart is the percentage change over 12 months in the industrial production index. This series provides information on the growth of the industrial sector and important insights into the growth of manufacturing employment. We will see how these numbers have a major impact on commodities, interest rates, inflation, and so on. This will be the subject of the next analysis.

Q How many charts do I have to follow to have an understanding of monetary policy?

A In order to follow monetary policy, you should follow all the data available from the Federal Reserve and all the monthly and weekly money supply data. The most important data to follow are two series. The first one is the percentage change over 12 months in MZM. This percentage change provides information on the amount of liquidity that the Federal Reserve is injecting into the system.

The second very important chart to be used, together with the change in MZM, shows real interest rates. This graph is computed by taking the rate of 13-week Treasury bills and subtracting from this number the change over 12 months in the consumer price index. For instance, if the 13-week Treasury bills rate is 6 percent and the change over 12 months in the consumer price index is 2.7 percent, then real short-term interest rates are 6 percent less 2.7 percent, which equals 3.3 percent. The direction of real interest rates provides information on whether the action of the Fed is toward tightening or toward easing. The level of real interest rates also provides clues about whether real interest rates are inflationary or noninflationary.

Q What is the essential chart I should follow to get a good understanding of interest rate developments?

A   You need only one chart: the chart that shows the levels of 13-week Treasury bills and the yield on 10-year Treasury bonds on the same graph.

Q   What about inflation data?

A   Inflation data are very important because, together with interest rates, they are lagging indicators. The most important chart on inflation is the change over 12 months in the consumer price index.

The next charts are those of the price of gold, the price of crude oil, and the price of copper. While the trends in gold prices and crude oil prices provide some indication on the future of inflation, the direction in the price of copper provides clues on the strength or weakness in the economy. Strength in copper prices suggests that the economy is strengthening, and a decline in copper prices suggests that the manufacturing sector is weakening.

Another commodity that is important is lumber. The price of lumber is very closely related to housing activity, so a weakening in the price of lumber tells you that the housing sector is weakening. Of course, the housing sector is a leading indicator and confirms whether the rise in interest rates is affecting negatively the housing sector. On the other hand, a rise in lumber prices is the result of a strengthening in the housing sector, mostly caused by declining or stable interest rates.

Another number that is important is the trend of the dollar against major currencies. The dollar index is traded on the New York Board of Trade. The value of the dollar is very important, because if inflation rises beyond certain levels that can only be brought under control with a recession, the dollar tends to anticipate this development and declines quite sharply. You may want to investigate overseas investments when the dollar is weak.

The CRB index of raw industrial materials (spot) is also an important commodity index to follow. These charts provide a very comprehensive but essential view of inflationary pressures. When they rise, inflationary pressures are increasing, and when they decline, inflationary pressures are decreasing. On the other hand, raw material prices also provide information on the strength and weaknesses of the economy. These graphs are used to confirm whatever conclusions one reaches from the analysis of the charts indicated in the economic analysis section.

Q   Trends in the stock market impact the economy. On the other hand, business and financial cycles impact the stock market. We still need to follow some charts about stocks. What are the minimum charts that will help me assess market trends?

A   There are two types of charts. The first is about the stock market and stock market trends. Of course, the more data you have and the more charts you follow about this subject, the better off you are. The second set of charts is about sentiment indicators.

Q   What are the most important charts?
A   The first set of charts gives information about the Standard & Poor's 500 index and the NASDAQ index. These two charts are the synthesis of what's happening to more than 5,000 stocks and the largest corporations in the United States. These two graphs, one of the S&P 500 and one of the NASDAQ, are a must.

There is a third chart that is crucial, and it's the chart of total volume traded on the New York Stock Exchange on a weekly basis. The weekly data should be smoothed by using a 15-week moving average. Total weekly trading volume on the New York Stock Exchange is a very important and critical leading indicator of stock market trends. Any market increase not accompanied by rising volume should be viewed with great suspicion. On the other hand, expanding trading volume should be a warning that the market is ready to head much higher. The point is that trading volume on a weekly basis on the New York Stock Exchange smoothed using a 15-week moving average is a crucial chart.

Q   Are there any other charts to determine how much the stock market is overbought or oversold?
A   Yes, the first chart is obtained using weekly advancing stocks, declining stocks, and total issues. The number of advancing stocks as a percentage of total issues and the number of declining stocks as a percentage of total issues should be used. Then take the ratio between the percentage of stocks rising divided by the percentage of stocks declining. This ratio should be smoothed using a 15-week moving average. The outcome is a graph that looks like an oscillator that moves between ranges. When the oscillator is close to the upper range, the market is overbought. When this ratio falls to the lower end of the range, the market is oversold. Please refer to Chapter 11 on technical analysis for the correct interpretation of overbought and oversold conditions. Another overbought-oversold indicator is computed using the volume of rising stocks and the volume of declining stocks as a percentage of total volume on a weekly basis. The ratio of the volume of rising stocks as a percentage of total volume divided by the volume of declining stocks as a percentage of total volume is also a useful overbought-oversold indicator. This too should be smoothed using a 15-week moving average and oscillates between two ranges. As in the advance-decline oscillator, this one too provides useful information on how much the market is overbought or oversold.

Q   What about sentiment indicators? Which one do you recommend?
A   *Barron's* publishes weekly a comprehensive table of sentiment indicators showing the percentage of investors who are bullish, bearish, or neutral. These data provide excellent information on the sentiment of the investment community.

Preparing the Forecasts

Q Why is it important that I prepare a forecast based on all of the analysis that I have done?
A You have to look at the future and develop an outlook of the possible scenarios available to you. It's like playing a game. The data that you have analyzed will provide you with some alternative outlooks, one of which is probably the most likely one. Then next week or next month, you evaluate the data again, reassess the options that are available to you, and readjust your strategies to the new outlook.

Q How do I start?
A The relationships that we will use to build an outlook or set of scenarios are based on the relationship between leading, coincident, and lagging indicators.

If you are trying to forecast a leading indicator, you can only use a lagging indicator for this purpose. If you are analyzing a coincident indicator, the only way to forecast its direction is to use a leading indicator. If you are forecasting a lagging indicator, then you have to use a coincident indicator to predict its trend.

Q Let me ask you the question again—how do I start?
A The most important market to forecast, of course, is the stock market, as it is measured by the S&P 500 or the NASDAQ. There are two issues in this forecast to be considered. One is the likely direction of the stock market. The other is the likely growth rate of the stock market—will its growth be very rapid or will it be slow? Those are two important issues that have to be dealt with.

Q The stock market is a leading indicator, isn't it?
A The stock market is an important leading indicator of the economy, together with the growth of the money supply. Since the stock market is a leading indicator, you can only forecast a peak in the stock market by using lagging indicators.

Q What you are telling me is to look at the charts of the lagging indicators, so that I can forecast the leading indicators, and everything is okay if the lagging indicators decline. I have to be careful if the lagging indicators bottom, and I need to recognize that there is rising risk if the lagging indicators increase. How do I recognize a bottom in a lagging indicator?
A The turning points in inflation and interest rates are exactly the same because they are lagging indicators. The issue is what are the conditions that allow you to forecast their trend? Rising inflation and interest rates have always been preceded by a rise in the growth of the money supply from levels of close to 0 percent to levels of 15 percent.

Inflation and interest rates are also preceded by strong growth in the coincident indicators, such as retail sales, industrial production, and employment. During such times, it's quite typical that the National Association of Purchasing Managers index and the National Association of Purchasing Managers deliveries index are all well above 50.

Q If the growth in the money supply has been increasing rapidly (between close to 0 percent and 15 percent), and the economy and all the coincident indicators are also growing rapidly (well above the long-term average rate), I should expect rising inflation and interest rates, right?
A That is exactly correct. If you see that the conditions arise and inflation and interest rates stop declining, the odds are that what you are experiencing is a very important bottom in both inflation and short-term and long-term interest rates.

Q So when I see inflation and interest rates bottom, I should be aware that the risk for stock prices is increasing, and I should be more cautious.
A That is exactly correct.

Q If, therefore, inflation and interest rates start rising, when should I expect them to decline?
A Inflation and short-term interest rates should be expected to decline only after a protracted decline in the money supply lasting from well above 10 to 15 percent to close to 0 to 3 percent, followed by very weak economic conditions, with employment, retail sales, and industrial production growing below their long-term average growth rate. In these conditions, it's quite typical to see the National Association of Purchasing Managers index and the deliveries index fall below 50. Under these conditions, you should look for a peak in both inflation and short-term and long-term interest rates.

Q When I see that the economy is weakening, preceded by slower growth in the money supply, and I see inflation and interest rates peaking, what am I supposed to look for as far as the stock market is concerned?
A Slow growth in the money supply, followed by weak economic conditions and declining short-term and long-term interest rates, and inflation are very powerful signals that the stock market has reached a major bottom and a new bull market will be under way. Under these conditions, risk is very low, and you should invest your money aggressively.

Q So, to forecast an indicator, the first thing to do is to recognize its cyclical timing. Therefore, to forecast the stock market, I have to start with the assumption that the stock market is a leading indicator. The only way to predict a turning point in a leading indicator is to use lagging indicators. I should use the trends in inflation and interest rates, and these techniques to predict

whether inflation and interest rates are rising or declining, thus increasing or decreasing stock market risk.
A That's quite right. Also, when you're not sure what the lagging indicators (in this case, inflation and interest rates) are doing, remember that the outlook for a lagging indicator is reached by looking at the coincident indicators.

Q Talking about lagging indicators, bonds could be a great investment at certain points in the financial cycle. How do I know when to buy and when to sell bonds, and can you give me a framework, using the charts that you suggested, to make that prediction?
A Bond yields are a lagging indicator, as are short-term interest rates and inflation. As a result, in order to forecast bond yields and short-term interest rates, look at what happens to coincident indicators. The typical behavior of bond yields and short-term interest rates is to decline sharply when the economy is very weak. This is characterized by industrial production growing below its average growth rate, employment and retail sales slowing down, GDP growing below 21/2 to 3 percent, and the National Association of Purchasing Managers index falling below 50.

Under conditions of weakness in the economy, there is a decline in bond yields and short-term interest rates and inflation. On the other hand, when the economy strengthens and the growth in industrial production rises sharply, when employment growth and retail sales growth rise close to their long-term average, and when the National Association of Purchasing Managers index improves and moves close to 50, you should expect bond yields and short-term interest rates to bottom out and begin to form a base process.

As the economy continues to strengthen and all the indicators grow more rapidly, with the National Association of Purchasing Managers index rising well above 50, then bond yields, short-term interest rates, and inflation will continue to rise.

Q Are commodities an asset that investors should consider as an investment?
A Commodity contracts can be purchased in the futures market, and they are used extensively to hedge purchasing activities in corporations.

Q Can you give me some guidelines on how I can assess the outlook for commodities?
A It's very important to always keep an eye on the chart showing real short-term interest rates. If real short-term interest rates are at or above their long-term average of about 1.4, then you should not expect sharply rising inflation, bond yields, or commodity prices, as happened in the 1970s. However, if in a business cycle, economic conditions are such that the Fed needs to ease monetary policy in an aggressive way, then you should expect com-

modity prices, inflation, and interest rates to jump quite sharply, due to the lagged effect of the easing by the Fed.

Q   Give me a framework to forecast commodities.
A   The first step in forecasting an indicator is to determine its cyclical timing, and commodities are a lagging indicator. As a result, their rate of change follows the rate of change in coincident indicators, such as the industrial production index, retail sales, employment, and the National Association of Purchasing Managers indexes. Since the prices of commodities are a lagging indicator, the only way to predict their trend is to examine the development of coincident and leading indicators and the most important leading indicators are the money supply, MZM, and the yield curve.

If the growth of the money supply has increased for two to three years from a low-growth rate of 0 to 3 percent to well above 10 percent, and if the yield curve steepens substantially, you should expect, after a year or a year and a half, an environment of strong economic conditions followed by higher commodity prices. On the other hand, after a one- or two-year decline in the growth of the money supply and a substantial flattening of the yield curve due to the sharp rise in short-term interest rates relative to long-term bond yields, you should look for lower commodity prices.

Developing an Investment Strategy

Q   The question now is how do I use these scenarios to develop an investment strategy throughout a financial cycle?
A   The first step in determining a strategy is to establish the current phase of the stock market cycle. Are you in phase one when everything is rosy and stocks can be expected to rise and the breadth of the market is quite considerable? Are you in phase two, which is the mature phase of the stock market cycle, when stocks rise but now selectivity becomes important? Or are you in phase three when all the conditions of the stock market are negative?

Q   What should I do in phase one?
A   Phase one, is the phase when everything goes up. You have to be aggressive in investing your money. However, it's always prudent not to invest your money all at once, but gradually. You have approximately two to three months to invest your money. On the other hand, you have to do it gradually and focus on the strong sectors—stocks and mutual funds. Diversification at this stage is also important.

Q   What about phase two of the stock market cycle?
A   Phase two of the stock market cycle is when some signs are beginning to appear that the market is in a mature stage. This usually happens when

inflation and interest rates are bottoming out and commodities are beginning to rise. These are all signs that now you have to become more selective. At this point, you are fully invested and you recognize that there are signs indicating caution. Technical indicators are also suggesting that the breadth of the market is decreasing.

Q Well, what should I do then?
A You need to be aware that the market is still going to rise, but not all the stocks will. You have to keep an eye on which sectors of the market are strong and which sectors are weak. Sell the stocks that are not performing and replace them with performing stocks in new emerging sectors.

Q So when the market is in a mature stage, I should be concerned about selling stocks that are not performing well. I should try to concentrate more of my money in the big-name stocks of companies that are well established and offer some protection on the downside if the market starts to have some corrections.
A That's exactly right. This is a phase where you are really getting ready for phase three of the stock market cycle.

Q What should I do in the next phase of the stock market cycle?
A Phase three of the market cycle takes place when inflation is already rising, commodities are on the way up, and short-term and long-term interest rates are clearly increasing. This is the time when you have to start implementing a defensive investment strategy. At this point, the focus should not be on adding new stocks, but on slowly reducing the exposure to the stock market by raising cash. This is done by gradually selling portions of the stocks in your portfolio that are not performing well. If you have 100 shares of a stock that has declined 5 to 10 percent, sell maybe 20 shares, and then if it continues to go down, sell more.

Q Can you give me some guidelines on how I should develop a strategy for bonds?
A Bond prices are a function of many, many factors, but one of the most important ones is the maturity of the bond. The longer the maturity, the more pronounced the price fluctuations are. If you see long-term interest rates declining, the greatest profit potential is offered by bonds with long-term maturity. On the other hand, if bond yields decline, bonds with very short-term maturities offer the least profit potential.

The trends in bonds can be divided into three phases: phase one when bond yields decline, phase two when bond yields bottom out and start trading in a range, and phase three when bond yields rise with inflation.

In phase one you want to have very long-term bonds. This is when bond yields decline. Your bond portfolio should consists mostly of long-term bonds because they will offer the largest profit potential.

Q What do I do when I see that bond yields seem to have bottomed because of strong economic conditions and inflationary pressures?
A In phase two of the bond cycle you should start selling and taking profits from bonds of long maturities and start shifting the money into shorter-maturity bonds so you can protect your portfolio. The reason for doing this is because you know that eventually yields are going to rise and you'll lose money if you hold bonds of a long maturity.

Q What should I do with my bond portfolio if I see that inflation has bottomed and bond yields are likely to rise?
A The strategy at this point should be to aggressively shift all your bonds to shorter-maturity bonds, bonds with maturities possibly less than two years. If interest rates rise, those prices change very little. In fact, most of the portfolio should be in 13-week Treasury bills that don't change in price. In phase three you have to take a very defensive strategy and put most of your money in cash. The money invested in Treasury bills will continue to provide higher returns because this is the phase when interest rates are rising.

When the time comes that bond yields peak, you will have all this money readily available to you to shift to longer-term bonds as soon as you recognize that bond yields are beginning to decline and enter phase one. At that point, you will move gradually and steadily from bonds with short-term maturities to longer-term maturities.

Q Is there an advantage for investing in commodities?
A The advantage of focusing on investments in commodities is that when commodity prices rise, usually the stock market and bonds do not perform well. So commodities offer a profit potential during a bear market in stocks and bonds. Also, strength in commodities is usually associated with strength in stocks that are commodity based, for instance, energy stocks or stocks of mining companies.

Taking Action

Q Let's say I just completed my weekly or monthly review of my forecast and I have updated the strategy that I should follow. At this point, I am ready to make my investment decisions. I think the first issue I need to face is whether I should be in mutual funds or stocks.
A The overwhelming majority of mutual funds are committed to being fully invested in stocks. The issue of risk is a personal issue and is not eliminated if the money is given to a mutual fund. It is a fact that when the stock market declines or performs very poorly, most of the mutual funds under management perform poorly.

Q If the stock market performs poorly and the mutual funds are not behaving well, what should I do?
A You should slowly sell shares of the mutual fund and place your money either in a money-market account earning returns or in another asset that you feel is going to get stronger.

Q I was under the impression that I should hold money in mutual funds for a long time.
A That probably is true. However, the risk is that if the market does not perform well for a protracted period of time, it's very difficult for the mutual fund to show great profits. Therefore, it is still the responsibility of investors to control the performance of their money and understand why their portfolio is or is not performing well.

Measuring Portfolio Performance

Q You mentioned that one of the important aspects of developing an investment program is measuring performance and the feedback that is derived from it. What do you mean?
A Measuring the performance of a portfolio is the most crucial aspect of investing your money. If investors do not have the time to evaluate their portfolio and plot its trend against the market, they should not manage their investment. Performance should be measured on a weekly basis, and investors should understand why the portfolio is or is not performing.

Q What should I do about it?
A Focus on what makes you lose money. If you have stocks that are not performing for a month, and they have declined more than 10 percent from the time you purchased them, they should gradually be sold. You need to correct mistakes, which is the most important aspect of this phase.

Q What should I do when a stock is not performing well and I am losing money?
A Take action right away! Don't think in terms of selling everything—just sell a little bit—and see what happens. If the stock continues to lose money for you, continue to sell. If you have chosen the wrong mutual fund, with the wrong portfolio manager investing in the wrong stocks, you should start selling it.

Q What should I do with the money that I've raised?
A That depends on your strategy. You should leave it in cash if you see risk ahead. You should reinvest it in stronger stocks or in stronger mutual funds if you feel you still have an opportunity to make money.

Index

271